Praise for *The New Secularism in the Muslim World*

Too often cultural, political and security insensitivities have blinded the eyes of well-meaning activists causing them to declare what's right wrong and what's wrong right. This is frequently the case regarding religious freedom and secular governance in Central Asia and Azerbaijan. As only he can, Svante Cornell asks the questions so few are willing to ask but whose answers are the missing link in the elusive pursuit of religious freedom, for all.

REV. JOHNNIE MOORE, President of the Congress of Christian Leaders, former Commissioner for the United States Commission on International Religious Freedom

Svante Cornell's new book is a must read for anyone interested in the relationship between Islam and the state. The former Republics of Central Asia and Azerbaijan, he reveals, have developed a unique model of the secular state, one that respects traditional forms of belief but works aggressively to keep religion out of politics. While admitting that religion has sometimes been over-securitized by the state, Cornell also suggests that the Central Asian and Azerbaijani approach has successfully countered the divisiveness of radical Islamist ideologies. The book lays the groundwork for arguing that American officials who seek to promote freedom of religion sometimes inadvertently assist religious radicals who seek to destroy the coexistence among Muslim, Christian and Jewish citizens that the Central Asian and Azerbaijani model seeks to protect.

MICHAEL DORAN, Senior Fellow, Hudson Institute, and former Senior Director for Near East and North African Affairs, National Security Council.

Rigorously written and rich in detail, this book deserves to enter the mainstream of debate over the current state and future development of relationship between the state and religion in Central Asia. Dr. Cornell traces the regional history of Islam with emphasis on the emergence of the Maturidi school and how secular views gradually spread across the region even before the Soviet rule. He masterly maps out how the Central Asian "model" of religious policy was formed and is functioning now across the region.

SENATOR SODYQ SAFOEV, Rector, University of World Economy & Diplomacy, Tashkent, Uzbekistan.

Religion, religious freedom, secularism, Islam, Islamism—these are subjects about which most people are less knowledgeable than they assume. They'd be well-advised to turn to Svante Cornell's new book which focuses a scholarly eye on them all, and delves deeply into Central Asia and the Caucasus, a fascinating and historically rich corner of the world that has been largely neglected by academics and journalists alike.

CLIFF MAY, President, Foundation for the Defense of Democracies and former Commissioner for the United States Commission on International Religious Freedom.

THE NEW SECULARISM IN THE MUSLIM WORLD

AFPC

The New Secularism in the Muslim World
Copyright © 2023 by Svante E. Cornell

All rights reserved under the Pan-American and International Copyright Conventions. This book may not be reproduced in whole or in part, except for brief quotations embodied in critical articles or reviews, in any form or by any means, electronic or mechanical, including photocopying, recording, or by any information storage and retrieval system now known or hereinafter invented, without written permission of the publisher, AFPC Press.

Library of Congress Control Number: 2022952260

Paperback - 978-1-956450-62-0
Hardback - 978-1-956450-63-7
Ebook - 978-1-956450-64-4

AMERICAN FOREIGN POLICY COUNCIL

AFPC Press
American Foreign Policy Council
509 C Street NE
Washington, DC 20002

in association with

Armin Lear Press Inc
215 W Riverside Drive, #4362
Estes Park, CO 80517

THE NEW SECULARISM IN THE MUSLIM WORLD

Religion and the State in Central Asia and Azerbaijan

Svante E. Cornell

AFPC

CONTENTS

Preface i
Introduction 1

1. The Problem:
State and Religion in the Muslim World 7
Is Islam the Problem? 9
Theological Context 15
Intellectual Currents in the Muslim World 19
The Intellectual Hegemony of Islamism 29
Implications of the Islamist Hegemony 37
Will Islamism Prevail? 47

2. The State and Religion:
Models of Interaction 53
The Emergence of Freedom of Conscience
and Separation of Church and State 55
Understandings of Secularism 71
Five Models 74
Between Ideal-Types and Reality 83

3. Religion in Central Asia and Azerbaijan 87
Central Asian Islam 87
Law and Creed: *The Development of Islamic Theology
in Central Asia* 89

Central Asian Sufism 98
  Between Two Empires: *Russian Rule, Ottoman Reforms, and Emergence of Secular Intelligentsia* 104
  Soviet Rule and its Unexpected Consequences 115

4. Independence and the Religious Question.. 121
  The Challenge of Statehood: *Central Asia at Independence* . 122
  The Challenge of Radical Islam 127
  Challenges and Responses 144

5. Devil in the Detail:
  Specific Challenges and Responses 145
  Tajikistan: *From Power-Sharing to Growing Restrictions*... 146
  Uzbekistan: *From Defensive to Proactive*................... 151
  Azerbaijan: *Sunni-Shia Relations and "Multiculturalism"* ... 158
  Kazakhstan and Kyrgyzstan: *The Limits of Openness* 164
  Turkmenistan 173
  Similarities and Differences 175

6. Is There a Model? 177
  Embracing Secularism 178
  The Legal Basis 185
  Traditional vs Novel Religion 208
  Residual Soviet Thinking and the Primacy of Security Structures 212
  Doubling Down: *Articulating Positive Agendas* 219
  Do Similarities a Model Make? 222

7. Central Asian Secularism
In Comparative Perspective 225
    Turkey's Declining Secularism 226
    Tunisia: *The Domestication of Islamism?* 232
    The Moderate Monarchies: *Jordan, Morocco, the UAE* .. 239
    Incomplete Secularism: *Laïcité in West Africa* 250
    Indonesia: *Democracy in a Religious State* 255
    Conclusion... 262

8. Looking Ahead

    Acknowledgments 287
    About the Author 289
    Index. 291

PREFACE

NO QUESTION HAS BEEN MORE CENTRAL to the Muslim world's politics and society over the past half century than the relationship between religion and state. This period coincided with the rise of political Islam as a dominant ideological movement, and the growing mixing of religion and politics that it helped bring about. The shape and form of this mix has been diverse. At worst, it has taken the shape of terrorist groups such as ISIS and Al Qaeda, and led to Islamic revolutions in Iran and Sudan. In other places, like Turkey, political Islam rose through electoral politics. Everywhere, the implications have been immense. Whereas secular ideas dominated the Muslim world around 1950, at century's end they had been largely marginalized. The impact of this development has been nothing but a disaster. The mixing of religion and politics has done great damage to the political life of Muslim societies, as well as to religion itself. At best, it has led to a new form of authoritarianism that has hit women and minorities hardest; at worst, it has contributed to civil war and the total destruction of societies.

This is the context in which the Muslim-majority states of the former Soviet Union – Azerbaijan, Kazakhstan, Kyrgyzstan,

Tajikistan, Turkmenistan and Uzbekistan – gained independence in 1991. Thirty years later, this book argues, these six states have developed a new model of secular statehood. While this model to some extent still carries remnants of Soviet practices, it is fundamentally different from Soviet-era atheism. And while it draws on the French understanding of laïcité and Kemalist Turkey's secularism, it has unique characteristics that derive from the region's own history and approach to religion.

Could this model – or a future, improved version of it – be of relevance to other Muslim nations that seek a way out from the destructive mixing of religion and politics? Many would find such a notion preposterous. For over two decades, a motley crew of officials, scholars and activists have decried the restrictive and indeed repressive aspects of government approaches to religion in Central Asian states and Azerbaijan. Worse, they argued, these approaches would only exacerbate the problem of Islamic extremism these states sought to counter.

Two decades later, those dire predictions turned out to be baseless. If anything, levels of radicalism across the region have declined, leading some of the region's states to dial back on restrictions and adopt a less defensive approach to religion. Meanwhile, statesmen and scholars from the rest of the Muslim world have increasingly taken an interest in the trajectory of Central Asia and Azerbaijan, countries that in their eyes appear to be success stories rather than cautionary tales. Meanwhile, the states of the region are constantly evolving, and are now engaging in much closer cooperation than at any time since independence.

The idea behind this book dates back more than a decade. For long, I had been intrigued by the cognitive dissonance between Westerners and Central Asians. Most Westerners took it for granted that the only way forward for these countries was through wholesale liberalization and the expansion of freedom of religion. Central Asian leaders, by contrast, viewed such advice as a recipe for disaster. As new and weak nations whose traditional religious institutions had been decimated by Soviet rule, they feared their societies would be overrun by well-funded propagandists of political Islam. Still, Westerners urged them to reach out to Islamist forces and accommodate them in their political systems. For their part, leaders in Central Asia and Azerbaijan could not understand why their Western interlocutors seemed to criticize their insistence on maintaining secular laws and secular education – something Westerners themselves took for granted in their own countries. Of course, this debate was not unique to Central Asia and Azerbaijan; it was taking place across the Muslim world, most prominently in Turkey. There, the country's Islamist movement deftly appealed to Western powers for support against the country's secularist establishment. And it obtained the blessing of the United States and European Union, helping it gain power in 2002.

At some point, I recall looking into whatever scholarship existed on the relationship between state and religion in Central Asia and Azerbaijan. A cursory survey showed that it was basically non-existent. True, entire shelves could be filled with articles and reports criticizing the approaches taken by these states. But hardly a single study existed that sought to analyze, or even describe, what the leaders of these states sought to achieve, and why they adopted the policies they did. To critics, perhaps, those questions were not relevant. But to a student of the region, they most certainly should be.

Against this background, my colleagues and I resolved

to fill this vacuum, beginning with the publication of country studies that aimed to describe the relationship between state and religion across the region. The Central Asia-Caucasus Institute & Silk Road Studies Program published successive studies in its Silk Road Papers series from 2016 to 2020, which the reader can consult online.

Following the publication of these case studies, it would have been easy to collect them and publish in book format. But that would not have answered the bigger need: placing the experience of Central Asia and Azerbaijan against the background of developments in the Muslim world as a whole.

That, then, is the purpose of this book. It does so by first painting the outlines of the problem: the broader evolution of the relationship between religion and state in the Muslim world. That question, discussed in chapter one, forms one part of this book's foundation. The other part, the focus of chapter two, is to look more conceptually into models of interaction between religion and state. Having thus established a foundation, the book then delves into the substance of the matter. Chapter three provides an overview of the religious history of Central Asia and Azerbaijan, looking particularly into the characteristics of Islam across the region. Chapter four explores the religious challenge the region's states faced at independence, and how they responded to it. Chapter five delves into the detail, country-by-country, of state approaches to religion. On this basis, the next two chapters move to the important question whether the diverse experience of these six states constitutes a model. Chapter six looks into the internal consistency of the model, exploring the similarities and differences between these states. Chapter seven, by contrast, compares them with other frequently touted models in the Muslim world to determine if they are sufficiently distinct from those experiences to be termed a model. Finally, the last chapter looks to the future, examining possible trajectories for the region, and implications for the region's Western partners.

INTRODUCTION

OVER THE PAST SEVERAL DECADES, the relationship between religion and politics in the Muslim world has been a central theme in world affairs. Most Muslim-majority nations have experienced the growth of assertive and often aggressive demands to realign their political systems, laws, and education systems along religious lines. The rise of the ideology advocating for this – Islamism – has taken many shapes: In some countries, such demands have been voiced in the political realm and through civic activism. In many others, they have been associated with political violence that has profoundly destabilized a long list of countries. Almost everywhere, Islamists have put forces that resist the growing mixing of religion and politics on the defensive. Islamism established itself as the most powerful ideology in the Muslim world, a development that has had real implications for the lives of millions. The implications have not been limited to Muslim countries: hatred of the United States and, more broadly, Western civilization is a centerpiece of the Islamist ideology. From Afghanistan in the east to Libya in the West, America and its European allies have been forced to fight the most militant among Islamist groups. Where

Islamists have secured power, they have shifted the foreign policies of their nations in the direction of greater antagonism toward the United States and Europe.

The one part of the Muslim world that has firmly bucked this trend is Central Asia and Azerbaijan, a cluster of six countries that played an important historical role as an intellectual center of the Muslim world but which, from the eighteenth century onward, were subjected to Russian and subsequently Soviet rule. Throughout the three decades of their independence, these countries have maintained a staunch attachment to secular government, which also enjoys the support of a considerable majority of their population. While firmly rejecting the demands of Islamists, leaders of these countries have emphasized the importance of keeping religion out of politics and have countered the divisiveness of Islamist ideology by showcasing the harmonious relations among their Muslim, Christian, and Jewish citizens. They have also applied restrictive and often repressive measures to deal with Islamist challenges within their societies, frequently casting a vast net in doing so. In the foreign policy realm, they have welcomed a partnership with the United States and Europe and played important roles in supporting Western efforts in Afghanistan and the Middle East.

Against this background, one could have imagined that the approaches of these states toward religion would have garnered Western interest and, perhaps, even qualified support. Curiously, the opposite has been the case. Western academia has yet to produce a substantial study of state approaches to religion in this region or even one of its component countries. By contrast, governmental and non-governmental advocacy groups, primarily based in the United States, have taken a harshly critical approach to their religious policies. Yearly reports of the U.S. Commission on International Religious Freedom, as well as publications of private groups such as Human Rights Watch, have invested considerable energy into detailing violations of individual religious freedoms in this region and in urging punitive action against them by Western governments.

Such violations have indeed occurred across the region, and advocacy groups cannot be faulted for calling attention to them. What is curious is that the United States and Europe have shown so little interest in what these states have been trying to achieve: the maintenance of a secular form of government with secular laws and secular education systems. What is even more puzzling is that Western advocacy groups (and Western governments) have frequently emerged in support of the efforts of Islamist forces to advocate *against* the very principles Americans and Europeans take for granted in their societies. This, in turn, has led to profound consternation in Central Asia and Azerbaijan. Leaders in these states have touted their secularism and opposition to Islamist ideology as a point of commonality with the West and anticipated that Westerners would support their endeavors. They are at a loss comprehending why Westerners oppose not just the methods by which they seek to maintain secularism but sometimes that very goal itself.

This cognitive dissonance inevitably leads to conspiracism, best expressed to this author by a retired Central Asian statesman during the ravages of the Islamic State in the Levant several years ago. As we rose to take leave following a lengthy conversation, the elderly statesman appeared to hesitate, then said: "Please do not do a Munich." He clarified: "Please do not sell us out to the Islamists in exchange for them leaving you alone." It dawned on me that he was referring to the infamous 1938 Munich agreement and suspected what he considered the Western appeasement of Islamism to be part of some grand bargain in which his homeland might be a pawn to be traded.

This book takes its starting point in the complex relationship between the state and religion in the Muslim world. It is that context – and the growing dominance of Islamist ideology – that makes Central Asia and Azerbaijan an outlier. Therefore, Chapter one will set the scene by mapping the interrelationship of state and religion in the past century. Chapter two, by contrast, examines the models of interaction between the state and religion at a more conceptual level and proposes a typology for understanding how state approaches to religion can evolve.

Following these introductory chapters, the volume then turns to the region itself. Chapter three surveys the development of Islam in Central Asia and Azerbaijan, focusing on the region's relative openness to other religions, rationality, and secular ideas. Chapter four dives deeper into the religious question during the transition from Soviet rule. Chapter five explores in greater detail the state policies toward religion in each of the six countries.

On the basis of this analysis, the book then seeks to determine whether the approaches of these six states, in turn, constitute an identifiable model of state approaches to religion. In other words, are their approaches similar enough to one another, and distinct enough from other states to be considered a model?

Chapter six explores the internal consistency of the model by drawing out the main themes that emerge from the study of individual countries.

By contrast, Chapter seven looks outside the region to

compare the Central Asian experience with other frequently touted models in the Muslim world.

Finally, the book seeks to look ahead. If this region indeed constitutes a model of secular statehood, there are two questions for the future. The first is whether it is sustainable. While the model is far from perfect, what improvements and adaptations would it need to be maintained in the longer term? The second question is whether it could hold any appeal to other parts of the Muslim world as they tire from the mixing of religion and politics. In other words, as the region's model of state approaches is improved and adapted, could it provide inspiration for those forces that seek to counter Islamist ideology elsewhere?

This book has been a long time in the making. It is the result of an initiative to study state approaches to religion in Central Asia and the Caucasus that began half a decade ago at the Central Asia-Caucasus Institute & Silk Road Studies Program Joint Center. As we decided to take a closer look at the issue, we realized that there was virtually no scholarship that sought to investigate what those states' approaches were and what considerations lay behind them. We resolved to begin to fill this void at first with a series of case studies. From 2016 onward, we published case studies of Azerbaijan, Kazakhstan, Uzbekistan, Kyrgyzstan, and Turkmenistan. In parallel, the idea emerged to produce a study of the region as a whole that situates it in the broader context of religion and politics in the Muslim world. This book is the result.

Many individuals have played roles in the several years of research that resulted in this book. First are the researchers that contributed to these case studies published in the past several years. These include Victoria Clement, Johan Engvall, Jacob Zenn,

Boris Ajeganov, Julian Tucker, as well as Johanna Popjanevski, who left this world too early.

Second, are the research assistants that helped procure materials and sources for this project. They include Diana Glebova, Braunny Ramirez, Jack Verser, and Kamilla Zakirova. Equally important are the scholars, diplomats, and friends whose ideas helped inspire this project during many animated conversations over the past two decades. Colleagues and friends that have been important interlocutors and sparring partners include Herman Pirchner, Ilan Berman, Brenda Shaffer, Elin Suleymanov, Gloria La Cava, Eldar Ismailov, Fariz Ismailzade, Eldor Aripov, Patrik Jotun, Ingrid Tersman and Åke Peterson. First and foremost among them, however, is S. Frederick Starr, the founding chairman of the Central Asia-Caucasus Institute, who has been perhaps the greatest supporter of this initiative and this book.

1. THE PROBLEM:
State and Religion in the Muslim World

FOR SEVERAL DECADES, the relationship between religion, state and society has been at the center of controversy within the Muslim world. The issue has had an outsize impact on Muslim-majority states, which have wrestled with the question of reconciling growing demands for adherence to religious precepts with the necessity of participating in the modern world.

The issue of concern here is not the secularization of *society* but the secular nature of the *state*. As the American example shows, the separation of state and religion does not preclude a society – or large parts of it – from remaining deeply religious. The issue is how a country's laws, politics, and education system – and other walks of life – are governed by religious principles or, conversely, the extent to which they are autonomous from religion.

In this respect, the Muslim world stands out in global comparison. Across the globe, the separation between religion and the state has become the norm. As the next chapter will discuss, this separation can take many forms. A minimum requirement, however, is that the state does not officially proclaim a particular religion as a state religion. Outside the Muslim world, only a minority of the world's countries presently proclaim a state religion. The separation of religion from the state is by no means a solely western phenomenon: while it is the norm in Europe and North America as well as Latin America, it is also the norm in Asia – across the Buddhist, Confucian, and Hindu cultural zones, as well as in sub-Saharan Africa. Furthermore, outside the Muslim world, the trend is unequivocally in the direction of greater separation: in the past twenty years, countries as distinct as Bolivia, Nepal, and Sweden have moved toward disestablishing religion.

Among Muslim-majority states alone, the opposite is true: it is a secular government that is the exception. An unbroken arc of states from Morocco in the west to Pakistan in the east has proclaimed Islam to be the religion of the state. What they mean by this in practice differs significantly. But whereas the rest of the world has moved toward greater separation, the trend in the Muslim world has been toward more, not less, mixing of religion and politics. Half a century ago, secular notions of politics prevailed across much of the Arab world, as well as in Iran and Turkey. Since then, secular government has been in retreat almost everywhere in the Muslim world. To a considerable degree, this state of affairs hampers the development of Muslim-majority countries. It contributes to their dysfunctionality, undermines their political stability, and handicaps them in their interaction with the world.

This chapter will discuss the relationship between religion and the state across the Muslim world. It will first view how this relationship has evolved in the past century, shedding light on the causes of the retreat of secular governance and the rise of religious politics. It will then move to the implications of this phenomenon, with the purpose of situating the experience of Central Asia and Azerbaijan in a comparative perspective.

Is Islam the Problem?

Why does the Muslim world differ so starkly from the rest? Why, when other cultural zones have opted for separation of religion and politics, have Muslim countries moved instead toward a greater intermixing between them? This question has been the subject of heated debates, and possible answers vary widely. Some Muslims and outsiders alike argue that the very nature of the Islamic religion does not predispose Muslim societies toward secular governance. Others claim that the answer, instead, lies in historical and socio-economic features: the history of colonialism and the dislocations and turmoil caused by urbanization and modernization – what Bassam Tibi summarizes as "a cultural-political response to a crisis of failed postcolonial development in Islamic societies under conditions of globalization."[1] Yet others argue that the Islamic world took a turn for the worse about a thousand years ago when a particular interpretation of the religion took hold. Ahmet Kuru, for example, makes a strong argument that the alliance in place since then between the state and the Ulama – the Islamic clergy – is largely to blame.[2] In other words, the problem is not Islam itself but how it has been interpreted and evolved.

While this discussion is not the subject of this work, touching upon it cannot be avoided because it affects the very rationale of this study. If the world of Islam is intrinsically different from the rest of humanity and destined for a fusion of the religious and

---
1 Bassam Tibi, *Islam and Islamism*, New Haven: Yale University Press, 2010, p. 3.
2 Ahmet T. Kuru, *Islam, Authorirtarianism and Underdevelopment: A Global and Historical Comparison*, Camrbidge University Press, 2019.

the political, then a study of secular government in Central Asia and Azerbaijan borders on the irrelevant. It would be, at best, a study of a peculiar historical parenthesis – a truly post-Soviet phenomenon bound to expire. If it were so, as the region gradually puts distance between itself and the Soviet experience, it will become more akin to the rest of the Muslim world and gravitate toward the mixing of religion and politics that is prevalent everywhere where Muslims form the majority.

This line of thinking is relatively popular and comes in at least three forms. The first is that of Islamists, who argue that secular government and Islam are fundamentally incompatible and that this is as it should be. A young Recep Tayyip Erdoğan, for example, argued in 1994 that "secularism and Islam are incompatible, like opposing magnets," because secularism "infringes on the sovereignty of God."[3] The second variant is that of western critics of Islam, who apply a similar culturalist argument. They argue that because Islam is an all-encompassing religion, secular government in the Muslim world is impracticable. While these two types are relatively predictable, there is also a third, more curious approach: that of some Western liberals, who claim that the imposition of secular government on Muslims is an inherently authoritarian and unnatural phenomenon and that the secularization that took place in the West should not be transposed to Islamic societies. Instead, these well-wishers argue those religious politics are a fundamentally democratic feature that should be encouraged. After all, if Muslims want more religion in their politics, why should anyone object?

While these three perspectives come from very different

---

3 "Recep Tayyip Erdoğan: "Hem laik hem Müslüman olunmaz." Youtube, https://www.youtube.com/watch?v=zJC-nUV4WrQ.

starting points, they all assume that Muslims entirely lack the agency to determine their future and to choose a secular form of government. Such historical determinism is certainly not warranted. After all, had this study been composed a thousand years ago, the tables would have been turned. At that time, Europe was in its "Dark Ages," with religious obscurantism holding the continent in a tight grip. Meanwhile, the Muslim world, mainly thanks to its Central Asian scholars, was indeed the intellectual center of the world –home to scientists, philosophers, and pundits of all stripes engaged in vigorous and heated debate.[4] As Bernard Lewis points out, "in most tests of tolerance, Islam, both in theory and in practice, compares unfavorably with the western democracies as they have developed during the last two or three centuries, but very favorably with most other Christian or post-Christian societies and regimes."[5]

That said, those like Lewis that have compared Christian and Islamic civilizations often make the valid point that the two religions emerged in fundamentally different ways.[6] Christianity was the religion of the oppressed, growing under conditions of hardship for three centuries until it achieved the Roman Empire's toleration. Islam, by contrast, was the religion of conquerors, with a Prophet that also came to lead a political entity in his lifetime and apply a law claimed to be of divine provenance. Islam does not have any equivalent to the Christian notion expressed in Matthew 22:21: "Ἀπόδοτε οὖν τὰ Καίσαρος Καίσαρι καὶ τὰ τοῦ Θεοῦ τῷ Θεῷ," or "Render unto Caesar the things that are Caesar's, and

---

[4] S. Frederick Starr, *Lost Enlightenment: Central Asia's Golden Age from the Arab Invasions to Tamerlane*, Princeton University Press, 2013.
[5] Bernard Lewis, *What Went Wrong? Western Impact and Middle Eastern Response*, London: Orion Books, 2002, p. 127.
[6] For example, Bernard Lewis, *What Went Wrong? Western Impact and Middle Eastern Response*, London: Orion Books, 2002, p. 108.

unto God the things that are God's." This phrase would seem to unequivocally separate the worldly realm from the Godly one. Quite to the contrary, early Muslim history did not distinguish between religious and worldly matters because the expansion of the Muslim religion and the Muslim empire were synonymous.

Yet religions are interpreted and implemented by humans. In the centuries that followed, the words in the Gospel of Matthew did not prevent the Christian world from developing a complete fusion of religion and state, for which eighteenth-century scholar Justus Böhmer coined the term "Caesaropapism." Conversely, Mohammed's establishment of a state in Medina did not prevent separation of worldly and Godly power from emerging in the Muslim world. Politics and religion were in some sense separated after the death of the fourth Caliph, Ali. Within a few hundred years, the Caliph in Baghdad was a mere figurehead, power resting with the Turkic conquerors that had swept into the Middle East from the Turkmen steppes. This contrast is a solid reason to reject an excessive emphasis on intrinsic differences between religions in explaining the divergent trajectories of the West and the Islamic world. As a result, modern scholars have termed such emphasis "essentialist" and reductive.[7] Indeed, they argue, social and economic factors in the past century have more important explanatory power than thousand-year-old theological differences. Furthermore, structural differences between the two religious traditions led in a different direction: The institutionalized Christian Church developed a strict hierarchical structure that proved adept at exercising worldly power. By contrast, Islam, at least in its majority Sunni variety, does not provide for any religious hierarchy

---

7 Eg. Nader Hashemi, *Islam, Secularism and Liberal Democracy*, New York: Oxford University Press, 2009, pp. 19, 39.

1. The Problem: State And Religion In The Muslim World

at all, thereby severely undermining the ability of clergy to emerge and grab worldly power. Of course, over time, such a hierarchy emerged, often thanks to its alliance with the state.

The validity of these points does not make the intrinsic differences between religions entirely irrelevant. Just as the circumstances of the birth of Christianity provide a strong argument for the separation of religion and the state, the early history of Islam constitutes a strong point of reference for those Muslims seeking to merge the two. Whatever the intrinsic nature of religion is, if it can even be determined, the way religions have been practiced and implemented does make a difference. A key distinction is that in the Christian world, there was never a "Christian state" comparable to the Umayyad or Abbasid Caliphate. Neither was there an application of "Christian law" similar to the application of Islamic law in domains ruled by the Islamic empire. When the Byzantine empire adopted Christianity, it did not vacate the long-standing Roman law and impose a new code. Roman secular law remained in force throughout, even if it was sometimes amended or modified to conform to religious principles.

Therefore, efforts to develop secular government in Christian societies did not immediately run into the obstacle of overcoming religiously based legal principles. By contrast, efforts to apply secular law and government in Muslim countries confront the presence of the Sharia. To cite just one example, the Qur'an is clear about inheritance law: daughters get half of what sons get. Even states that have sought to apply secular law, like Senegal or Tunisia, have tended to shy away from overturning traditionally applied Islamic family law. Outside the post-communist area, only Turkey made a clean break with this in the 1920s and handled the problem by importing Swiss family law wholesale.

It seems incontrovertible to argue that there are elements of Islamic history that complicate the separation of religion and the state. Equally incontrovertible is the fact that, at times, human beings have interpreted religious scripture in more liberal ways in the Muslim world than was the case in the Christian world. The problem, then, lies not in Islam in the sense of a static or immutable tradition because no religious body is static or unchangeable. As Kuru argues, the main body of religious thought took a turn for the worse at a particular time in Islamic history; as Bassam Tibi makes clear, the problem today is compounded by the modern ideology of Islamism, which "is not a revival of Islam... but rather constructs an understanding of Islam" that is, in fact, an "invented tradition."[8]

Islamic and Christian history shows us that there is nothing predetermined about the relationship between religion and the state in either civilization. Only fifty years ago, a powerful wave of secularization was sweeping across the Muslim world. The dominant forces were Kemalist Turkey, Pahlavi Iran, Nasserist Egypt, and Baathist Syria and Iraq. The proponents of Islamic statehood seemed marginal at best. And fifty years from now, the same might again be true. But in recent decades, Islamism has become by far the most powerful ideological force in the Muslim world, gaining a near-hegemonic position in many countries. How did this happen? There is no simple answer, but several factors have played a role. One is how the interpretation of Islamic doctrine has developed. A second is the broader evolution of dominant ideologies in the Muslim world. A third is the stagnation or failure of secular regimes and the concomitant rise of a resurgent Islamism to intellectual hegemony.

---

8 Tibi, p. 1.

1. The Problem: State And Religion In The Muslim World

Theological Context

Islamic history has seen its share of tension between literalist and rationalist interpretations of religious tenets. In the first few centuries following the death of Muhammad and his companions, an assertive rationalist school of thought known as the Mu'tazila, heavily influenced by Greek rationalism, emerged as the dominant theological force. Proponents of this school held that reason and logic should be used to resolve religious problems. They were skeptical of the practice of finding answers in the deeds and sayings of the prophet, the *hadith*, as they lacked confidence in the ability to know for certain what stories of the prophet's life were indeed true and suspected that *hadith* were either made up or misconstrued to advance various interests.

Further, they opposed literalist interpretations following the letter of the holy book. The Mu'tazilites rejected the notion that the Qur'an was eternal and uncreated, arguing that logically, God must have come before the Qur'an and that it must have been created. They also believed that the doctrine of the unity of God meant God was pure essence and could not bear any likeness to creation. Therefore, they concluded that anthropomorphic verses in the Qur'an – speaking of God's hands, face, or sitting on a throne – cannot be understood literally but must be interpreted metaphorically. On this basis, they also advanced the need for metaphorical interpretation when various parts of the Qur'an appeared to contradict each other. Likewise, the Mu'tazilites applied logical reasoning to the notion of divine justice and predestination. If God is both benevolent and omnipotent, how is it that evil exists? For the Mu'tazilites, this was only possible if human beings had free will. To be sinners, individuals had to choose to disobey God. They also argued that humans had the inherent ability to tell right from wrong *without* the help of divine revelation.[9] This type of thinking made it possible to accept the existence of natural laws and for humans to engage in the study of them.

By contrast, opponents of the Mu'tazilites rejected all these tenets. Their most literalist detractors, known as the *Athari* – the antecedents of today's Salafis – simply argued that the Qur'an should be followed literally without asking questions and that all theological speculation was in itself harmful. Others, primarily the *Ashari* school of theology, did engage in theological reasoning, but only to prove the Mu'tazilites wrong. To them, the Qur'an was eternal; and their understanding of God's omnipotence led them to reject the notion of human free will, as well as the existence of any laws of nature. They constructed a complex theory of human "acquisition" of God's will but, by and large, argued that both free will and the notion of any laws of nature would contradict God's omnipotence: if humans acted independently of God, that would deny him absolute power. Thus, if humans speak, it is not, in fact, the human who speaks but God who makes him speak. Likewise, as the detractors argued in a famous refutation of the Mu'tazilites, it is not a law of nature that leads fire to make cotton burn. It is, at every instance, God who makes cotton burn at contact with fire, and God could equally decide not to make cotton burn. Any other conclusion would deny God's omnipotence.

While these issues might seem arcane, they have powerful implications. The beliefs of the *Asharis* logically lead to a rejection of modern science as something forbidden and harmful because it implies the study of something rejecting the omnipotence of God. Conversely, the Mu'tazilite understanding of Islam would seem to

---

9 A concise overview of Mu'tazilism is in Richard C. Martin et. al., *Defenders of Reason in Islam: Mu'tazilism from Medieval School to Modern Symbol*, London: Oneworld, 1997.

accommodate the idea of man-made laws and popular governance, whereas neither the *Athari* nor the *Ashari* conception of religion would accept anything other than Islamist government. After all, if humans do not have free will and cannot tell right from wrong, how could they be allowed to form governments or make laws independent from divine revelation and divine law?

Chapter three will discuss how Central Asian theologians of the Maturidi school sought to find a middle way between the unabashed rationalism of the Mu'tazilites on one hand and the austere anti-intellectualism of the *Asharis* and the *Athari* literalists on the other. But the key to our understanding of the development of the Muslim world is the fact that the Mu'tazilite school was roundly defeated by the late ninth century and that subsequently, the differences between the Ashari and Maturidi schools of theology were deliberately downplayed – with the Ashari interpretation dominating to such an extent that until recently, scholars' knowledge of Maturidi thought came mainly from Ashari sources.[10] The Mu'tazilite school never completely died: it saw a brief renaissance in the nineteenth century, and there are forces today seeking to revive it.[11] Similarly, Maturidi's thinking survived in the former Ottoman lands but under growing *Ashari* influence.

The fact remains that heavily anti-intellectual forces have dominated Islamic orthodoxy for over a thousand years. Crucially, the development of canonic collections of *hadith* in the ninth century shifted the balance toward the traditionalist position; and the contemporaneous codification of four schools of Sunni jurisprudence gradually led to a push toward consensus on most

---
10 Jeffry R. Halverson, *Theology and Creed in Sunni Islam*, New York: Palgrave MacMillan, 2010, p. 22.
11 Rachid Benzine, *Les Nouveaux Penseurs de l'islam,* Paris: Albin Michel, coll. "L'islam des Lumières," 2004.

outstanding issues of Islamic law, and a gradual effort to stress the commonalities between these schools rather than their differences. It thus came to be accepted that Islamic scholars should now refer (through the process called *taqlid*) to the consensus within their respective schools of jurisprudence rather than engage in independent reasoning known as *ijtihad*. The famous saying was that the "gates of *ijtihad*" had now closed.[12] Importantly, this closing did not apply among the Shi'a.

In the past two centuries, efforts to introduce secular laws, secular education, and secular government have faced vigorous opposition from religious clerics bred in this anti-intellectual tradition. So have efforts to reinterpret Islamic tenets in the light of modern conditions that differ from the medieval conditions when the scholarly consensus was reached. Of course, it is well known that the Christian experience also saw the Church seeking to stifle the development of science, Galileo's travails being the most famous case. It took the renaissance and reformation to force the Church into retreat. That said, science developed in the Christian world because, as scholars have noted, the underlying culture was "uniquely humanistic in the sense that it tolerated, indeed, protected and promoted those heretical and innovative ideas that ran counter to accepted religious and theological teaching."[13] While the Church for long worked to stifle independent inquiry, from the late thirteenth century onward, there was no concerted effort by the church to proscribe the study of philosophy or the use of reason. In the Muslim world, by contrast, a philosopher like Ibn Rushd (known in the West as Averroes) by the twelfth century had to forcefully defend his right to engage in the same study of philosophy and logic. However, these disciplines had been present

---
12 Edward Schacht, *An Introduction to Islamic Law*, Clarendon Press, 1964, p. 70.
13 Toby E. Huff, *The Rise of Early Modern Science: Islam, China and the West*, Cambridge University Press, 2003, p. 11.

in the Muslim world for centuries. In other words, just as the Western mind was opening, the Muslim mind appeared to be closing.[14] In centuries that followed, Europe took quantum leaps in intellectual and technological development and established its domination over the world, while the Muslim world descended into a gradual decline.

Intellectual Currents in the Muslim World

The eighteenth and nineteenth centuries saw a powerful encounter between an expanding West and the Muslim world. Ever more Muslim lands were overrun by European powers. The Ottoman Empire, the seat of the Caliphate since 1517, survived until the first world war, but it began to shrink after its failure to capture Vienna in 1683. It lost territory first in Europe, subsequently in the Middle East, and in addition, had to accept "capitulations" – special privileges granted to Europeans living or working in the Empire. Iran was essentially overrun by Russians from the north and British from the south. Muslim India, the vestiges of the Mughal empire, came under the British Raj. And in the Arab world, European powers advanced following Napoleon's campaign in Egypt and Syria in the late eighteenth century. The British, in particular, took a dominant role, ensconcing themselves in Egypt and the Persian Gulf, while France established colonies in North Africa.

This encounter with the West made the decline of the Muslim world painfully obvious. It came as a shock to Muslims that had been convinced of their religious superiority as the people of the last prophet of God. While elites had been aware of a

---

14 Edward Grant, *The Nature of Natural Philosophy in the Late Middle Ages,* Washington: The Catholic University of America Press, 2010, p. 266. See also discussion in Hillel Ofek, "Why the Arabic World Turned Away from Science," *The New Atlantis*, Winter 2011. (https://www.thenewatlantis.com/docLib/20110605_TNA30Ofek.pdf)

certain decline compared to the glory days of the past, it was the encounter with the West that really showed how significant, in relative terms, that decline really was. The blatant differences in power and technological development between the Christian and Muslim worlds generated a paramount question, succinctly formulated in the title of Bernard Lewis's book: "What went wrong?"

Starting in the nineteenth century, thinkers from the Maghreb to the Indian subcontinent developed bodies of thought in an attempt to bring their homelands out of their decline and compete with the West. The issues these thinkers focused on were, in one scholar's words, "remarkably invariant": they related to the relationship between Islam and the rational, empirical sciences; the relationship between religion and politics, and thus forms of government; national identity and the relationship to the outside world; and the status of women in society.[15]

These thinkers agreed on the questions at hand and also agreed that the Muslim world's traditional approach to learning and politics was obsolete. In particular, they identified the traditional Ulama and their emphasis on the doctrine of *Taqlid* – the imitation or blind following of preceding scholars – as inadequate. However, they diverged strongly in terms of the solution to the problem.

The political ideas that developed were manifold but can be divided into two key camps, which in turn each subdivide into two further groups. The first division concerned the role of religion: where one group gravitated toward nationalism and promoted entirely secular solutions, another advocated for retaining Islam as the key point of reference. The secular camp further divided

---

15 Mansoor Moaddel, *Islamic Modernism, Nationalism, and Fundamentalism: Episode and Discourse*, University of Chicago Press, 2005, p. 7.

into a more liberal group and a more authoritarian one, while the Islamic camp split into modernist and Islamist wings.

Liberal nationalists essentially adopted the Western understanding of the nation and of liberal democracy. They defined the national community in territorial or ethnic terms, ; an issue complicated in the Arab world by the dissonance between emerging national boundaries and the larger Arab nation. The first liberal nationalists emerged in Egypt, the Arab country with the strongest separate national identity, and subsequently in Syria and Iran. Liberal nationalist ideas also arose in Turkey and among Muslims in the Russian empire, as discussed in chapter 4, and British India. But liberal nationalism did not develop a wide enough following and did not prove robust enough to meet the challenges of the colonial and post-colonial periods. More assertive, indeed more authoritarian ideologies were better prepared to wage the struggle against colonialism and to fill the vacuum left in the turmoil of the post-colonial period.

The second group consists of secular authoritarian nationalists. This group is rather broad and can be said to include as diverse forces as the hardline Kemalists in Turkey, the Pahlavi regime in Iran, and Arab socialist movements such as those in Egypt under Nasser, the Baath party in Syria and Iraq, as well as in Algeria. They include traditional right-wing authoritarian forces and those more inclined toward redistributionist economics. It should be noted, though, that Arab socialists tended to be distant from purely Marxist ideological perspectives. Over time, secular nationalism in the Muslim world tended to be dominated by this more authoritarian tendency. There were exceptions: in countries like Turkey, Iran, and Pakistan, a more liberal, democratic version of secular nationalism did gain ground. But everywhere, they struggled mightily to find oxygen when squeezed between advancing Islamist forces and retreating authoritarian nationalists, both of which were skeptical if not hostile to free inquiry and independent intellectual life.[16]

Islamic modernists emerged in particular in Egypt and India in the nineteenth century. They differed from secular nationalists by maintaining Islam as their crucial point of reference. But unlike the Islamists, their ambition was to reform the ossified understanding of Islamic principles in a progressive direction. In particular, their aim was to reconcile Islam with modernity and science. The most radical among them held what Pakistani scientist Pervez Hoodbhoy calls the "reconstructionist" line, which argues that early Islam was "revolutionary, progressive, liberal and rational" while they ascribed the Muslim world's decline into "stultifying rigidity and reactionary dogmatism" to the "triumph of *taqlid* (tradition) over *ijtihad* (innovation)."[17] In India, the principal leading proponents included Sir Syed Ahmed Khan, who proposed to reinterpret the Qur'an allegorically to remove any contradiction with scientific evidence. He suggested a methodology by which any part of scripture that conflicts with scientific fact be interpreted metaphorically rather than literally. Not staying at that, Khan favored the complete abolition of Islamic law.

The most influential modernists did not go that far. In Egypt, the leading voices were Jamaluddin Afghani and, in particular, Muhammad Abduh, who eventually became Chief Mufti of Egypt in the late nineteenth century.[18] Abduh argued, similarly to the reconstructionists, that true Islam was fully compatible with

---

16 Kuru, *Islam, Authoritarianism and Underdevelopment*.
17 Pervez Hoodhboy, *Islam and Science: Religious Orthodoxy and the Battle for Rationality*, London: Zed, 1991, p. 55.
18 Mark Sedgwick, *Muhammad Abduh*, London: Oneworld, 2010.

reason and science. He argued that reason preceded revelation and that the latter came to confirm and clarify the former – and on this basis, that Islam was much more receptive to science and reason than Christianity. Abduh, however, rejected separation of religion and politics, noting that this was unnecessary in Islam because the Muslim world never faced an institution like the papacy with its claims to temporal power.[19] Abduh, however, advocated strongly for the improvement of women's rights, maintained the equality of men and women, and supported women's education. As Chief Mufti, for example, he issued a fatwa declaring the use of face covering for women un-Islamic.

Because they sought to fundamentally reform the traditional Islamic approach to jurisprudence and make it compatible with rationality and science, the Islamic modernists display obvious similarities to the Mu'tazilite tradition a millennium ago. As Mansoor Moaddel puts it, the modernists' approach "was nothing short of an outright rebellion against Islamic orthodoxy, displaying astonishing compatibility with the ideas of the Enlightenment."[20] Confusingly, however, Afghani and Abduh are frequently included among the forebears of the Salafi movement, despite their conclusions being diametrically opposed to those of present-day Salafis. This misunderstanding stems from their single commonality with Salafis: the urge to cut through centuries of the "stultifying rigidity" and imitation (*taqlid*) of the Ulama and to base theology on the Quran itself. Beyond that, the modernists have no commonality with the Salafis because their approach to the Quran and theology more broadly could not be more different,

---

19 Josef Linnhoff, *'Associating' with God in Islamic Thought: A Comparative Study of Muslim Interpretations of Shirq*, Edinburgh: University of Edinburgh Ph.D. Dissertation, 2020, p. 140. https://era.ed.ac.uk/bitstream/handle/1842/36935/Linnhoff2020. pdf?sequence=1&isAllowed=y
20 Moaddel, p. 2.

emphasizing reason and logic the Salafis content themselves with blindly following the letter of the Qur'an as early-day literalists would say, "without asking questions."[21] The confusion stems, in part, from the tendency of some of the modernists to embrace Salafism following the creation of Saudi Arabia in the 1920s. Lebanese scholar Rashid Rida, in particular, started as a follower of Abduh but gradually embraced the Saudi and Salafi tendency as the most promising vehicle for countering western colonialism – a political rather than theological goal.[22]

The modernists continued to have influence, in particular in monarchies like Jordan and Morocco, where Kings with strong traditional Islamic legitimacy have adopted many modernist ideas, as viewed in detail in chapter eight – a model increasingly adopted in the Gulf, with the United Arab Emirates taking the lead. Similarly, Habib Bourguiba and his successor Zine al-Abidine Ben Ali sought to modernize Tunisia by adopting a version of state-controlled Islamic modernism rather than outright secularism, which they judged inapplicable in an Arab context.[23] However, while Islamic modernist ideas have remained influential with a set of intellectuals across the Muslim world, they have more recently struggled to have widespread political influence.

The final group is the Islamists. Unlike the liberal nationalists, authoritarian nationalists, and Islamic modernists, they had no interest in emulating the advances of the West or reconciling Islam with reason, science, and modernity. They rejected

---

21 On the misunderstanding of Abduh as a Salafi see Henri Lauzière, "The Construction of Salafiyya," *International Journal of Middle East Studies*, vol. 42, 2010, pp. 369-89, and Lauzière, "What We Mean Versus What They Mean by 'Salafi': A Reply to Frank Griffel," *Die Welt Des Islams*, vol. 56, 2016, pp. 89-96.
22 Henri Lauzière, *The Making of Salafism*, New York: Columbia University Press. 2016, pp. 60-94.
23 Rory McCarthy, "Re-Thinking Secularism in Post-Independence Tunisia," *Journal of North African Studies*, vol. 19 no 5, 2014, pp. 733-750.

1. The Problem: State And Religion In The Muslim World

modernity and the West entirely, with the possible exception of some technological advances that could prove helpful. (That said, they opposed the scientific spirit that made these technological advances possible in the first place.) To the Islamists, the answer lay solely in a full embrace of Islam as an all-encompassing system governing society, economy, and politics. But unlike the modernists, they viewed this return to Islam very much in the vein of the *mujaddids*, the frequently recurring figures calling for a return to principles and a purging from Islam of alien influences. Such role models included the eleventh-century theologian Abu Hamid al-Ghazali, the thirteenth-century scholar Ibn Taymiyyah, the sixteenth-century Sufi Ahmad Sirhindi, and the eighteenth-century firebrand Muhammad ibn al-Wahhab.

All these figures arose to claim that pure Islam had been corrupted by alien influences, and Muslims needed to revert to the purity of the original creed. Al-Wahhab was particularly influential because of his alliance with a local chieftain in Najd in the center of the Arabian Peninsula, Muhammad bin Saud. This alliance would eventually give birth to the Kingdom of Saudi Arabia, governed by this austere interpretation of Islam, which developed into modern-day Salafism. Focusing on strict textualism, an extremely narrow understanding of monotheism, and a strong antipathy toward Christians, Jews, Sufi mystics, and Shi'as, the Salafis' ideological antecedents go back in a straight line to the thirteenth-century scholar and agitator Ibn Taymiyyah, and further to the jurisprudence of the ninth-century Ahmad bin Hanbal and the original *athari* school. While initially marginal in the Muslim world, it grew to prominence thanks to the legitimacy Saudi Arabia derived from its custody of Islam's holiest sites, the fact that Saudi Arabia escaped colonialism, and the billions of petrodollars Saudi Arabia fed to Salafi movements across the globe.

While Salafism has become increasingly influential, the modern-day ideology of political Islam owes most of its influence to the thinking of several ideologues of the first half of the twentieth century. Among them were Hassan al-Banna, Abu A'la Mawdudi, and Sayyid Qutb. Banna was the son of a Hanbali preacher in the Nile delta, who was attracted to the efforts of Islamic reformers but rejected their interest in modernizing the religion. Instead, he advocated the rejection of Western lifestyles and values and urged a return to the purity of early Islam. He saw this purity in very different terms than Abduh – in a fundamentally traditional and inward-looking way and Islam as an all-encompassing system that governed everything from politics and economics to social questions. Banna's historical role lies in his founding of the Muslim Brotherhood, the *Ikhwan-al Muslimeen*, a society that aimed to liberate the whole Muslim world from foreign domination and to establish a unified state in the Muslim world that would govern based on Islamic law and propagate the message of Islam to mankind. Crucially, he saw violence as an entirely legitimate instrument for the spread of Islam.

Equally significant was Mawdudi, born three years before Banna in Hyderabad. Mawdudi would establish the Jamaat-i-Islami, which remains the primary Islamist organization in South Asia. Mawdudi, who was even more prolific than Banna, similarly saw the decline of Islam as a result of corruption by non-Islamic tendencies and urged a return to purity. A true millenarian, Mawdudi redefined the concept of jihad, previously mainly seen as meaning defensive war, to legitimize a war that would enable Islam to take over the world. He also redefined the Islamic concept of *Jahiliya* (the age of ignorance) from meaning the pre-Islamic Arab society to signifying any place and time where an Islamic state has yet to be implemented. His argument was succinct:

> Islam is a revolutionary ideology and programme which seeks to alter the social order of the whole world and rebuild it in conformity with its own tenets and ideals... Islam wishes to destroy all States and Governments anywhere on the face of the earth which are opposed to the ideology and programme of Islam regardless of the country or the Nation which rules it.[24]

These radical innovations, and the widespread influence they had on Islamist movements, have led Mawdudi to be counted as the perhaps most influential of Islamist thinkers. The only possible rival for this honor is Egyptian Sayyid Qutb, born like Banna in 1906, who only joined the Muslim Brotherhood later in life and became its chief ideologue, driving the movement in a radical and violent direction.

Qutb built on Mawdudi's ideas on *Jahiliyah*, concluding that present-day rulers in Muslim countries were insufficiently pious. He declared true Islam to be, for all purposes, extinct – much like the Saudi Wahhabis, who termed Muslims that disagreed with them unbelievers and offered them to "accept Islam." Qutb thus ruled that the opponents of the Islamist "vanguard" were not Muslims at all and could therefore be excommunicated through *Takfir* and killed – without violating Islamic precepts that prohibit the killing of Muslims. This breathtaking liberty with Islamic

---

24 Abul A'la Maududi, *Jihad in Islam*, Beirut: Holy Quran Publishing House, 1980, p. 5. (http://www.muhammadanism.org/Terrorism/jihah_in_islam/jihad_in_islam.pdf)

precedent laid the ground for the various violent extremist groups in the Muslim world today that declare *takfir* against anyone they perceive as insufficiently Islamic, including, frequently, each other. Another critical contribution of Qutb's was to solidly integrate what Bassam Tibi calls genocidal anti-Semitic ideas borrowed from European fascism with the traditional antipathy toward Jews that had long existed in Islamic thought. Qutb devoted an entire book to the subject.[25] He injects into Islamist ideology the notion of a Jewish world conspiracy, blaming Jews for everything from atheistic materialism to the destruction of the family and urging for their complete annihilation.[26] As Tibi has argued, Qutb and his followers gave "antisemitism a religious imprint and aim to make it look like an authentic part of traditional Islam, not an import from the West."[27]

The Islamist ideology, then, is a thoroughly modern phenomenon inspired by European totalitarian ideologies like communism and fascism. Tibi is correct in making a firm distinction between Islam and Islamism: Islamism's obsession with political domination distinguishes it from traditional religion's focus on deliverance in the afterlife rather than in the present. But as Robert Reilly notes, "the infection of Western millenarian ideological thought from Nietzsche and Marx would not have made Islamism the attraction it is unless Islamism was not also able to claim legitimacy by drawing upon something within the traditions

---

[25] Sayyid Qutb, *Past Trials and Present Tribulations: A Muslim Fundamentalist's View of the Jews*, Pergamon Press, 1987.
[26] Matthias Küntzel, *Jihad and Jew-Hatred: Islamism, Nazism and the Roots of 9/11*, New York: Telos Press, 2007.
[27] Bassam Tibi, *Islamism and Islam*, New Haven: Yale University Press, 2012, p. 57. Also Tibi, "From Sayyid Qutb to Hamas: The Middle East Conflict and the Islamization of Anti-Semitism", ISGAP Working Paper, 2010. (https://isgap.org/wp-content/uploads/2013/08/Tibi.pdf)

of Islam itself."[28] Reilly concludes that this something was the denigration of reason, a commonality shared by *Athari* and *Ashari* thought with fascism and communism. As we have seen, the *Athari* and *Ashari* interpretation of Islam holds that the essential characteristic of God is not his reason but his omnipotence. They maintain that one cannot impose any rationality on God because that would negate his omnipotence. The logical conclusion of this understanding of God is, quite naturally, a preference for compulsion and the use of force over persuasion and dialogue.

This helps explain the appeal of Islamism, a phenomenon similar to the rise of totalitarian ideologies in Europe in the first half of the twentieth century. Compared to rival ideologies, Islamism was initially at a disadvantage, eclipsed by secular ideas. As will be seen below, however, the superior determination and organizing ability of Islamists helped them gradually eclipse other currents of thought.

The Intellectual Hegemony of Islamism

While the main powers of the Muslim world were decidedly secular in the middle of the twentieth century, that would change as Islamism began its rise to prominence in the 1970s.

Turkey was after the short-lived first Azerbaijani republic, the first Muslim country to establish a secular republic. The move meant a clean break from the past, as it carried with it the abolition of both the Sultanate and the Caliphate. Not staying at that, the Constitution proclaimed the country a secular state and replaced the Sharia with European legal codes imported wholesale and integrated into Turkish law. Atatürk adopted the Latin alphabet

---

28 Robert R. Reilly, *The Closing of the Muslim Mind: How Intellectual Suicide Created the Modern Islamist Crisis*, Wilmington, DE: ISI Books, 2011, p. 179.

in place of the Arabic, banned religious orders and seminars, and prohibited the wearing of clerical outfits. In the perhaps most symbolic move, the language of the call for prayer was (for a time) changed from Arabic to Turkish. Unlike communist countries, however, Kemalist Turkey never abolished or repressed religion per se. As Turkish secularists point out, nothing was done to prevent Muslims from fulfilling the demands of their faith. The state, as former President Süleyman Demirel once told this author, only sought to ensure that pious Muslims could not force others to follow their example.[29] But already by 1946, faced with the advance of communism, the state began to relax some of its most ardent secularist policies. By 1950, democratic elections led to the rise of the Democratic Party, which appealed to conservative voters that sought an easing of restrictions on religion. For the next forty years, Turkish politicians walked a tight balance between maintaining the secular state and responding to growing demands in society for a greater role for religion. The 1980 military coup actively sought to infuse religion into Turkish nationalism in an attempt to counter the growth of left-wing ideas. In the 1990s, the mainstream political parties lost legitimacy due to in-fighting, corruption, and mismanagement that culminated in the severe financial crisis of 2000-2001. This prompted the rise of Islamist politics to the fore, with Erdogan's AKP winning a majority in parliament in late 2002.

Iran followed a path that is, in some respects, both similar and very different. Reza Shah Pahlavi, who crowned himself in 1925, similarly sought to modernize and Europeanize Iran. As in Turkey, he sought to change the legal and educational system of

---

29 Author's interview, Ankara, 2007.

the country as well as symbolic matters like dress. The shift in Iran was more gradual and piecemeal in the academic field. The government only gradually took over schooling and allowed the clergy to retain schools of its own, though the government managed to exert control over their curriculum. Similarly, the legal reforms in Iran were more gradual than in Turkey. The government at first set out to standardize Islamic law, then allowed religious courts to maintain authority over family matters while being taken under the control of the ministry of justice. Sharia courts were only abolished and replaced with a European-modeled civil code in 1939, two years before Reza Shahs forced abdication.

But in contrast, symbolic measures were more aggressive than those in Turkey: the laws passed in the 1930s outlawed the wearing of the veil and imposed western dress for both men and women. While Turkish laws also famously sought to change how the population dressed, it never went as far as the Iranian campaigns to forcibly unveil the country's women. Iran's political instability also complicated matters: the abdication of Reza Shah allowed the clergy to make a comeback in the 1940s and 1950s. Then followed the more liberal regime of Mossadegh before its overthrow in 1953, which led to a restoration of authoritarian monarchic rule. While Mohammad Reza Shah continued to seek to modernize and westernize Iran, several factors caused him to fail. One was the ostentatious opulence and arbitrariness of his rule, which differed from the more participatory civilian rule that prevailed in Turkey, with the exception of short-lived military interventions. More importantly, perhaps, Iran's government faced "a fairly institutionalized and financially independent clerical establishment outside the control of the state,"[30] which stands in sharp contrast to Turkey, where the state took control over the country's mosques and religious institutions through the Directorate of religious affairs. Iran never did, and as a result, the religious communities became a center of resistance to the Shah, whereas in Turkey, they were largely under state control until the late 1980s.

Across the Arab world, a secular nationalist ideology with socialist undertones became increasingly powerful in the middle of the twentieth century. While it was no unified movement, it rested on Arab nationalism as its main facet, which its proponents saw as entirely congruent with socialism. Arab socialism, thus, was never Marxist in orientation and was opposed to the communist notion of class struggle. Its main proponent was the Baath party, which emerged in Syria in the 1940s, from where it also spread to Iraq and other Arab states. But Arab socialism gained ground first in Egypt following the Free Officer's coup, which brought Gamal Abdul Nasser to power. While Nasser was not a Baathist, he shared the ideology of secular Arab nationalism coupled with socialist ideas. By the 1960s, Baathists came to power first in Syria and then in Iraq and built authoritarian regimes that remained in power until 2003 in Iraq and continue to rule Syria today. While the regimes that emerged in Algeria and Libya sought to mix Islamic ideas with socialism, the Baath party remained secularist in its orientation. In Egypt, by contrast, secularism receded following Nasser's death, as his successor Anwar Sadat loosened restrictions on the Muslim Brotherhood and other Islamist organizations in the wake of the 1967 defeat in the war

---

30 Birol Baskan, "State Secularization and Religious Resurgence: Diverging Fates of Secularism in Turkey and Iran," *Politics and Religion*, vol. 27, 2014, pp. 28-50.

against Israel. The 1971 constitution cited Sharia as "a source of legislation," which in 1980 was amended to read the "principal" source of legislation. From the 1980s onward, the secular regimes in the Arab world began to ossify and stagnate, both in ideological terms and in their ability to deliver public goods to their citizenry. Meanwhile, Islamist ideology was mounting its challenge to the established order.

As already mentioned, the late 1970s turned out to be the turning point in Islamism's rise to intellectual hegemony in the Muslim world. Islamist movements had begun to organize and gain traction, pushing secular leaders on the defensive and forcing them to make concessions to Islamists. In Egypt, the Brotherhood and the even more radical Gama'a al-Islamiyya expanded their footprint, and Islamist extremists assassinated Anwar Sadat following his decision to make peace with Israel. In Pakistan, the secular Zulfiqar Ali Bhutto began bowing to Islamism, declaring Islam the state religion in 1973. Similarly, in Malaysia, the rather liberal understanding of Islam among the Malay majority gradually shifted in a more radical direction in the 1970s. In Turkey, Necmettin Erbakan created an Islamist political party in 1971 and throughout the decade that followed, formed part of several coalition governments. In all these cases, more secular or liberal elites chose to make concessions to Islamist sentiment to co-opt the Islamic movement and prevent more radical Islamists from gaining ground. In all cases, this strategy failed: concessions only whetted the appetite of Islamists for further Islamization.

The end of the 1970s was a turning point. The rise of Khomeini and the Iranian revolution was undoubtedly the first and most dramatic shift. Khomeini's unorthodox interpretation of

Islamic government[31] broke with traditional Shi'a theology. But it showed that the creation of an Islamic state was not a pipe dream: it could happen in real life. This provided enormous inspiration to Islamist movements in the Sunni world: both the Muslim Brotherhood and the Turkish *Milli Görüs* movement, previously rather prejudiced against the Shi'a, developed a considerably more pro-Iranian stance.

The second was the siege of the Grand Mosque in Mecca by religious radicals, whose importance in Saudi Arabia's exportation of Salafism remains poorly understood. The event is most eloquently explained in Yaroslav Trofimov's 2008 book, *The Siege of Mecca*.[32] To obtain the Ulama's approval for their effort to repress the siege, the Saudi monarchy was forced to accept many of the demands of the ultra-orthodox clergy – and, in particular, give it a free hand in spreading Salafi ideology across the globe.

Third, the 1980 Turkish military coup purposefully opened the floodgates for the Islamization of society by ushering in the Turkish-Islamic synthesis, an idea that would form the background for the meteoric rise of political Islam in Turkey in the 1980s and 1990s.[33] This notion was employed to shore up Turkish nationalism with greater Islamic content to fend off the growing leftist mobilization among Turkey's urban youth. It led the Turkish state to begin sponsoring an Islamic revival through greater Islamic content in education and a laxer attitude toward Islamist mobilization in society. This included the growing

---

31 Hamid Dabashi, *Theology of Discontent: The Ideological foundation of the Islamic Revolution in Iran*, London: Routledge, 2017; Nikki Keddie, *Iran and the Muslim World: Revolution and Resistance*, New York: NYU Press, 1995.
32 Yaroslav Trofimov, *The Siege of Mecca: The 1979 Uprising at Islam's Holiest Shrine*, New York: Random House, 2008; Behlül Özkan, "The Cold-War Era Origins of Islamism in Turkey and Its Rise to Power," *Current Trends in Islamist Ideology*, November 2017.
33 Banu Eligür, *The Mobilization of Political Islam in Turkey*, New York: Cambridge University Press, 2010, pp. 85-135.

presence of Saudi-financed publishing houses. Yet, in Western academic and policy thinking, this episode remains largely neglected, hidden behind the mistaken notion of the Turkish army as a bastion of secularism. This only became the case in the 1990s when the Turkish military felt it had lost control over the Islamist movement and sought to repress it.

Fourth and finally, the rise of Zia ul-Haq in Pakistan following his military coup in 1978 formed the backdrop for the Islamization of that country, as he sought to implement full Sharia law. It was also a key step without which the international mobilization of *mujahideen* for the war in Afghanistan could not have happened. Indeed, the Afghan resistance to the Soviet occupation was initially relatively moderate and traditional. It was mainly because of Pakistan's insistence, with Saudi and American funding, that the bulk of the resources and fighters for the resistance shifted in a radical Islamist direction.

It is noteworthy that, at least in the cases of Turkey, Pakistan, and Afghanistan, American foreign policy inadvertently contributed to the rise of radical Islamism. American planners appear to have seen politicized Islam as a workable bulwark against Communism.[34] While this has evaded mainstream analysis, it was implicitly acknowledged by President Carter's late National Security Advisor Zbigniew Brzezinski when asked by a French journalist whether it had been a smart move to support Islamists that would subsequently cause so much trouble. "What is more important in a world-historical perspective – the Taliban or the

---

34 Robert Dreyfuss, *Devil's Game: How the United States Helped Unleash Fundamentalist Islam*, New York: Henry Holt, 2005; John Cooley, *Unholy Wars: Afghanistan, America and International Terrorism*, London: Pluto Press, 1999.

fall of the Soviet Empire; a few frantic Muslims or the liberation of central Europe and the end of the Cold War?"[35]

In the decades that followed, these "frantic Muslims" advanced everywhere. The more extreme versions founded Al Qaeda, which sought to take the battle directly to the "far enemy," the United States, and later gave birth to ISIS. With the same end goal but abstaining – for now – from the use of violence was Hizb-ut-Tahrir, a global movement that emerged in Lebanon in the 1950 but is headquartered in London. It spread rapidly among educated youth in many Muslims countries and the Muslim diaspora in the West. In Sudan, an Islamist regime emerged in the late 1980s, which supported militant Islamist causes far and wide. In Egypt, Syria, and Jordan, the Muslim Brotherhood emerged as the key opposition movement to the established regime. In the Palestinian territories, the formerly leftist ideology of the Palestinian resistance to Israeli rule gave way to an increasingly Islamized agenda, Hamas being the most visible beneficiary of this shift. In Algeria, Islamist extremists failed to gain power in 1991 and instead waged a bloody civil war against the military-backed government that lasted for a decade. In Turkey, Islamists won power in a 2002 election under the guise of a moderate, "Islamic conservative" movement but gradually reverted to their ideological origins once they had consolidated power. As far away as Indonesia, the traditionally liberal Islam practiced in the archipelago began to give way to a Middle Eastern-inspired, more orthodox interpretation of Islam with greater political ambitions.

The list goes on. But the point is the following: in the past several decades, Islamism has emerged as the dominant political ideology in the Muslim world, surpassing and outmaneuvering

---
35 *Le Nouvel Observateur*, 15-21 January 1998, p. 76.

1. The Problem: State And Religion In The Muslim World

Islamic modernism and all secular ideologies. The 2011 Arab upheavals were symptomatic of this trend: while liberal youth started the Egyptian revolution, it was the Muslim Brotherhood that possessed the organizational wherewithal to emerge victorious in elections, and soon sought to take this opportunity to seize power for good. Where civil confrontation deteriorated into civil war, as in Syria or Libya, more moderate groups rapidly became irrelevant, and power shifted to the more extremist, militant movements.

> Underlying this development is the fact that the urge for a secular government has never been as strong in the Muslim world as among Christians. As Lewis notes, the Muslim world had nothing remotely comparable with such epoch-making Christian events as the Schism of Photius, the Reformation, the Holy Office of the Inquisition, and the bloody religious wars of the sixteenth and seventeenth centuries, which almost compelled the Christians to secularize their states and societies. . . Muslims encountered no such problem and therefore required no such answer.[36]

Furthermore, religious reformation preceded the introduction of secularism in the Christian world – a process that appears inversed in the Muslim world.[37] And finally, the fact that the introduction of secular ideas coincided with colonial and post-colonial regimes undermined public receptivity to them.[38]

---
36 Lewis, *What Went Wrong?* p. 115-116.
37 Abdou Filali-Ansary, "The Challenge of Secularization", in Larry Diamond, Marc Plattner and Daniel Brumberg, eds., *Islam and Democracy in the Middle East*, Baltimore: Johns Hopkins University Press, 2003, 232-237.
38 Hashemi, *Islam, Secularism and Liberal Democracy*, pp. 133-170.

Implications of the Islamist Hegemony

The merger of politics and religion has serious implications for both realms. The implications for religion are not our primary concern here. Let it be noted that the mixing of religion and politics has a strong corruptive tendency on religion itself, as the experience of Iran and, more recently, Turkey both attest to.[39] The implications of the marriage of religion and politics in broader Muslim society are nevertheless central to this book's focus on Central Asian and Azerbaijani secularism. The failure to adopt secular government in most of the Muslim world mirrors the rejection of rationality and undermines the emergence of science and the pursuit of knowledge. This, in turn, is one key reason why Muslim societies have proven unable to compete in a world economy that puts a premium precisely on knowledge. Finally, the political implications of the fusion of religion and politics condemns states to continued illiberalism and authoritarianism while also complicating their ability to interact with the world.

The starting point is epistemological. What schools teach children to be legitimate sources of knowledge will determine the basis of the people's education. That, in turn, determines a society's outlook on life and the filter through which it interprets events. Islamists decry the West's excessive focus on reason and experience as sources of knowledge at the expense of divine revelation. The influential scholar Syed Hossein Nasr of George Washington University, for example, rejects the Islamic modernists' notion that Islam and science are compatible: even devout scientists "cannot

---

[39] The Iranian Islamist regime has led to a decrease in religious observance in the country, and to the perhaps strongest secularist movement in the Muslim world. Similarly, the first Sunni country to go through an Islamist revolution is also the first in modern times to officially separate religion from politics and embrace secularism – a condemnation of religious politics if any. And finally, in Turkey, the more President Erdogan tries to force Islam on the people, the more he faces popular resistance.

prevent their activity from ... from emptying the Islamic intellectual universe of its contents unless this science is shorn away from its secular and humanistic matrix."[40] The problem for the Islamists, then, appears to be modern science's reliance on empirical and rational sources of knowledge at the expense of divine revelation, which Nasr claims to be superior.

In the same vein, Ahmet Davutoglu, a leading Islamist intellectual before serving as Turkey's Foreign Minister and Prime Minister, is illustrative in this regard, not least because he supposedly hails from a "moderate" Islamist tradition. Davutoglu claims that Western civilization suffers from an "acute crisis" exactly because of its "modernist paradigm" that imposes the "peripherality of revelation."[41] In Davutoglu's view, the problem of the West is that it distinguishes between reason and experience on one hand and revelation on the other. It relegates revelation to the sidelines, emphasizing only the validity of reason and experience. He hails, instead, the Islamic concept of "tawhid," "the unity of truth and the unity of life which provides a strong internal consistency."[42]

Davutoglu, at least, allowed that reason can be an acceptable source of knowledge, which is more than can be said for more extreme currents of Islamism that reject it outright. Pakistani physicist Hoodbhoy has detailed in excruciating detail the consequences, when implemented, of the Islamist approach to life. As Hoodbhoy documents, during Zia's Islamization efforts, Islamists complained that weather forecasts contradicted God's omnipotence. How could scientists pretend to know what the

---

[40] Quoted in Hoodbhoy, p. 70.
[41] Ahmet Davutoglu, *Civilizational Transformation and the Muslim World*, Kuala Lumpur, 1994, p. 13-14.
[42] Ahmet Davutoğlu, *Alternative Paradigms: the Impact of Islamic and Western Weltanschauungs on Political Theory* (Lanham, Md.: University Press of America, 1993), p. 195.

weather would be in the future since God could decide something completely different? As a result, weather forecasting was actually banned for some time before practical necessity dictated it be discretely restored.[43] This is only one of the most spectacular and patently absurd consequences of Islamist ideology, and there are many more.

More broadly, the problem with Islamism is the refusal to accept the primacy of reason and the insistence instead on a literalist reading of scripture. A metaphorical reading of scripture would allow a scientific worldview to coexist with religion. But a literalist one does not: if there is something in scripture that conflicts with scientific evidence – such as Jesus turning water into wine, Moses parting the red sea, or Muhammad's night journey to Jerusalem – the literalist view leads to the suppression of science, which would contradict revelation. As we have seen, precisely because pursuit of science could lead human beings to adopt views that are incompatible with revelation, the literalist approach discourages humans from engaging in science at all unless scientific pursuits are under close Islamic supervision.

The rejection of rationality profoundly affects society's understanding of cause and effect.[44] In a society where a premium is put on rationality, people will seek rational explanations for events and pursue rational solutions to problems. But if people are taught to reject rationality, the result will be a tendency toward fatalism, superstition, and conspiracy. All of these problems are visible in the Muslim world today.

Observers have long remarked on the prevalence of fatalism in large parts of the Muslim world, coupled with widespread

---

43 Hoodbhoy, *Islam and Science*, p. 47.
44 Reilly, *The Closing of the Muslim Mind*, p. 1.

belief in predestination.⁴⁵ While Pew research surveys found that an average of ca. 40 percent of Western Europeans and two-thirds of East Europeans believed in fate, the figure in most Muslim-majority countries was over 90 percent.⁴⁶ In recent years, the practical implications of such attitudes have led scholars to emphasize the need for education to reduce "fatalistic attitudes" toward earthquake preparedness and road accidents.⁴⁷ Western societies also have their share of fatalism, but the openness to reason has gradually allowed educational efforts to develop a sense of individual responsibility. Similarly, belief in superstition continues to be widespread where rationality is not the foundation of knowledge. While superstition is present in every civilization, an epistemology that emphasizes rationality will help push superstition to the fringes, whereas one that rejects rationality will have a much harder challenge to root it out.

The same goes for conspiracism. As the popularity of trutherism, birtherism, and theories of election fraud in the United States indicates, a propensity toward conspiracy theory as an explanation exists in all societies. But it has long been clear that belief in conspiracy is more prevalent in the Middle East than in many other societies.⁴⁸ For example, while up to a third of Americans have

---

45 Eg. Edmund Power, "Fatalism and Free Will in Islam," *Studies: and Irish Quarterly Review*, vol. 2 no. 5, 1913; Helmer Ringgren, "Islamic Fatalism," in Ringgren, ed., *Fatalistic Beliefs in Religion, Folklore, and Literature*, Stockholm: Almqvist and Wiksell, 1967, pp. 52-62.
46 Pew Research Center, "Eastern and Western Europeans Differ on Importance of Religion, Views of Minorities, and Key Social Issues," October 29, 2018 (https://www.pewforum.org/2018/10/29/eastern-and-western-europeans-differ-on-importance-of-religion-views-of-minorities-and-key-social-issues/); Pew Research Center, *The World's Muslims: Unity and Diversity*, Aug. 9, 2012, p. 41. (https://www.pewforum.org/2012/08/09/the-worlds-muslims-unity-and-diversity-executive-summary/)
47 Hoda Baytiyeh and Mohamad K. Naja, "Can education reduce Middle Eastern fatalistic attitude regarding earthquake disasters?" Disaster Prevention and Management, vol. 23 no. 4, 2014; Ahsan Ul Haq Kayani, Mark King, and Judy Fleiter, "Fatalism and Road Safety in Developing Countries, with a Focus on Pakistan," *Journal of the Australasian College of Road Safety*, vol. 22 no. 2, 2011, pp. 41-47.
48 Daniel Pipes, *The Hidden Hand: Middle East Fears of Conspiracy*, New York: St. Martin-Griffin, 1998.

expressed belief that the U.S. Government had advance warning of the 9/11 attacks, and up to ten percent thought it was complicit in them, in a survey of Egypt and Saudi Arabia, over half of respondents believed Jews were behind the attacks, and over two-thirds thought the U.S. had actively helped the Islamic State take power in Syria and Iraq.[49] The widespread belief in conspiracy directly relates to the rejection of reason. If citizens are not led to seek evidence for their beliefs or to challenge irrational explanations, the natural human propensity toward conspiracy theories will remain unchecked.

The prevalence of conspiracism impedes the development of society. Problems are sourced to evil actors over whom one has no influence, instead of concrete causes that have rational solutions. They also have strongly harmful consequences, most prominently for minorities – typically Jews, but also minorities like Yezidis, Copts, and Alevis – that are exposed to violence and death as a result of conspiracy theories they are blamed for being part of.

The resistance toward the pursuit of intellectual freedom has noticeable and measurable effects on levels of education, knowledge, and economic development. While the most developed western countries spend three to four percent of their GDP on research and development, Muslim-majority countries on average spend far below one percent. Only Malaysia and Turkey spend over one percent of GDP, and aside from them, only the UAE and several North African countries surpass half a percent of GDP.[50] No university in any Muslim country is included in the top 200

---

49 Brenda Nyhan and Thomas Zeitzoff, "Conspiracy and Misperception Belief in the Middle East and North Africa," *Journal of Politics*, vol. 80 no. 4, 2018.
50 OECD, *Gross Spending on R&D*, 2019.

1. The Problem: State And Religion In The Muslim World

universities ranked worldwide.[51] Pervez Hoodbhoy documents in detail the impediments put by religious figures and Islamist politicians against the pursuit of science, including efforts to force all science into an Islamic mold. Naturally, there has been a push to remove from curricula scientific findings that appear to contradict literalist readings of the Quran – for example, the Turkish Islamist government in 2017 stopped teaching the theory of evolution in schools.[52]

The reluctance to support science is one problem; but in most Muslim-majority countries, there is an acceptance of the need to engage in the "hard sciences" in order to be economically competitive. A perhaps more serious underlying problem is the deeper antagonism toward the intellectual freedom that provides the environment in which scientific advances emerge. As Osama and Ghuessoum observe in a survey of science in the Muslim world, the publication of scientific papers increased noticeably from the late 1990s to the late 2000s, particularly in Turkey, Malaysia, Iran, Saudi Arabia, and Pakistan, where governments have invested in education to boost economic development. They have yet to reach high levels of quality, at least if ranked by citation indices: with the exception of Turkish and Iranian-based scholars, few scholars in Muslim countries have high levels of citations. The survey authors emphasize the absence of "broad, liberal, holistic education in science" and particularly identify that the "weakness in the teaching of science in the Muslim world is the absence of philosophy and even history of science from the university curricula."[53]

[51] Times Higher Education, *World University Rankings 2020*, at www.timeshighereducation.com.
[52] Tuvan Gümrükçü, "Turkey to Stop Teaching Evolution Theory in High Schools: Education Board," *Reuters*, June 23, 2017.
[53] Athar Osama and Nidal Ghuessoum, "The Dark Age of the Muslim World," *MIT Technology Review*, 2016.

This is eerily reminiscent of Bernard Lewis's analysis of Muslim translation efforts in the medieval era. As Lewis notes, the "criterion of choice was usefulness", leading to translation of works on medicine, hard sciences, and philosophy, "which at the time was considered useful" – but no works of "literature of any kind."[54] As Lewis puts it, "this was clearly a cultural rejection: you take what is useful from the infidel" but not their "absurd ideas .. inferior literature ... or meaningless history."[55] The UNDP's successive reports on Arab human development have shown the lack of interest in outside knowledge. In a much-cited conclusion, the 2002 report found that:

> The Arab world translates about 330 books annually, one-fifth of the number that Greece translates. The cumulative total of translated books since Caliph Maa'moun's time (the ninth century) is about 100,000, almost the average that Spain translates in one year.[56]

It is difficult to disagree with Saudi critic Turki al-Hamad, who cautioned that the Arab approach of seeking only to "adopt the good things [from the West] and ignore the bad" does not work: "these are all products of a certain philosophy, a certain way of thinking. If you adopt the product but ignore the producer – you have a problem."[57]

The effect of Islamism on political systems and international

---

54 Lewis, *What Went Wrong?*
55 *Ibid.*
56 United Nations Development Program, *Arab Human Development Report 2002: Creating Opportunities for Future Generations*, p. 78
57 "Reformist Saudi Intellectual Turki al-Hamad: I'm 'Pessimistic' About the Possibility of Making Real Changes", MEMRI Special Dispatch no. 1868, April 9, 2008. (https://www.memri.org/reports/reformist-saudi-intellectual-turki-al-hamad-im-pessimistic-about-possibility-making-real)

relations is so clearly harmful that it merits only a brief discussion. The insistence of the extremist groups on the use of force, and their urge to declare other Muslim infidels, has been a leading cause of the descent of many Near Eastern countries into civil war and sectarian strife. The radicalization of the Afghan resistance led directly to the country's civil war in the 1990s and the rise of the Taliban. More recently, Iraq, Syria, Yemen, and Libya have followed suit, with considerable sectarian violence in many of these conflicts. Where Islamists have secured power – as in Iran or Pakistan in the 1980s – their application of Sharia has inevitably caused problems. Aside from the human rights issues involved, rulers applied Islamic law as understood by their specific sect, which did not coincide with that of the Sunni minority in Iran or the Shi'a in Pakistan. Of course, fully developed Islamist regimes like those in Iran and Sudan also became hosts to and sponsors of like-minded groupings abroad, thereby destabilizing entire regions.

The problem, however, goes beyond the extremists. Western observers are preoccupied with whether Islamist movements are prone to violence or not, which resulted, in the aftermath of September 11, in an embrace of a purported "moderate" Islamism as a counterweight to extremism. The self-proclaimed moderates reject the most extreme ideologies within political Islamism and use the rhetoric of democracy and human rights to advance their cause in the face of authoritarian regimes they seek to replace. Westerners who had come to identify authoritarian rulers as the main problem of Middle Eastern societies pinned great hope on this moderate Islamism, which appeared to be popular and democratic in nature. But these Islamist movements have shown a tendency to support the *mechanism* of democracy to achieve power, and to the extent they have embraced democratic ideas, it appears limited to a majoritarian approach that ignores the liberal constitutionalism that calls for foundations of functioning democracy such as checks and balances and the respect for minority rights. Seeing themselves as representatives of a pious majority that others should obey, they are at best akin to the "illiberal democrats" identified by Fareed Zakaria.[58] In practice, they remain fundamentally undemocratic. At the very basic level, their faith in the notion that the people, rather than God, is the source of sovereignty and the legitimacy of a government appears questionable.

Furthermore, moderate Islamists have a pronounced tendency to excuse, or at best fail to condemn, the extremists in their midst. The Egyptian Muslim Brotherhood and Turkey's Justice and Development Party both, once in government, showed a willingness to interact with much more radical movements, be it Hamas or jihadi groups in Syria, the Sinai, or Libya. Simply put, they do not seem to share the Western preoccupation for drawing a red line between groups that use violence and those that do not. Moreover, they adopted a strongly illiberal approach to the rights of those they do not consider representatives of the "majority" of Muslims, be they Copts in Egypt, Alevis in Turkey, or secularists in general. As Turkish scholar Ihsan Dağı has argued, this is a form of "postmodern authoritarianism'" that "is not justified by a reference to the 'text' but to the 'people' and its 'will,'" and is "'democratic and representative' in justification and process but authoritarian in content and outcome."[59]

---

58 Fareed Zakaria, *The Future of Freedom: Illiberal Democracy at Home and Abroad*, New York: W.W. Norton, 2003.
59 Ihsan Dağı, "Pursuing Islamism with Democracy" *Today's Zaman*, December 9, 2012. (http://www.thefreelibrary.com/Pursuing+Islamism+with+democracy.-a0311455555)

1. The Problem: State And Religion In The Muslim World

Finally, Islamist regimes and movements have had profound destabilizing effects on regional and international stability. The role of Iran and Sudan in hosting international terrorism is well-known, as are the earlier Saudi efforts to propagate Salafi ideology around the globe and Pakistan's effort to use Islamist extremists against Indian interests in Kashmir and Afghanistan. With the exception of Iran, sponsors of extremist organizations gradually lost control over their offspring. This led in the Pakistani case to frantic efforts to reassert control over radicals while working to physically eliminate those groups that appeared uncontrollable. In the Saudi case, there seems to have been a full U-turn, with a younger leadership now embracing the notion of "moderate Islam" and engaging in social reforms, while closing the spigot to Salafi groups abroad.[60]

But as then-U.S. National Security Advisor General H.R. McMaster stated in 2017, Turkey and Qatar appear to have replaced Saudi Arabia as the most prominent sponsors of radical Islamist ideology.[61] In the complex geopolitics of the Middle East, those two countries have led a faction motivated by political Islamism and stand in opposition both to the conservative *status quo* alliance led by Saudi Arabia, the UAE, and Egypt and to an Iranian-led alignment that includes the Syrian regime and a host of paramilitary forces in countries like Lebanon, Iraq, and Yemen. While it is clear that steps taken by the status quo bloc in conflicts like Yemen and Libya have contributed to the destabilization of those countries, these moves have essentially been defensive, an

---

[60] Hassan Hassan, "The 'Conscious Uncoupling' of Wahhabism and Saudi Arabia," *New Lines*, February 22, 2022. (https://newlinesmag.com/argument/the-conscious-uncoupling-of-wahhabism-and-saudi-arabia/)

[61] Joyce Karam, "US National Security Adviser: Qatar and Turkey are New Sponsors of Radical Ideology," *The National*, December 13, 2017.

attempt to thwart the efforts by either the Shi'a Islamist bloc (in Yemen) or the Sunni Islamist bloc (in Libya) to assert control over those countries.

Will Islamism Prevail?

The ideology of political Islam has been at the center of world politics for over 40 years. Islamists have never looked back from their advances in the late 1970s. In a sense, they have been wildly successful: from Morocco in the west to Pakistan in the east, an unbroken chain of countries proclaiming Islam to be the religion of the state. Even in countries like Turkey, which maintains a nominally secular government, Islamists established themselves as the dominant political force, as they have sought to do in Malaysia and Indonesia.

The Arab upheavals of 2011 led Islamists to advance further. They seized power in Egypt and sought to do the same in Tunisia, Syria, Libya, and Yemen. Results differed: they were beaten back in Egypt, integrated into the political system in Tunisia, and helped start civil wars in the other three states. But everywhere, the language of political Islam continued to set the agenda across the Muslim world.

As this chapter has noted, it was not always this way. And if one takes a longer view, it is by no means clear that Islamism's march to success will continue unhindered. Quite to the contrary, there are numerous indications that they may have overplayed their hand, just as other radical ideologies before them. Perhaps the ravages of the Islamic State were a wake-up call. Perhaps Muslims got tired of the sectarian violence perpetrated in their religion's name. Possibly the failure of Islamists to live up to their rhetoric of purity once in power is beginning to do them in. But there is now a growing list of developments that suggest the tables have been turned and that Islamists are on the defensive.

First among these is the defeat, for the time being, of the Muslim Brotherhood. On the ascendant a decade ago, this the oldest and most archetypical Islamist organization appeared on the cusp of securing control over Egypt, as well as other Arab states, in the aftermath of the 2011 upheavals. But it was not to be: Despite ardent Turkish and Qatari backing, the Brotherhood's rise and missteps led to a strong popular movement against it in Egypt and, eventually, a military intervention that proceeded to severely repress the movement. This power grab also mobilized a strong reaction across the region, led by the UAE and supported by Saudi Arabia, which had historically been relatively friendly to the Brotherhood. While the appropriateness of the methods used by Arab rulers to suppress the Brotherhood can be the subject of much debate, it remains a fact that the movement itself is a shadow of its old self.

Equally important is the reform process in Saudi Arabia. That country is crucial because it is home to Islam's holiest sites and because it played a key role in bankrolling extremist Islamism across the world. But the Kingdom changed its approach – first slowly, when it found itself targeted by the likes of Osama bin Laden, and more recently in a more dramatic fashion. The shortcomings – indeed, recklessness – of Saudi Crown Prince Mohammed bin Salman have been the subject of much commentary. But while those are certainly clear, it is also a fact that he has presided over a wave of liberal reforms in the social sphere that are unprecedented and would have been unthinkable a decade ago. Not only do women now drive cars, the religious police have been abolished, and women are, at least in modern urban areas, no longer forced to cover their heads and faces. The Crown Prince has denounced the ultra-conservatism of the past and proclaimed to return Saudi Arabia to "moderate" Islam. Departing from decades of anti-Semitic propaganda, one of Saudi Arabia's top clerics recently visited Auschwitz and has spoken of religious coexistence. This shift in Saudi Arabia also paved the way for the UAE, Bahrain, and Morocco to normalize their relationship with Israel formally.

Further north, one of the main victories of Islamism was the gradual dismantling of Turkey's secular regime. Recep Tayyip Erdogan, with roots in Turkey's Islamist movement, has worked to make Turkey's state and society more Islamic while making support for the Muslim Brotherhood a keystone of Turkish foreign policy. Erdogan has repeatedly vowed to raise "pious generations." Among many other steps, he has made Turkey's education system more Islamic and built an enormous religious bureaucracy. But he has failed. Opinion polls show that Turks, and particularly younger Turks, are distinctively more secular and less observant of Islamic mores than their parents' generation. Compared to 2008, for example, fewer Turks define themselves as religious conservatives, fast during Ramadan, or require their children to marry someone of the same religion. It is no wonder that in domestic politics, Erdogan has been forced to tone down his Islamism and instead adopt more nationalist rhetoric to maintain public support.

The 2020 Abrahamic accords are another telling example. While it had long been known that many Gulf Arab states maintained relations with Israel because of their common antipathy toward Iran, these ties had been largely covert because Arab rulers feared Islamists would successfully mobilize the public against them. Clearly, rulers in the United Arab Emirates and Bahrain no longer saw this as a major concern. Even in Saudi Arabia, the government has spoken favorably of the accords. Thus far, Islamist leaders in Turkey, Iran, and the Muslim Brotherhood have raged against the Accords; but the famed "Arab street" appears to have met them with a shrug.

Last but not least was the stunning announcement in early September 2020 that Sudan had resolved to separate religion from the state and become a secular state. This development was momentous: not only did Sudan play a largely overlooked role in the spread of Islamism, turning into a bastion of radical Islam following a 1989 coup d'état – Americans may recall the country hosted Osama bin Laden for several years. But while it has been common for formerly secular states in the Muslim world to proclaim Islam a state religion, Sudan is the first case of a country that *reversed* this decision, essentially concluding that the mixing of religion and politics was the wrong way to go.

It is, of course, too early to proclaim the demise of the Islamist ideology. It remains the most powerful intellectual movement in the Muslim world and remains on the offensive in countries like Indonesia. But that is the case mainly because of the weakness of its rivals and because of Islamists' willingness to intimidate and kill their detractors.

What if Muslims tire of Islamism and begin to identify the fusion of religion and politics as a key problem that needs to be overcome? It is by no means certain that this will happen. After all, it took Europe centuries of sectarian warfare to arrive at this conclusion. And as already discussed, Islamic history, in general, did not provide, thus far, as powerful an argument for the separation of religion and politics as was the case in Christian Europe. Still, there is no reason for the Muslim world to make the same mistakes the Christian world did for as long a period. If, indeed, the balance has begun to shift, what are the models from which Muslim-majority countries could learn as they seek to separate religion and politics? In the not-too-distant past, Kemalist Turkey would have served as the primary model. But Kemalism proved unable to adapt itself to the changes of the twenty-first century and has given way to Erdogan's rule. As a result, there is no prominent successful secular model in the Muslim world today. Of course, Muslims could look at past examples and learn from them – be it to bring back Muhammad Abduh's liberal ideas, the socialism of Nasser, or Kemalist nationalism. As will be seen, they could opt to emulate models that embrace moderation of religion but not full secularism – with Indonesia, Jordan, Morocco, and the UAE providing relatively successful models.

But as this book will show, there is a distinct model of secular statehood emerging in Central Asia and Azerbaijan. These states, now independent for over three decades, have steadfastly sought to buck the trend in the Muslim world and build a modern form of secular statehood. This model is hardly recognized as such: it is seldom viewed as a cohesive model and is derided both as authoritarian and dependent on the atheist Soviet legacy. But it is also attracting greater interest as countries like Azerbaijan, Kazakhstan, and Uzbekistan develop their relations with the rest of the world and seek to improve and modernize their understanding of secular government. No one has sought to examine whether this is indeed a model or whether it has the potential of developing into one. That is the task of the remainder of this volume.

2. THE STATE AND RELIGION:
Models of Interaction

WHEN THE SOVIET UNION BROKE UP IN 1991, leaders of newly independent countries faced numerous challenges in the creation of new states. This included models of political and economic governance. But it also included more fundamental issues of the form of nationhood these states embraced, as well as the relationship between religion and the state. Everywhere, Soviet-era atheism was discarded. But remarkably, leaders in all six Muslim-majority states – Azerbaijan, Kazakhstan, Kyrgyzstan, Tajikistan, Turkmenistan, and Uzbekistan – opted to adopt a secular model for their emerging states. And in the thirty years that have passed, all have maintained this course, in several cases doubling down on it. In fact, these Muslim-majority states have been less acceptant of religious influence on state institutions than Christian-majority states such as Armenia and Georgia. But having established that the state should be secular did not amount to a stroke of magic: what would this mean in practice? Far from describing a specific form of government, in different countries, the term secularism is interpreted to mean widely divergent state approaches to religion.

While most industrialized states and many developing nations have adopted a secular form of governance, the forms of relations between the government and religion take many different shapes. At its heart, the key question is what influence religious institutions and beliefs should have on the state and society. Most definitions of secular government focus on two principles: separation and neutrality. In other words, the separation of the state from religious institutions and the state's neutrality toward religious denominations. In practice, however, the reasons why states resolve to regulate the domain of religion diverge. One is to maintain the state's autonomy *from* religious institutions; another is to promote the freedom of conscience for all believers irrespective of denomination.

Because definitions of secularism diverge, as do the goals of its promoters, misunderstandings often arise. For Americans, secularism means that the state is neutral toward all religions, following the American Constitution's First Amendment's proclamation that Congress "shall make no law respecting an establishment of religion, or prohibiting the free exercise thereof." But in France, *laïcité* emphasizes the protection of state and society from the influence of religious institutions. Proponents of French *laïcité* question whether America is secular at all, pointing to the influence of religious organizations on American politics. And in Turkey, the archetypical secular state in the Muslim world, at least until recently, defenders of *laiklik* ensured that the state controlled organized religion to preserve the secular nature of the country's laws and education. They see both America and France as dangerously permissive toward politicized religion. They blame Americans and Europeans for having supported, in the name of democracy, the takeover of the state by Recep Tayyip

Erdoğan's Islamists. Americans would retort that France's secularism "became fundamentalist"[1] and that Turkey's is authoritarian. Clearly, these three states do not have the same understanding of secularism.[2] Neither do the constitutional monarchies in Europe. These all had an established state religion, but gradually reformed their government toward increasing separation between the state and religion, while vestiges of this past remain, for example, the British and Swedish requirement that the Monarch be of the protestant faith.

This chapter will begin with a brief overview of the development of state-religion relations globally to seek to extract, on a more conceptual level, the different models – or in Weberian parlance, ideal types – of state approaches to religion.

The Emergence of Freedom of Conscience and Separation of Church and State

Western observers frequently see the development of freedom of conscience and secular government as a specific Western invention, spurred by the European wars over the reformation that, by sheer exhaustion, led to the development of religious toleration and, eventually, secular governance. But centuries before this happened, the Mongol Empire fiercely enforced the freedom of religion, allowing the coexistence of Christians, Muslims, Manicheans, and Buddhists, among others, in the lands it controlled.[3] And while the Ottoman Empire relegated Jews and Christians to the status of second-class citizens, from the mid-fifteenth century, the Millet

---
1 Eg. Robert Zaretsky, "How French Secularism Became Fundamentalist," *Foreign Policy*, April 7, 2016. (https://foreignpolicy.com/2016/04/07/the-battle-for-the-french-secular-soul-laicite-charlie-hebdo/)
2 Ahmet Kuru, *Secularism and State Policies toward Religion: The United States, France, and Turkey*, Cambridge: Cambridge University Press, 2009.
3 Jack Weatherford, *Genghis Khan and the Quest for God: How the World's Greatest Conqueror Gave Us Religious Freedom* (New York: Viking, 2016).

system recognized their autonomy in internal communal affairs – a considerable contrast to most of Europe, where proponents of freedom of conscience only went so far as to urge toleration of other Christian denominations. The idea of officially recognizing the existence of other religious traditions remained anathema almost everywhere.

Still, the modern understanding of the separation of church and state developed in tandem with the development of the nation-state in the Western world. Before the reformation, the relationship between the state and religion was unproblematic: the Catholic Church was established across western Europe and wielded enormous power over both rulers and societies. This did not mean that Europe was in any way monolithically Catholic: aside from the continent's large Jewish population, the persistence of sects such as the Cathars, Lollards, and Hussites – despite the dire consequences of heresy – testify to the restiveness of Europeans and the strength of resistance to the established church. Still, Catholicism maintained its hegemony, and the Vatican increasingly sought to enforce religious uniformity, illustrated most infamously by the Spanish inquisition.

But the rapid spread of Protestantism challenged the Church's role and ushered in two centuries of warfare that engulfed Germany, France, the Low Countries, and the British Isles. As Europe slowly recovered from the devastation of the wars of religion, the continent's rulers – spiritual and temporal alike – grappled with the new realities of a continent upon which religious homogeneity could no longer realistically be forced. Practical necessity dictated finding ways for religious communities to coexist rather than seek to annihilate each other, and the efforts to seek such compromise is what led to the growth of tolerance and

2. The State And Religion: Models Of Interaction

Europeans slowly departing from St. Augustine's encouragement of the persecution of heretics.[4]

A starting point was the Peace of Augsburg of 1555, which regulated religion by introducing the principle of *Cuius regio, eius religio*, stipulating that the ruler of a territory had the right to determine which religion – Catholicism or Lutheranism – was practiced in his realm. As such, it did not provide religious freedom and limited itself to two denominations. But it did allow "heretics" to emigrate to territories where their religion was official, and provided for religious coexistence in specific cases, cities where Lutheranism had been practiced for a long time.

As historian J.H. Burns puts it, "experience showed that to attempt the imposition of uniformity was to threaten or destroy the solidarity of the state, the authority of government, perhaps the very existence of ordered and civilised life."[5] In the case of France's religious wars, an influential group emerged to argue that loyalty to the state – that is, to the monarch – must come first, and politics must take precedence over religion. The Edict of Nantes, issued in 1558, maintained the role of the Catholic Church as the established religion, but it provided for the toleration of Protestants, again under particular conditions.[6] Even while this was far from providing full freedom of conscience, the Edict tore a hole in the notion of religious unity that had dominated the continent.

Meanwhile in the northern Netherlands, Calvinism had become the established religion, while it only commanded the loyalty of a fifth of the population. The Union of Utrecht of 1579, which united the northern Dutch provinces, specified that "each

---

4 John Coffey, *Persecution and Tolerance in Protestant England 1558-1689*, London: Routledge, 2000, p. 6.
5 J. H. Burns, "The Birth of Toleration in the Sixteenth Century," *Institute of Intellectual History*, St. Andrews University, n.d., p. 14.
6 Elie Benoist, *Histoire de l'Édit de Nantes*, 1693. (https://bit.ly/3dl2ov8)

person shall remain free in his religion and that no one shall be investigated or persecuted because of his religion."[7] The Union explicitly sought to prevent the re-establishment of Catholicism and in many ways, accepted religious freedom because the Calvinist church – itself hardly a paragon of tolerance – was unable rather than unwilling to suppress other denominations.[8] Still, the Netherlands was unique in Europe attracting considerable Jewish immigration as a result.[9] Across Europe, Calvinism became recognized only with the 1648 Peace of Westphalia, and minority worshipers were now allowed to practice their faith, establishing a principle of religious toleration. But this still did not extend to other denominations like Anabaptists, and certainly not to non-Christian groups.

The seventeenth century saw growing religious pluralism, but not necessarily toleration. As historian Mark Goldie notes, religious groups remained focused on establishing their control and suppressing those they viewed as a heretic:

> Luther was ferocious against the Anabaptists, calling down the wrath of the German princes upon them. At Geneva, Calvin burned Servetus for heresy. In England, the regime of Elizabeth and the early Stuarts drove religious nonconformists to flee to the Netherlands and America; in the Netherlands, Calvinists harassed those

---

[7] English text at https://www.constitution.org/cons/dutch/Union_Utrecht_1579.html. See also Lucy M. Salmon, *The Union of Utrecht*, Washington: American Historical Association, 1894, p. 141.

[8] Evan Haefeli, *New Netherlands and the Dutch Origins of American Religious Freedom*, Philadelphia: University of Pennsylvania Press, 2012, p. 20.

[9] Jo Spaans, Religious Policies in the Seventeenth-Century Dutch Republic, in Ronnie Po-chia Hsia and Henk van Nierop, eds., *Calvinism and Religious Toleration in the Dutch Golden Age*, Cambridge University Press, 2002, pp. 72-86.

who deviated into Arminianism; and in Massachusetts, separatists were punished.[10]

Britain and particularly its American colonies, now developed into the new testing ground for reforming the relationship between the state and religion. In Virginia, the Anglican church was the established religion. Massachusetts was under the control of Puritan Calvinists, who wholeheartedly embraced religious coercion and viciously punished what they considered heresy. Notably, given that they had escaped religious persecution in England, they showed no intention to extend to others the freedoms they had crossed the Atlantic to enjoy. This put them at odds with dissenting figures that resisted the theocracy being established in Boston.[11]

Most significant among these was Roger Williams, himself a Puritan minister, who rejected the very notion of coercion in religious matters. His main concern, at least initially, was not the fate of government but of religion itself. He vehemently opposed forced worship as something that "stinks in God's nostrils" and feared a society built on religious coercion would corrupt not just the state but the church itself.[12] This led Williams to a revolutionary conclusion: the state must be separated from all religious matters. His thought emphasized the centrality of freedom of conscience, which temporal powers had no right to interfere with.

---

10 Mark Goldie, "Introduction," in Mark Goldie, ed., *John Locke: A Letter Concerning Toleration and Other Writings*, Indianapolis: Liberty Fund, 2020, p. ix.
11 Timothy L. Wood, *Agents of Wrath, Sowers of Discord: Authority and Dissent in Puritan Massachusetts, 1630-1655*, New York: Routledge, 2006.
12 John M. Barry, *Roger Williams and the Creation of the American Soul: Church, State and the Birth of Liberty*, New York: Viking, 2012; Barry, "God, Government, and Roger Williams' Big Idea," *Smithsonian Magazine*, January 2012. (https://www.smithsonianmag.com/history/god-government-and-roger-williams-big-idea-6291280/)

Such ideas put Williams in direct confrontation with Massachusetts leaders, who banished him in 1636.

That same year, he founded the colony of Rhode Island, which promulgated full religious freedom. Uniquely for its time, this included non-Christians: Williams believed that all humans had the same faculties for conscience, and thus the colony provided civil rights to Quakers, Jews, and native Americans alike. In 1644, he secured a royal charter for the colony, which confirmed the separation of church and state. Of course, Williams was no modern-day libertarian: he did consider the responsibilities of government to include the maintenance of public order and public morality.[13] Thus, while his colony welcomed Quakers, he strongly objected to key Quaker beliefs and spent considerable efforts toward the end of his life savaging Quaker theology and principles, including a momentous multi-day debate with leading Quakers at Newport in 1672 and a "venomous diatribe" against Quakerism published thereafter.[14] Still, Williams' Rhode Island was a forerunner among the American colonies and would influence the American conception of separation of Church and State.

Williams was a controversial figure in his day, and Rhode Island was a small colony. The example set there did not immediately have a significant impact on other colonies. It did, however, influence thinkers like John Milton and John Locke, and several colonies would also provide for religious freedom to different degrees. In 1649, Maryland's assembly passed an "Act Concerning Religion" that guaranteed religious freedom but limited it to

---

13 Martha C. Nussbaum, "The First Founder," *The New Republic*, September 10, 2008. (https://newrepublic.com/article/61558/the-first-founder)
14 LeRoy Moore, "Religious Liberty: Roger Williams and the Revolutionary Era," *Church History*, vol. 34 no. 1, 1965, p. 64. Also Robert J. Lowenherz, "Roger Williams and the Great Quaker Debate" *American Quarterly*, vol. 11 no. 2, 1959, pp. 157-165

"Trinitarian Christians," reflecting its sponsors' intention to guarantee the rights of Catholics in the colony. Two decades later, John Locke assisted in the writing of the Fundamental Constitutions of Carolina, which extended religious freedom to non-Christians, including Jews and Native Americans.

Meanwhile, back in England, the aristocrat turned Quaker William Penn wrote *The Great Case of Liberty of Conscience*, arguing that any form of religious coercion is an affront to God, not just to man. When he secured a charter to found Pennsylvania in the early 1680s, he established an example of a colony with "as robust a separation" between Church and State "as could practically be achieved at that time and place."[15]

This line of thinking began to attract greater number of adherents in England, not least because of the tumultuous and bloody wars of religion that saw frequent shifts in power between Catholics and Protestants. By the late seventeenth century, the pendulum had appeared to swing back toward religious intolerance: in France, Louis XIV in 1685 revoked the Edict of Nantes, ordered the destruction of protestant churches, and sent several hundred thousand Huguenots into exile, primarily in the Netherlands. At the same time, the brief reign of James II in England spurred fears that he would seek to re-establish Catholicism, thus leading to a new wave of religious conflict. But he was deposed in the Glorious Revolution of 1688, an event that established the primacy of Parliament in the Kingdom and codified basic civil rights in the 1689 Bill of Rights. More importantly, drawing on the ideas of John Locke, the 1688 Toleration Act provided for the

---

15 Nicholas P. Miller, *The Religious Roots of the First Amendment: Dissenting Protestants and the Separation of Church and State*, Oxford University Press, 2012, p. 62. Also Arlin M. Adams and Charles J. Emmerich, "William Penn and the American Heritage of Religious Liberty," *Journal of Law and Religion*, vol. 8 no. 1/2, 1990, pp. 57-70.

full right of worship to nonconformist Protestants. Like Locke, however, the Act withheld such rights to atheists, who were seen to have no moral principles, as well as to Catholics, on account of their presumed loyalty to the Pope. Restrictions on Catholicism were not eased until the nineteenth century.

In France, the seventeenth century saw the rise of Enlightenment thinkers, many of whom took a more radical approach and sought to eradicate religious authority. Such ideas would lead to the French Revolution, which briefly disestablished the Catholic Church before it was partly restored by the Concordat. But it was in America that the ideas of the Enlightenment first found root. Following the American revolution, Virginia experienced a strong debate on the matter of religious policy. Jefferson and Madison succeeded in passing a Statute on Religious Freedom that prohibited government taxation for religious purposes. Jefferson borrowed heavily from Enlightenment thinkers in arguing for the Statute while also noting the precedent of other colonies, starting with Rhode Island. This Virginia Statute became crucial in the formulation and passing of the First Amendment to the U.S. Constitution, which prohibits the Establishment of religion at the Federal level. Some state constitutions continued to have privileges for established churches, but eventually, in 1940, the Supreme Court ruled that the First Amendment was also applicable at the State level.[16]

Europe, by contrast, would have to wait until the twentieth century for the separation of Church and State. In the United Kingdom, restrictions on Catholics continued until 1871. In

---

16 John Ragosta, "The Virginia Stature for Establishing Religious Freedom," in Francis D. Cogliano, ed. *A Companion to Thomas Jefferson*, Blackwell, 2012, 75-90; Daniel Dreisbach, "Virgnia's Contributions to the Enduring Themes of Religious Liberty in America," in Paul Rasor, and Richard E. Bond, eds., *From Jamestown to Jefferson : The Evolution of Religious Freedom in Virginia*, University of Virginia Press, 2011.

Denmark, religious freedom came with the 1849 constitution; Swedish citizens were not allowed to convert to Catholicism until 1873, and Catholics would have to wait until 1951 to be able to serve as doctors and teachers. In half of the European Union's countries, constitutions continue to provide privileges for specific churches to this day.

France, of course, played a crucial role in the shifting landscape of the relationship between state and religion in Europe. The 1789 French revolution was motivated heavily by anti-clerical thinking, and the revolutionary decade would deal a body blow to the Catholic church. Soon after the July revolution, all Church property was nationalized, the taxing power of the church was abolished, and the record-keeping duties of the church were taken over by the state. The clergy's privileges were abolished, and clergy were forced to swear allegiance to the Republic. Catholic practice was curtailed, and up to thirty thousand clergy members were forced into exile. The leaders of the revolution sought to replace the Catholic faith with alternative, new beliefs, such as the Cult of Reason and, subsequently, the deistic Cult of the Supreme Being.[17] This was an unprecedented assault on the role of the Catholic Church and religion in society, as it meant not only the disestablishment of the Catholic Church, which had occurred in Protestant countries but the appropriation by the state of many of the key roles of religious officials in society.

It was not to last, however: the revolution self-destructed within a decade, and by 1801, Napoleon Bonaparte entered into the Concordat with the Catholic Church. While this restored

---

17 Jean Baubérot, *Histoire de la Laïcité en France*, Paris: Presses Universitaires de France, 2010; Michel Vovelle, *1793: La Révolution contre L'Église: De la Raison à l'Être Suprême*, Paris: Éditions Complexe, 1988; Frank Tallett and Nicholas Atkin, eds., *Religion, Society and Politics in France Since 1789*. London: Hambledon Press, p. 1–28.

the Catholic Church to a central role in society, it should not be mistaken for a re-establishment. Rather than recognizing the divinity of the Church, as the pre-revolutionary regime had done, the state now simply accepted Catholicism as the religion of the great majority of French citizens and accorded it certain privileges. This did not stop the state from similarly establishing organic laws defining state relations with the Protestant and Jewish faiths. And the state kept the assets confiscated from the church, refused to make the Catholic clergy state employees, and secularized the legal system through the *Code Civil*.[18] Going further, Bonaparte enforced the separation of medicine and secondary education from the clutches of the church while leaving alone, for the time being, the Church's influence on primary education.

The nineteenth century would see a tug-of-war between the conservative church and its supporters and the growing anticlerical sentiment of the country. The Catholic Church was briefly re-established after Napoleon's defeat in 1814, but already by 1830, its position as state religion was abolished. The failure of the restored monarchy in the 1870 war against Prussia ushered in the Third Republic, in which the power of anticlerical forces grew visibly. The Catholic church, despite its numbers, failed to translate its size into power, in part because the church "focused on trying to replace the republic with a new monarchy, instead of supporting conservative politicians."[19] As a result, anticlericalism grew stronger and gained a stronghold on parliament. In 1881-82, laws were passed to make primary schooling compulsory and secular.

When the law on "separation of the churches from the state" was passed in 1905, it was the more liberal of several proposed

---

18 Baubérot, *Histoire de la Laïcité*, loc. 229.
19 Kuru, *Secularism and State Policies Toward Religion*, p. 144.

versions that carried the day. More extreme versions, one seeking to de-Christianize the country and another seeking total state control over the church, were set aside, opening the way instead for a model that built on the separation of church and state. The law begins by affirming the freedom of conscience noting that the republic neither recognizes nor supports or salaries any religion. The law was built on French politicians' studies of the system employed in several American states.[20] As French historians have argued, the 1905 law is hardly an intellectual heir to the French Revolution: it borrows much more from John Locke's liberalism.[21] In practice, however, it dealt a serious blow to the Catholic church, as it unilaterally abrogated the Concordat, and ended state funding of churches and clergy. This led some observers to question how liberal it was.[22] This law did not end the state-church battles in France: only World War II would do that, not least because the Church's association with the reactionary Vichy regime finally led French Catholics to accept defeat and stop fighting the secular republic.[23]

The French struggle with the Catholic Church would be repeated in a number of countries. After the 1910 revolution, Portugal's republicans instituted a law on separation of church and state inspired by the French 1905 law, and introduced numerous measures to suppress the Catholic Church. Jesuits were exiled from the country, religious orders and monasteries were suppressed,

---

20 Maurice Larkin, *Church and State after the Dreyfus Affair: The Separation Issue in France*, Basingstoke: MacMillan, 1974.
21 Isabelle Agier-Cabanes, "La laïcité, exception libérale dans le modèle français," *Cosmopolitiques*, no. 16, November 2007.
22 Kuru, *Secularism and State Policies Toward Religion*, p. 145-146.
23 Claude Singer, "1940-1944: La Laïcité en Question sous le Régime de Vichy," *Raison Présente*, no. 159-150, 2004, pp. 41-54; Nicholas Atkin, "The Challenge to Laïcité: Church, State and Schools in Vichy France, 1940-1944," *The Historical Journal*, vol. 35 no. 1, 1992, pp. 151-169.

divorce legalized and religious teaching in schools banned.[24] Similarly, the 1917 Mexican revolution was motivated by "radical anticlericalism," and that year's constitution aimed to undo all forms of religious power over society.[25] It prohibited all forms of religious education, transferred all religious property to the state, and denied legal status to churches. While these provisions were so revolutionary that they could not immediately be implemented, the Mexican state would move even further in a socialist, anticlerical direction in the 1930s.[26] In Spain, the introduction of the Second Republic in 1931 brought an anticlerical government to power, which promulgated a constitution along similar lines to that in France and Portugal: separation of church and state, closure of religious orders, and secularization of education.[27] Among major European Catholic states, only Italy evaded a process of this kind. The Catholic church was disestablished following the second world war and the 1947 Constitution, but fully lost its privileged status only in 1984.[28]

The beginning of the twentieth century saw considerable controversy over these matters, but by the late twentieth and early twenty-first centuries, the question of managing the Catholic church, or relations among protestant churches, became increasingly a non-issue as religion lost its grip on western societies.

---

24 Silas Cerqueira, "L'Église Catholique et la Dictature Corporatiste Portugaise," *Revue Française de Science Politique*, vol. 23 no. 3, 1973, pp. 473-513

25 Roberto Blancarte, "Laïcité au Mexique et en Amérique Latine", *Archives des Sciences Sociales des Religions*, no. 146, April-June 2019, p. 33.

26 Richard Roman, "Church-State Relations and the Mexican Constitutional Congress, 1916-1917," Journal of Church & State, vol. 20 no. 73, 1978. Also Roderic Ai Camp, *Crossing Swords: Politics and Religion in Mexico*, New York: Oxford University Press, 1997.

27 Stanley G. Payne, *A History of Spain and Portugal*, vol. 2, Madison: University of Wisconsin Press, 1973, pp. 630-632.

28 Alessandro Ferrari and Silvio Ferrari, "Religion and the Secular State: The Italian Case," in Javier Martínez-Torrón and Durham W. Cole, eds., *Religion and the Secular State: National Reports,* Prov, UT: Brigham Young University International Center for Law and Religion Studies, 2010, pp. 431-448.

2. The State And Religion: Models Of Interaction

Across Europe, and particularly France, attention instead shifted toward handling the rise of Islamic consciousness among the continent's large Muslim population. This shift resulted in great part from the failure of European nations to integrate, let alone assimilate, many of their immigrants from Muslim-majority countries. The extent to which European states actually sought to assimilate these immigrants, of course, is a matter of debate. Germany's use of the term *Gastarbeiter*, guest worker, for its growing number of immigrants from southern Europe and Turkey is telling: both the German state and the German population expected immigrants to go back to their home countries after having worked for a given number of years in Germany. This, of course, did not happen. Britain and France, as well as the Netherlands, saw an influx of migrants from their former colonial possessions, who were expected to integrate into majority society.

What this meant, however, was not clear, because the experience of the 1930s had turned European leaders away from nationalist discourses and led them to desist from asking immigrants to assimilate into the majority culture. The ideology of multiculturalism then gained strength, suggesting that cultures do not combine in a melting pot, as traditionally imagined in the United States, but as a "salad bowl" or "cultural mosaic," in which the components maintain their uniqueness rather than blend together.[29] But this notion rested on the expectations of modernization theory, which projected that economic and social development would relegate religious identities to the past. Instead, the opposite happened: second-generation Muslim immigrants experienced an upswing in religious identification,

---
29 Peter Baofu, *The Future of Post-Human Migration: A Preface to a New Theory of Sameness, Otherness, and Identity*. Newcastle: Cambridge Scholars Publishing, 2012, p. 22.

a process that had distinct political implications. This was due to the influence of radical Islamist ideology, which established a direct challenge to western democracy and the western lifestyle as a whole. Rather than integrating, thus, a considerable portion of Europe's Muslim population – and particularly those born in Europe – were segregating.

That in turn forced European states to consider how to deal with the inherently separatist demands of portions of the Muslim population: the wearing of the hijab in schools, requests for provision of food conforming to Islamic dietary laws, demands for the separation of the sexes in various contexts such as swimming classes. Were such demands compatible with the secular nature of Western statehood? How did they relate to the gender equality that western societies had come to take for granted? Most western states sought to make accommodations for Muslim demands, but several, such as France and Denmark, went the other way: they determined that the secular nature of their state and society required pushing back against demands that undermined public order as they saw it, as well as challenging the rights of individuals, particularly underage children, to equality before the law. As a result, France in 2004 imposed a ban on ostentatious religious symbols in schools, and this was followed by debates in several European countries on banning the all-encompassing Islamic veil, the Niqab or Burka.

These debates were not new: they reprised many of the themes that had been litigated in Turkey for close to a century. When Kemal Atatürk created the Turkish republic in 1923, he was motivated by a strong modernist urge that saw religion as a key reason for the country's backwardness. As viewed in the previous chapter, Turkey embarked on the most sustained effort at state-led secularization in the Muslim world outside the Communist bloc. This included the full purging of religious influence from the education system and the legal realm; the closing of religious orders and brotherhoods; and restrictions on religious garb. Unlike in the Communist states, however, the Turkish state did not seek to eliminate religion as such: Turkey never closed mosques, nor did it interfere with religious life-cycle rituals, aside from removing the right to conduct marriages from religious officials, shifting it to the state.

However, the Turkish form of secularism did not stay at separating religion from the state: cognizant of the compact resistance against its efforts at secularization, the Turkish state saw the need to institute state control over religion, in order to maintain the autonomy of the state from religious influence. In other words, much like nineteenth-century French secularists, Turkish leaders did not see a path for peaceful and separate coexistence between the state and Sunni Islam: one necessarily would control the other. As a result, all mosques were made state property, and all imams salaried civil servants.

This order of things came to be challenged when Turkey began to democratize starting in the 1950s. Anticlerical sentiment was much less widespread among the population than in France; and as a result, religious liberalization was key to the appeal of conservative political parties, and enabled them to successively weaken elements of the secular state in ensuing decades. In this the Cold War played an important role, as both Turkey's leaders and their American allies came to see a controlled boosting of religious sentiment as a useful bulwark against the spread of Communist ideology and Soviet influence. As noted, the 1980 military coup leaders introduced the idea of a Turkish-Islamic synthesis, which sought to infuse Turkish nationalism with Sunni Muslim content. In the post-cold war era, this process saw its logical conclusion in the arrival to power of Recep Tayyip Erdoğan's Islamists, who, having been forced out of office after a brief stint in power in the mid-1990s, sought to portray a more moderate approach. Erdoğan has not formally tampered with the secular foundation of the country's constitution, and nominally the AKP has only claimed to reform Turkish secularism from a negative and restrictive version to a more positive version resembling the American system. In reality, having taken over the reins of the state, Erdoğan made good use of the institutions the state had created to control Islam, but now shifted the objective to boosting religious identity and consciousness in the country – not least by infusing ever more religious content into the education system.

As the discussion above has shown, secular government became hegemonic in the Western world following World War II. There is general consensus on the virtue of providing religious freedom, and on separating church and state. That said, at least three different versions have emerged on how to implement this in practice. The United States proposes a model where the state observes strict neutrality toward religion, but in general views religion as a positive social institution and sees little if any challenge to the state's autonomy from religion. The northern European monarchies have instead gradually liberalized a system involving a dominant religion wedded to the state. Finally, the French model, which Turkey followed and adapted to its conditions, continues to espouse a form of secularism that is more skeptical of organized religion, and to allow the state a much greater leeway of intervention to reduce religious influence on either state or society. The next section looks more closely at these differences, to distill a conceptual model of various forms of interaction between religion and the state.

Understandings of Secularism

While Westerners have come to take secular governance for granted, misunderstandings arise as a result of diverging definitions of secularism. The existence of two dramatically different ideal-types of secularism, in particular, generate confusion. The dominant form presently is what the French term the "Anglo-Saxon" model of secularism, which emerged with the American Constitution. This model arose from the sectarian conflicts between religious denominations in England and the American colonies. The main aim of this model is to secure religious freedom for the individual. It follows that the state must observe *neutrality* between different religious dogmas. In no sense does this make the state anti-religious; quite to the contrary, it emerged from the very notion of protecting the freedom of all different communities to worship without state interference.

The gradual liberalization model of northern European monarchies in practice emulates the American model, while not taking it to its full, logical conclusion. In the technical sense, some of these states – like the United Kingdom, Denmark and Norway – continue to have established state churches. One could thus argue they are therefore not fully secular. But that would be like arguing that they are not fully democratic because they continue to espouse a constitutional monarchy. That may in theory be a fully legitimate claim. But just a glance at any index of democracy indicates that the North European constitutional monarchies are among the most democratic states in the world, and similarly their established state churches have not prevented their laws, education system, and societies from being the most secularized in the world. Their political systems merely recognize that there are vestiges of a dominant religion in their society. In other words, a political system can be secular for most practical purposes while recognizing the continued existence of a dominant religious tradition.

In spite of the borrowings of the 1905 law, the French model of *laïcité* has a different background and also different aims. It does not primarily result from an attempt to regulate conflict and coexistence between religious denominations. Rather, it is focused on disagreements in a predominantly Catholic society over the role of religion in the state. In other words, *laïcité* was devised to shield the state – and by extension, the individual – from a dominant institutional religion. It sought not to protect a right *to* religious freedom but a right *from* religious oppression. The Turkish adaptation of this model – *laiklik* – went even further: in order to secure the autonomy of the state and society from religion, it sought to assert state control over religion. But in so doing, perhaps inadvertently, it also got wedded very closely to the very religious tradition it sought to control: Turkish religious institutions were focused solely on Hanafi Sunni Islam, and during the Cold War in fact came to aid the hegemonic aspirations of this religious tradition in society, contributing to the forces that came to undermine *laiklik* itself.

The different models of secular governance have divergent goals, and therefore, the relationship between the state and religion differ considerably. The European monarchies and the U.S. model of state neutrality do not tend to see religion *per se* as a

2. The State And Religion: Models Of Interaction

challenge to the state or to the freedom of society. Quite to the contrary, they tend to view state efforts to control expressions of religion as more problematic than those expressions of religion. In turn, they tend to be acceptant of individual and collective displays of religious identity. By contrast, the French and Turkish models view institutionalized religion as a threat to the freedom of the society and to the integrity of the state. As a result, they promote state intervention in the area of religion, in order to regulate the organization of religious communities and displays of religiosity in the public realm. Where the United States and north European models are comfortable with a society where public displays of religiosity are ubiquitous, the French and Turkish models would prefer a society where religion is strictly personal, exercised in private, and minimized in the public realm.

There are, of course, other models. The socialist atheist model actively sought to repress religion altogether, not just to reduce it to the private realm. While *laïcité* and *laïklik* differ from Anglo-Saxon secularism in having a healthy dose of skepticism for organized religion, they are not in and of themselves anti-religious. Neither France nor societies that have followed the French model – which we can term laicist systems – have razed churches or sought to restrict the exercise of religious rites. Laicist states share with socialism the fear of a threat to the state from organized religion; but socialist atheist societies view religion in itself as incongruent with modernity and progress, as an archaic belief system incompatible with their own that must be rolled back. This model has largely been abandoned in formerly Communist Eastern Europe or the Soviet Union, as well as in the Arab world, where Arab socialism in its Baathist and Nasserist forms are relics of the past.

This background serves, in part, to make sense in subsequent chapters of the policies adopted by Central Asian states. For this purpose, this chapter will now provide a conceptual continuum detailing the possible variations of a state's relationship to religion, from the closest fusion of worldly and spiritual realms to the most hostile relationship possible.

Five Models

While there are innumerable variants of the approaches a state can take toward religion, these all operate along a continuum. There is, however, no generally accepted categorization of state relationship with religion. Various scholars have offered different categories, particularly in seeking to distinguish different secular systems from one another.

Juan J. Linz models the relationship between state and religion in a circle, where positions such as theocracy, caesaropapism, and political religions can be found. In addition, he proposes two versions of secular government: a "friendly separation" of church and state on the American model, as well as "hostile laicizing" as in France.[30] This theme appears in several typologies: for example, Elizabeth Shakman Hurd distinguishes between "laicism" and "Judeo-Christian secularism." But in the category of "laicism," Hurd lumps together systems as distinct as the French and the Soviet Communist models: she argues that "laicism is a powerful organizing principle of modern politics that has been influential in France, the former Soviet Union, Turkey, China, and elsewhere,"

---

30 Juan J. Linz, "The Religious Use of Politics and/or the Political Use of Religion: Ersatz Ideology versus Ersatz Religion," in Jodi Bruhn and Hans Maier, eds., *Totalitarianism and Political Religions*, London: Routledge, 2004, p. 109.

and that its aim is to push religion into the private domain.[31] But this ignores the very different aims of two models: the Soviet, which sought to destroy religion, and the French and Turkish, who seek merely to confine it to the private realm in order to contain excessive religious influence on the public domain. To paraphrase former Turkish President Süleyman Demirel's words quoted in chapter one, the Soviet model seeks to prevent the exercise of religion, while the French and Turkish model only seek to prevent religion from being forced upon the individual. This difference is very significant.

Ahmet Kuru's model of state-religion regimes includes four types: religious state, state with established religion, secular state, and antireligious state. This is a much more useful typology, and Kuru further distinguishes between "passive" and "assertive" secular system, though he subsumes them under a single heading of secular systems.[32] But this does not fully reflect the diversity of secular systems, which can be neutral, as in the United States; be skeptical towards it and seek to insulate state and society from it, as in France; or to seek to directly control and regulate a dominant religion, as in Turkey.

For the purposes of this study, we will distinguish between a model of state-religion interaction that is skeptical toward organized religion and seeks to insulate the state from it, and the model that is hostile towards religion as such. We will also consider the skeptical model of secular governance as separate from the model focusing on state neutrality toward religion to warrant their own category. As a result, a continuum emerges, with an infinite number of combinations between full fusion of

---

31 Kuru, Elizabeth Shakman Hurd, *The Politics of Secularism in International Relations*, Princeton University Press, 2008.
32 Kuru, *Secularism and State Policies toward Religion*, pp. 8-14.

religion and politics on one end, and total state hostility toward religion on the other. Along this continuum, we can distinguish three ideal-type models of secular government applicable in the present day. Between the extremes, which we term "Fusion" and "Hostile," we find "Dominant Religion," "State Neutrality," and "Skeptical/Insulating."

Model	Fusion	Dominant Religion	State Neutrality	Skeptical/insulating	Hostile
Characteristics	State religion, no religious freedom	Privileged religion, religious freedom	No privileged religion	No privileged religion, religion confined to private realm	Religion suppressed
Historical Examples	Byzantine Empire	European monarchies	Mongol Empire		Revolutionary France
Modern Examples	Saudi Arabia, Iran, Vatican	United Kingdom, Denmark, Norway	United States, Germany, Singapore, Japan	France, Turkey, Mexico, South Korea	Soviet Union, Communist Albania

Fusion

The "**Fusion**" model presupposes that the political and spiritual realms are merged – often in the person of a leader holding ultimate worldly as well as religious power. In this system, the state seeks to impose one particular religion on the population. Other religions tend to be prohibited, actively discouraged, and repressed. Their adherents are expelled, forced to convert, or repressed. Needless to say, the state religion permeates law and education, both of which are explicitly based on religious principles. This system can either subordinate political power under religious institutions, or the inverse.

Historical and contemporary examples of the fusion model are many. The Byzantine empire was ruled by a system later termed *caesoropapism*, which features a state-controlled church where religious matters became part of state administration. In Europe, counter-reformation Spain is a prominent case, but most of pre-Westphalia Europe exhibited elements of this model. So did the Massachusetts theocracy set up in the 1630s. Europe only gradually and reluctantly abandoned this model, France with the Edict of Nantes, and the continent more broadly with the Peace of Westphalia. Vestiges of this system remained until the twentieth century, while the continent gradually moved along the continuum to the Dominant Religion model.

Further east, the Seljuk and Ghaznavid empires enforced their understanding of Sunni Islam upon their population. The Ottoman empire, by contrast, did not enforce religious homogeneity. But just as Pope Innocent III called the Cathars "more evil than the Saracens,"[33] the Ottomans had greater tolerance for infidels than for heretics. They accorded *millet* status to Jews and Christians, but not to any Muslim minorities, and particularly repressed the heterodox Alevis.

Today, states enforcing the Fusion model are rare: aside from the Vatican, which does not really have a lay population, Saudi Arabia is the closest example that comes to mind, since the state officially tolerates only one religion, all others being banned. Even there, the initiatives of Crown Prince Muhammad bin Salman, if successful, would gradually transition away from this model. Post-1979, Iran also, in part, approximates the fusion model, given the introduction of the novel doctrine of *velayet-e-faqih*. Yet Iran tolerates certain religious minorities, such as Christian Armenians, while ferociously repressing others, such as the Baha'i. The

---

33 Malcolm Barber, *The Cathars: Dualist Heretics in Languedoc in the High Middle Ages*, London: Routledge, 2014, p. 107.

short-lived Caliphate of the Islamic State in Syria and Iraq, too, qualifies as a particularly brutal example of the Fusion model, as does Taliban Afghanistan in the late 1990s.

Dominant Religion

The **"Dominant Religion"** model is superficially similar to the Fusion model in that it elevates one religious doctrine as a privileged religion. But it differs in that it tolerates, and sometimes provides a level of autonomy, for minority religious groups. In other words, while it does privilege one religious doctrine, it provides individual religious freedom, which the Fusion model does not. As a result, it allows for a separation of the state from religion, meaning that some states with a Dominant Religion have introduced secular laws, courts and education systems. Nineteenth-century European monarchies are good examples of states shifting from the "Fusion" model to the Dominant Religion model.

To some extent, the Ottoman Empire's *Millet* system also fits in this model. Whereas the empire was based on Sunni Islam and the Sultan was also the Caliph, merging worldly and spiritual power, the Ottoman empire provided relatively wide-ranging autonomy to its non-Muslim subjects. They were allowed to settle disputes internal to the religious community autonomously; but any dispute between a Muslim or non-Muslim would be settled according to Sharia law. As noted, heretics were accorded no privileges, and Sultan Selim the Grim massacred up to 40,000 Alevis as a result. And importantly, even the millet *system* hardly amounted to *individual* religious freedom, as individuals remained hostage to their particular religious communities and leaders. The

Ottoman state was thus a hybrid between the fusion model and the dominant religion model.

Moghul India also adopted the Dominant Religion model. Here, the added twist was that the Dominant Religion was actually in the minority, in a subcontinent that remained majority Hindu. Finally, Meiji Japan can be added to the list, as the state integrated Shintoism into the state bureaucracy, while continuing to permit the exercise of religious freedom.

State Neutrality

The Third model, occupying the middle point of the continuum, is the **"State Neutrality"** model, which to most western observers today is synonymous with "secularism." The most notable example emerged with the American Constitution. The main aim of this model is to secure religious freedom of the individual; it follows from this that the state must observe *neutrality* between different religious dogmas. Thus, it seeks to separate the state from religion. As noted, it does not make the state anti-religious, as it emerged from the very aim of protecting the freedom of all different communities to worship without state interference. Today, most European states – Germany in particular – have gravitated toward this model. European monarchies may retain, for mostly ceremonial purposes, formal links to what once was a privileged state church; for some of these, the distinction between the dominant religion and state neutrality model can be too small to identify.

But this model is not exclusively western. Most notably, the Mongol Empire fiercely enforced freedom of religion hundreds of years before Westphalia, and allowed the coexistence of Christians, Muslims, and Buddhists – among other – in the lands it controlled. The state privileged no religious doctrine.[34] Today, a number of Asian democracies, such as Singapore and Japan, have similarly adopted neutrality in religious matters.

Skeptical / Insulating

The fourth category is the **"Skeptical/Insulating"** model. Pioneered by Third Republic France, this model goes further than the neutrality model in seeking to insulate the state – and often society – from religious influences, taking a skeptical approach toward religion. This model is best known by its French term, *laïcité*, which – because it is seldom translated into English – is frequently confused with American-style "secularism." *Laïcité* serves not to protect a right *to* religious freedom, but a right *from* religious oppression.

As a result, its goals differ considerably from the State Neutrality model. It tends to be very sensitive to religious institutions' efforts to enforce homogeneity among their followers. Thus, in stark contrast to the state neutrality model, the model tends to view ostentatious public expressions of religion as more problematic than state efforts to control expressions of religion. Unlike the American model, where politics and official ceremonies frequently feature references to a general deity, the French model refrains from including references to God in official circumstances.

The Skeptical/Insulating model in fact views institutionalized religion as a threat to the freedom of the society and the individual, and to the integrity and autonomy of the state. As a result, it provides for state intervention in the area of religion, in order to regulate both the organization of religious communities

---

34 Jack Weatherford, *Genghis Khan and the Quest for God: How the World's Greatest Conqueror Gave Us Religious Freedom*, New York: Viking, 2016.

2. The State And Religion: Models Of Interaction

and displays of religiosity in the public realm. In particular, it actively discourages any mixing of religion and politics.

Outside France, this model is prominent among former French colonies, but has also been adopted in other countries. South Korea, for example, adopted elements of the model in the post-second world war modernization process in order to regulate religion. While it enhanced provisions guaranteeing religious freedom in the 1980s, the state continues to involve itself in religious affairs to "encourage harmony among different religions so that they may wield a sound influence on society."[35]

As discussed, a prominent example of the Skeptical/Insulating model is post-1923 Turkey, which adopted the doctrine of *laiklik* to manage and control the role of the dominant religion in society, Sunni Islam, and minimize its influence over politics.[36] But particularly after 1950, Turkey gradually combined its skepticism of organized religion and efforts to insulate the state with an effort to promote a dominant religion. Thus, the state's Directorate of Religious Affairs has exclusively busied itself with Sunni Islam, and in practice promotes the Hanafi-Maturidi understanding of that religion. While a majority of the population belongs to this tradition, large minorities do not – including millions of Shafi'i Kurds, heterodox Alevis, and Azerbaijani Shi'as. From the 1980 military coup onward, Turkish schools taught compulsory classes on religion, which exclusively covered Sunni Islam. Since the Justice and Development party came to power in 2002, Turkey has

---

35 Matthias König, "Religion and the Nation-State in South Korea: A Case of Changing Interpretations of Modernity in a Global Context," *Social Compass*, vol. 47 no. 4, 2000, 560-61.
36 Niyazi Berkes, *The Development of Secularism in Turkey*, Montreal: McGill-Queen's University Press, 1964.

rapidly drifted away from the Skeptical/Insulating model toward the Dominant Religion model.[37]

Hostile

The fifth and final category is the **"Hostile"** model. Forming the other end of the continuum, it actively and often forcefully discourages both private and public manifestations of religion. This model is associated with states controlled by atheist ideologies, most prominently socialist and communist states of the twentieth century. Communist states are the primary examples of the "Hostile" model, but others, such as Nazi Germany, can be added to the list – with many historians believing the Nazi ambition to be the eradication of Christianity had they won the war.[38]

"Hostile" states tend to be motivated by totalitarian ideologies that in fact compete with religion for the devotion of the population. In a sense, they seek to replace religion. Scholars have termed this phenomenon the "sacralization of politics," leading to the domination of "political religions" or "secular religions."[39] The Communist ideology, for example, itself had distinctly religious connotations. It saw religion as a direct threat to its intellectual hegemony. In so doing, one must ask whether the end of the continuum does not bring it back to its beginning, making it a circle: if Communism is understood as a religion rather than just a political ideology, the state was hardly atheist at all, but sought to replace pre-existing religions and enforce the sole authority of

---

37 Eric S. Edelman, Svante E. Cornell, Aaron Lobel, Halil Karavel, Blaise Misztal, *Turkey Transformed: The Origins and Evolution of Authoritarianism and Islamization under the AKP*, Washington: Bipartisan Policy Center, 2015. (http://bipartisanpolicy.org/wp-content/uploads/2015/11/BPC-Turkey-Transformed.pdf)
38 Eg. George L. Mosse, *Nazi Culture: Intellectual, Cultural and Social Life in the Third Reich*, Madison: University of Wisconsin Press, 2003, 235-262.
39 Emilio Gentile, "Political Religion: A Concept and its Critics - A Critical Survey," *Totalitarian Movements and Political Religions*, vol. 6 no. 1, 2005.

Communism. Such an understanding would bring us back to the Fusion model, with the Communist Party merging worldly power and spiritual authority derived from Marxism-Leninism.

Between Ideal-Types and Reality

The five models discussed above are ideal types. As such, in the real world, few states will fall squarely and neatly into a single category. Many states will manifest characteristics of more than one model. While some writings of history might assume that the world is inexorably moving in the direction of state neutrality toward religion along with the development of liberal democracy, in reality there is active contention today between the Dominant Religion, State Neutrality, and Skeptical/Insulating models. The first and last models – Fusion and Hostile – are increasingly rare, but around the globe states are moving along the continuum among the remaining three models, often borrowing elements of several.

Ignoring this complexity, western observers often use the term "secularism" interchangeably for government policies that differ in fundamental ways. In particular, when Western governments and organizations assess the practices of other states and design foreign policies in this field, the distinction between these models tend to be glossed over. Thus, American government agencies and many organizations promoting freedom of religion tend to assume that the only legitimate form of secular government is the State Neutrality model aimed at ensuring religious freedom. But because of historical links and their own proper experiences, many non-Western countries have in fact adopted religious policies that have much more in common with the Skeptical/

Insulating model, while occasionally maintaining aspects of the Dominant Religion model.

This is particularly the case in the Muslim world. The conditions that gave rise to secular ideas among political leaders shared more in common with the French than with the American experience. The urge to regulate relations between different Islamic communities certainly exists, particularly in societies like Azerbaijan that are split between Sunni and Shi'a communities. But this is dwarfed by the anti-clerical objective, much as in Catholic France, to protect the state from religious forces perceived to be large, monolithic and distinctively political in nature. Thus, the driving force behind secular governance has been the perceived need to prevent religious dogma from influencing the state and society. It should therefore come as no surprise that "secular" states in the Muslim world have drawn from the French, and subsequently Turkish, the experience of regulating religion. Since these states have democratic traditions that are less advanced than France, their policies have often been more restrictive than the French and even repressive in nature.

Where do Central Asia and Azerbaijan fit into this? All these models are relevant in this region. The international environment today strongly emphasizes religious liberty, and all regional states pay lip service to it. But the conditions that gave rise to secular ideas among political leaders shared more in common with the French and Turkish than with the Anglo-Saxon experience. Thus, the driving force behind secular governance has been to prevent religious dogma from influencing the state and society. Leaders of majority-Muslim post-Soviet societies – the five states of Central Asia and Azerbaijan – shed the atheist Soviet model upon independence, but rapidly gravitated toward a model inspired by the Turkish and French examples – one that ensured the sensitive state-building project they embarked upon would not be hijacked by the religious revival that began to sweep their societies.

But there is a twist: the new states differed from both France and Turkey in an important way. France and Turkey had strong traditional religious institutions, and their brand of secularism was based on the urge to regulate and control the Catholic church and the Sunni Ulama and orders, respectively. In Central Asia and Azerbaijan, the problem was the opposite: the weakness of traditional religious institutions as a result of seventy years of Soviet atheism. Traditional religion was not the key challenge: alien, politicized expressions of religion imported from abroad was what they feared. This meant that the state did not fear traditional religion – quite to the contrary, the state saw a need to work to strengthen traditional religion as an antidote to alien and radical ideas.

3. RELIGION IN CENTRAL ASIA AND AZERBAIJAN

THE WIDER CENTRAL ASIAN REGION appears on the fringes of the Muslim world, as it is understood today. Geographic distance and two centuries of Russian rule both contribute to this perception. But historically, the region was a core area of the Muslim world, one where some of the most important Islamic theologians developed doctrines that continue to be revered today. But Central Asia is also one of the parts of the Muslim world that have been exposed to the most assertive secularization. This puts the region in a unique position, as it seeks to develop a new relationship between state and religion – building on its historic traditions, but largely unaffected by the track record of the Middle East in the past half century.

Central Asian Islam

To the untrained eye, Central Asia may appear peripheral to the Muslim heartland in the Middle East. But the region occupies a central position in the history of Islam. Following the Islamization of Central Asia from the eighth century onward, the oases of the region developed a stunning intellectual environment unrivaled elsewhere in the world at the time.[1] Most of the most spectacular advances occurred in such secular fields as mathematics, science, and medicine, but the field of religion was by no means neglected. The most authoritative collection of *hadith* – accounts of the Prophet's life and sayings – were recorded by Muhammad al-Bukhari, a native of Bukhara.[2] Central Asia also became the center for the development of the largest Islamic legal school, the Hanafi branch of Sunni Islam, and home of the founder of the influential Maturidi school of theology. Orthodox theology was not the only religious field in which Central Asia played a prominent role: the region also figured centrally in the development of the mystical, esoteric forms of Islam known as Sufism. Several of the largest Sufi orders with a global presence originated in Central Asia – most prominently the Naqshbandiyya order, which presently extends from the Balkans to Indonesia.[3]

As this suggests, Islam in this region was never homogeneous or uniform: mystical and scriptural practices coexisted, while pre-Islamic beliefs and folk customs have continued to remain a part of religious life into the present. The religious environment has also been enriched by Central Asia's Hellenistic heritage, the philosophers of its "Lost Enlightenment," and the continuing presence of Christian and Jewish minorities. In part, this pluralism was possible because it was tolerated, to some extent, by the formal Islamic authorities. The dominant Hanafi school of jurisprudence and Maturidi school of theology gave Central Asian Islam a highly distinctive character that stands in stark contrast

---

1 This is described vividly in S. Frederick Starr, *Lost Enlightenment: Central Asia's Golden Age from the Arab Invasions to Tamerlane*, Princeton: Princeton University Press, 2013.
2 Jonathan Brown, *The Canonizaton of Al-Bukhari and Muslim: The Formation and Function of Sunni Hadith Canon*, Leiden: Brill, 2007.
3 Martha Brill Olcott, *Sufism in Central Asia*, Washington: Carnegie Endowment for International Peace, Carnegie Papers no. 84, May 2007. (http://carnegieendowment.org/files/cp84_olcott_final2.pdf)

to the practices in the core areas of the Middle East. Grounded in this tradition, Central Asian *Ulama* were tolerant of mystical practices, which stricter *madhabs* like the Hanbali considered un-Islamic. They were also more tolerant of pre-Islamic beliefs, which they sought to integrate and cloak in an Islamic shroud rather than systematically suppress. This facilitated the spread of a distinct and local form of Islam across the region.[4]

Law and Creed: The Development of Islamic Theology in Central Asia

A full understanding of the distinctive nature of Central Asian Islamic traditions requires a brief excursion into the evolution of Islamic law and theology. Following the death of the prophet there was and remains general agreement that the Quran was the word of God, while the life and sayings of the prophet (Sunna) were the practice and embodiment of the word of God. Thus, the Quran itself and the Sunna are the highest sources of authority. But for those seeking to organize society – or even their personal lives – along Islamic principles, this is hardly sufficient. The Qur'an is not a legal handbook or even a clear guide to life. It is adamant on some issues, silent on some, and appears contradictory on others. As for the Sunna, also known as the collection of *hadith*, it was fairly straightforward during the time of the prophet's companions, who could report first-hand on his life and messages. But after their departure, the Muslims depended on the transmission of *hadith* either orally or in written form. The major collections of *hadith* were not compiled until the ninth century AD, over two centuries after Muhammad's death. By that time, there was great confusion on what traditions about the prophet's life were genuine, and which

---
4 Starr, *Lost Enlightenment*.

ones were merely rumors or outright falsifications. That forced the collectors to trace the origin and transmission chain of each story, seeking to build criteria for determining their authenticity. This remains a serious controversy even today.

Even then, the Quran and Sunna could not easily define what Islam was and what it meant. The absence of a clerical hierarchy exacerbated this problem and led to myriad controversies and revolts that split the Muslims into irreconcilable groups within a few decades after Muhammad's death. The Sunni-Shi'a split is the most well-known of these, but other sects like the Khawarij and Murjiah, among other, compounded the picture. Even among the majority of Sunnis, however, key questions remained: what was permissible and what was not? And on a more abstract level, what consisted of correct Muslim doctrine, and what beliefs were orthodox or heretic? This gave birth to what we now call the Islamic "sciences," with two main branches: law and theology, or *fiqh* and *kalam*. In a process that took centuries, the Sunni Muslims eventually agreed that there were four madhabs, or accepted schools of jurisprudence, as well as two schools of *kalam*. Islamic sources tend to paper over these differences and understate them in the interest of Islamic unity. However, the differences between them are significant and largely underrated, and have deep implications for how Muslims approach each other, society at large, and not least non-Muslims.

Abu Hanifa and the Hanafi School

Islamic schools of law wrestled with many things, including how to deal with the many situations where neither the Quran nor the Sunna provided clear answers. Over time, two additional sources of law were recognized: consensus and analogic reasoning – *ijma* and *qiyas*. Some have included the discretion of jurists, as well as local custom as subordinate sources of law, on the basis of Muhammad's statement that the Islamic community as a whole would not do wrong. The Shi'a have added *aql*, reason, as a separate category. Where the main schools differ is when to depart from the Quran and Sunna and use secondary or tertiary sources of law.

Abu Hanifa (699-772), born in Kufa in present-day Iraq of a wealthy Persianate trading family with roots in Kabul, was the first of the founders of the four *madhabs*. Malik Ibn Anas (711-795) of Medina was the second. They were followed by Idris al-Shafi'i (767-820) of Gaza, a student of Malik's, and lastly Ahmad ibn Hanbal (780-855) of Basra. Abu Hanifa is credited with being the first significant scholar to put to use the method of analogic reasoning in Islamic law, as well as to seek legal solutions that take into consideration the needs of society.

Abu Hanifa was cautious not to focus too rigidly on the strict and literal application of texts: he urged consideration for the spirit of the teachings of the religion and argued that rulings should be guided by the public interest. He was also the person to develop the notion of *istihsan*, discretion of jurists, in order to "ease hardship" and apply tolerance and moderation to rulings.[5] The application of *urf*, customary law, was introduced primarily by his disciple Abu Yusuf (735-798), who served as chief judge under the rule of the fifth Abbasid Caliph, Harun-al-Rashid.[6] These measures hardly make the Hanafis liberals or democrats by modern-day standards. But in comparison with the other schools of law, the Hanafi school is considerably more open than the other

---
5 Ahmad Hasan, "Early Modes of Ijtihad: Ra'y, Qiyas and Istihsan," *Islamic Studies*, vol. 6 no. 1, 1967. Karachi.
6 Mohammad Khalid, *Islamic Law and Legal Change: The Development and Significance of 'Urf in the Hanafi "Usul al-Fiqh," with Special Reference to Ibn 'Abidin's "Risala" on 'Urf*, Ph.D. Dissertation, University of Manchester, 2009.

three schools to accepting non-scriptural sources of Islamic law, particularly the independent reasoning of Islamic jurists (*ra'y*).[7]

On the opposite side of the spectrum lies the austere Hanbali school, which seeks to the extent possible to rely solely on the literal text of the Quran and the Sunna. Hanbalis are extremely restrictive in the extent to which they resort to analogic reasoning, seeking to find *hadiths* to help them decide a case instead. They firmly reject the application of local custom. In terms of defining consensus, the difference could not be clearer: Ahmad Ibn Hanbal took the term to mean a consensus only among Muhammad's companions, whereas the Hanafi tradition defines it as the agreement of contemporary jurists. As will be seen, these contrasts also apply to the theological disputes that marred the Islamic world. In between these two extremes lie the Maliki and Shafi'i schools. The Maliki, in particular, are considerably more flexible than the Hanbalis, while the Shafi'is are in many ways in agreement with the Hanbalis on key matters while not taking their literalism to the same lengths.

It should be noted that the differences between the four schools have been reduced overtime, through active efforts of reconciliation and, not least, the effects of the codification of "authentic" hadiths in the ninth century by classic scholars Muhammad al-Bukhari and Muslim al-Hajjaj. Because there was now a canon of *hadith*, the hand of the literalists urging the use of *hadith* was strengthened at the expense of the proponents of using reason or considerations of public good. Still, the underlying

---

[7] The Hanafi school dominates in former Ottoman lands and Central Asia; the Shafi'i school is followed in Kurdish-populated areas, Southeast Asia, and East Africa; the Maliki school is dominant in the rest of Africa, while the Hanbali school is followed in Saudi Arabia and some Gulf monarchies. For more details about differences in jurisprudence, see Mohammed Hameedullah Khan, *The Schools of Islamic Jurisprudence: A Comparative Study*, Delhi: Kitab Bhavan, 1991; Irshad Abdal-Haqq, "Islamic Law: An Overview of Its Origins and Elements", *Journal of Islamic Law and Culture*, vol. 7 no. 27, 2002.

divergence in worldview remains to this day, and the geographic distribution speaks to the different needs of Islamic populations. The followers of the Hanafi school dominate in areas of Eurasia that are not ethnically or culturally Arab, and where Islam has sought to incorporate indigenous traditions and culture. Here, the Hanafi school has adapted to ways of life that have tended to be more open to modernity than their Hanbali and Shafi'i counterparts.

The Development of Kalam and Imam Maturidi

The early centuries of Islam were rife with deep theological debates. These concerned fundamental questions, such as whether the Quran was created or is eternal; and whether humans have free will, or their actions are, at all times, determined by God. As discussed in chapter one, the Mu'tazilite school, at one extreme, as a heavily rationalistic sect that dominated during the rule of Caliph Mamun (776-833). The Mu'tazilites believed in the application of reason rather than literal readings of texts, and argued, on the basis of logic, that the Quran must have been created by God, because God must have existed before he announced the holy book to Muhammad. They also strongly supported the notion of free will, again on logical grounds: if God is both just and wise, evil must be a result of human errors, and thus a result of human free will. They also believed that the notions of good and evil were knowable to man without the aid of divine revelation.

On the other side were the literalists, dominated by Hanbali followers, who rejected not only the notion of human free will, but of the application of reason as such. This tendency, known as the *ahl al-hadith* or colloquially as the *athari* school, did not stay at arguing that the Quran was eternal and uncreated, and that the

Quran and Sunna were the sole legal and theological authority: they held that the very exercise of rational thinking in religious matters, which they termed speculation, was prohibited – even if it upheld scriptural "truth." Likewise, they urged that scripture should be accepted in its literal meaning without asking questions. Therefore, for these traditionalists, the very exercise of *kalam*, or theology, was harmful, since there was no reason to speculate on theological matters when the text of scripture was sufficient.

Caliph Mamun's endorsement of the Mu'tazilite school as a state religion was, in fact, its undoing. In hindsight, we may wonder what would have happened had Mamun succeeded in imposing a rationalist interpretation of Islam. But his policies had the opposite effect, emboldening the opposition, simply because the Mu'tazilites never succeeded in cultivating enough of a following among Islamic scholars to gain prominence. Many viewed them as on or beyond the verge of heresy. Yet the *atharis*, whose austerity and literalism was impractical, did not manage to gain predominance either, although they remain an important minority even today: the Salafi movement is a direct descendant of the *atharis*.

Enter two ninth-century theologians, Mansur al-Maturidi of Samarkand (853-944) and Hasan al-Ashari of Basra (874-936). Working independently of each other and apparently unaware of each other's existence, both sought a middle ground between the liberal Mu'tazilites and the austere atharis. They were most vehement in rejecting the heterodoxy of the Mu'tazilites, but contrary to the atharis, they resolved to use rational theological arguments, *kalam*, to refute the Mu'tazilite positions. They also used it to defend Sunni doctrine from other deviant sects, and to refute criticism of Islam coming from other religions. In so doing, they enforced a more orthodox Sunni Islam than the Mu'tazilites, but by applying rationalistic methods. This eventually led Ashari and Maturidi to be recognized as the founders of the two accepted theological schools of Sunni Islam.

Muslim scholars tend to minimize the differences between Asharis and Maturidis, and it is frequent to come across statements, including by Western scholars, suggesting there were only "minor differences" between them.[8] This view prevailed until the second half of the twentieth century. But recent scholarship suggests this is simply wrong. As Maturidi's biographer Ulrich Rudolph puts it, "it can be soberly stated that there are no real deep consensuses between the [Ashari and Maturidi]. The differences are actually vast ... the view that both professed related teachings is actually an illusion."[9]

While they shared the same objective – defending Orthodox Sunni creed from heresy and unbelief – they took different positions on questions of key importance. One key reason was personal: while Maturidi was firmly in the Sunni camp from the start, Ashari was an ardent Mu'tazilite until he turned forty. Whatever the reasons of his change of heart – which he attributed to seeing the prophet in his dreams, but others attribute to efforts to "conspicuously procure, if not outright apply for, Hanbalite recognition"[10] – it led him to move much closer to the positions of the atharis in his efforts to rebuild his legitimacy as an orthodox Muslim. Maturidi's life, by contrast, had no such u-turns, leading him to feel more confident in taking positions that could subject him to traditionalist criticism. Another key reason was their

---
8 See Rudolph, 12-13.
9 Ulrich Rudolph, *Al-Maturidi and the Development of Sunni Theology in Samarqand*, trans. Rodrigo Adem, Leiden: Brill, 2015, p. 318.
10 Rudolph, *Al-Maturidi*, p. 318.

diverging traditions and perspectives: Maturidi was firmly in the Hanafi tradition, bred in the more liberal intellectual environment of Central Asia. Ashari, by contrast, aligned himself with the stricter Shafi'i tradition, and this divergence is clear in their respective work.

The perhaps most important difference lies in the concept of reason. A key question for Muslim theologians was whether humans have the capacity to identify right and wrong without divine revelation. This question goes to the heart of the relationship between the state and religion. If humans do not have the ability to discern what is right, then there can be no tolerance for *any* government that is not guided by divine revelation, let alone democratic government. In other words, only a theocracy can safeguard morality. But if, by contrast, humans have the ability to discern what is right independently, then a separation of church and state becomes fully legitimate, paving the way for a compatibility of Islam with both secularism and democracy.

For Ashari, this idea was "completely alien."[11] To Ashari, any notion of human free will, or ability to tell right from wrong independently, is a direct affront to God's omnipotence. There is no objective right and wrong: something is right only because God has ordered it to be so. If God orders the opposite, it is by definition also right. Therefore, only divine revelation can tell what is right or wrong. As one scholar summarized Ashari's thought, "no other being than Allah possesses any act at all."[12] As Ashari himself put it, if a man picks up a pen to write, "it is God who creates in him the will to write, the power to write, and motion of the hand to the paper with the pen. Allah then also causes the

---
11 Ulrich Rudolph, "Ḥanafī Theological Tradition and Māturīdism," *Oxford Handbook of Islamic Theology*, ed. Sabine Schmidke, 2016, p. 288.
12 Duncan B. Macdonald, *Aspects of Islam*, New York: MacMillan, 1911, p. 136.

figures to appear on the paper as the pen touches it."[13] The implications of this is that there are no laws of nature either, because the existence of such laws would – again – deny the omnipotence of God. As we saw in chapter one, the highly influential Ashari scholar Hamid al-Ghazali observed that it is wrong to say that fire causes cotton to burn. It may appear to humans that this is a natural law because it seems to happen every time cotton and fire are in contact with one another. But in fact, it is only God that leads the cotton to burn; and if God decides that it will not happen, it will not.

By contrast, Maturidi espoused the Hellenistic tradition that influenced Muslim philosophers like Ibn Sina, Al-Biruni, and Al-Farabi. He accepted the notion of man as a rational being, the only created being "who reflects on and understands" the wisdom of God.[14] He accepted, like Ashari, that God is omnipotent and determines what is good and bad; but also argued that God holds himself to the norms he has himself created, and therefore there is a "stable and intelligible system of norms." Because God has established such a system, and humans have the capacity to understand God's wisdom, humans can also learn to understand that system.[15] In this perspective, the pursuit of modern science and rational inquiry is fully compatible with Islam.

Comparing Ashari and Maturidi, Rudolph concludes that their aims and perspectives were completely different. Ashari made use of theology to "defend a position which, in its basis, corresponds to Sunni Traditionism" whereas Maturidi tried to find

---

13 Robert R. Reilly, *The Closing of the Muslim Mind*, Wilmingon, DE: ISI Books, 2011, p. 85.
14 Rudolph, *Al-Maturidi*, p. 297.
15 Rudolph, *Al-Maturidi*, p. 298.

"a meeting point between the religious ideas of the Traditionists and a type of thinking characterized by rationality."[16]

As Robert Reilly has argued, the Ashari belief in the total omnipotence of God essentially led his many followers to deny reality, causation, and the meaning of any scientific inquiry. The success of Al-Ghazali in hammering home these essentially nihilistic ideas goes a long way to explain the what Reilly calls "the closing of the Muslim mind."

Today, the Sunni Islamic world is essentially divided into at least four worldviews. One is the purely secular and modernist perspective espoused by a minority of Muslims, but an influential and growing segment. Pitted against them is another minority: the most austere Hanbali worldview represented by the Salafi movement. The most influential, certainly in the Middle East, is the Ashari worldview, which for most practical purposes is as opposed to modernity, rationality, and science as the Hanbali-Salafi one. Finally, there is the Hanafi-Maturidi tradition, which provides a middle way: it remains accepted as within the mainstream of Sunni Orthodoxy, but remains open to rational thinking, human agency, and a scientific worldview. The fact that this is the Central Asian religious heritage has important implications for the embrace of secular government in the region.

Central Asian Sufism

Maturidi sought to find a middle way between the emphasis on Islamic law and texts on one hand and reason and free will on the other. But an entirely different dimension of Muslim life in Central Asia is the spiritual mysticism known as Sufism. Sufism is present across the Islamic world and varies considerably in shape

---
16 Rudolph, *Al-Maturidi*, p. 319.

and form – and not least, in its relationship with formal, Orthodox Islamic doctrine. Sufism is known in the West mainly through the writings of the thirteenth century poet Jalaluddin Rumi. Born in Vakhsh in present-day Tajikistan, Rumi has been termed the best-selling poet in the United States.[17] In this shape and form, Sufism is an open-minded form of Islamic mysticism that puts the individual quest for communion with God above the literalism of the Sharia, and has very little to do with the rule-bound practice of Islam in much of the Muslim world. But as we shall see, there are also Sufi groups that remain strictly within the realm of Sunni Orthodoxy, and view mysticism only as a second story on top of strict religious observance. That said, the intolerance of Hanbali-style literalists for Sufism is well-known, and Sufism is in general a force that stands in opposition to the most extreme tendencies in Islam. But that does not necessarily make Sufism a force for reason and rational inquiry: Sufism in fact emphasizes intuitive knowledge of God at the expense of reason.

Central Asia was an important breeding ground for Sufi movements, and Sufism in Central Asia and Azerbaijan developed in several stages. The Central Asian environment was conducive to the emergence of Islamic mysticism for two reasons: first, the region's preference for the Hanafi school of law made Central Asian Islam more tolerant of non-Orthodox practices. Equally important, the rich intellectual history of Central Asia and Azerbaijan and their exposure to Hellenism, Buddhism, Christianity, Judaism and local religious traditions such as Shamanism made their inhabitants prime candidates for adopting an understanding of the new Islamic religion that was spiritual and mystical. As

---

17 Jane Ciabattari, "Why is Rumi the Best-Selling Poet in the US?" *BBC*, October 21, 2014. http://www.bbc.com/culture/story/20140414-americas-best-selling-poet

Starr puts it, the "Islam of strict rules, rote memorization, and conformity" did not appeal to Central Asians.[18] Furthermore, Sufi practices made it possible for them to mesh their pre-Islamic traditions with conversion to Islam, rather than abandoning their ancient traditions and adopting an alien, stern Arab creed.

Tellingly, one of the earliest Sufis was Al-Hakim al-Tirmidhi (d. 869) from Termez in southern Uzbekistan, who was at once a Hanafi jurist and an accomplished Sufi. Organized Sufi orders would develop in the twelfth century, when the Kubrawi and Yasawi orders emerged. The Kubrawi order is now almost extinct in Central Asia, but spread in particular to South Asia, where it remains influential. As for the Yasawi order, it was founded by Ahmad Yasawi, one of the first poets in the Turkic languages, who lived and died in the city of Turkistan in southern Kazakhstan. Yasawi began to spread the Sufi way beyond the urban areas of southern Central Asia, into areas populated by mainly nomadic Turkic tribes. He adopted an approach that one scholar calls "unusual even among Sufi standards," as he integrated Turkic Shamanistic practices into Sufism and showed openness to other religious traditions, and included unveiled women in religious ceremonies that were otherwise exclusively male.[19] The Yasawi order, relatively loosely organized and composed of many wandering mystics, would play an important role in spreading Islam among Turkic tribes not only in Central Asia, but into present-day Turkey.[20] There, it helped spawn the even more blatantly heterodox Bektashi order, which blends Islamic beliefs with Shamanistic

---

18 Starr, *Lost Enlightenment*, p. 473.
19 Renato Sala, "Ahmed Yasawi: Life, Words and Significance in the Kazakh Culture," Al-Farabi University, Journal of History, no. 2, 2018. p. 123.
20 Mehmet Fuat Köprülü, *Islam in Anatolia after the Turkish Invasion*, Salt Lake City: University of Utah Press, 1993.

and Christian traditions. The Bektashi was highly influential in the Ottoman Empire until purged in 1826.

This early line of Sufism was fundamentally open to mixing Islam with local traditions and customs and was in no sense in contradiction with rationality and scientific inquiry. It just happened not to be focused on such endeavors, instead seeking spiritual knowledge of God. But by the thirteenth century, when a second wave of Sufism began to emerge, things had changed. In the late tenth century, the aforementioned Al-Ghazali had played a critical role in shutting down philosophical and scientific inquiry, not least through his diatribe entitled *The Incoherence of the Philosophers*. But Ghazali tried to fill the void that he had helped create by reconciling Sufism with Islamic Orthodoxy. Making common cause with the literalists against the adherents of reason, he argued that "science itself bred a kind of rationalism that leads to skepticism and atheism," and instead embraced mysticism as "a superior form of cognition, a step above reason."[21]

This paved the way for the success of the Naqshbandi order, which emerged following the Mongol conquest of Central Asia. Mongol rule had spurred a popular resistance to alien rule that led Sufi orders to emerge as focal points. It also spurred a departure from the original Sufi emphasis on an inner path to God, instead developing a tendency of social and political activism. The order emerged in the Bukhara oasis in the late twelfth century, but would be known globally by the name of Baha-ad Din Naqshband, who formally added a rejection of asceticism and an embrace of what we would today call socio-political activism into the order's doctrine. He did so within the confines of Sufism by urging followers

---

21 Starr, *Lost Enlightenment*, 382-4.

to seek "seclusion within society," in other words to be active in society while maintain seclusion from it within their hearts.[22]

The Naqshbandi order also differs from other orders such as the Yasawi in its relationship with Orthodox Sunni Islam. All Sufi orders claim a lineage of transmission of the secret, inner meaning of the Quran that stretches back to Muhammad himself. But while the Yasawi, like most Sufi orders, trace their chain back to Ali, Muhammad's son-in-law and the focus of veneration of the Shi'a branch of Islam, the Naqshbandis stand out by tracing their lineage to Abu Bakr, Muhammad's companion and immediate successor. As a result, Sunni orthodoxy views most Sufi orders with some level of suspicion, but not so the Naqshbandis, who have always remained firmly in the Sunni orbit and emphasized the importance of observing Sharia. The Naqshbandi order came to epitomize Ghazali's feat of marrying Sufism with orthodoxy. It should be said, however, that the Naqshbandis have traditionally kept a firm line between themselves and the Salafi-style currents that have existed in Islam since the time of the Kharijites, and which are hostile to mysticism as such.

As long-time Central Asia scholar Martha Olcott observes, the Naqshbandi order "managed to reappear in different forms again and again after periods of stagnation."[23] At several times in its history, the order has emerged as a central rallying cry for resistance to alien rule, or alien social influences, and for an emphasis on Sunni orthodoxy against foreign impulses. Under Timurid rule in the fifteenth century, Naqshbandi Shaykh Khoja Ahrar of Samarkand rejected the rulers' jurisprudence that elevated customary law above Sharia, and their taxation of the population for

---

22 Martha B. Olcott, *Sufism in Central Asia*, p. 5. (https://carnegieendowment.org/files/cp84_olcott_final2.pdf)
23 Olcott, p. 4.

military purposes. In the late sixteenth century, similarly, Ahmad Sirhindi of Punjab emerged as a Naqshbandi renewer, opposing the syncretism of Mughal emperor Akbar, who had sought to fuse Islam and Hinduism into a new religion he called the "Religion of God." Finally, in the early nineteenth century, Khalid Baghdadi of Sulaymaniyah emerged to reject the western influences on the Ottoman empire and seek a return to Sharia as well as a purification of the order itself.

Khalid Baghdadi would prove particularly influential in driving the Naqshbandi order in the direction of political activism and Islamist militancy. He established a new branch of the order, which has come to be known as the Naqshbandi-Khalidi order. He strengthened the authority of the Shaykh and instilled in his followers the key duty of Khalidi Shaykhs to "seek influence upon rulers and to bring them to follow *shari'a* rules."[24] As Hamid Algar puts it, what was new about the Khalidi branch was "the vigor with which" Baghdadi propagated the Naqshbandi message, and how it inculcated "its message of Shari'a-oriented militancy almost everywhere it went."[25] This was certainly the case in the North Caucasus, where the Naqshbandi order played an important role in the revolt against Russian rule, and in Turkey, where Khalid's disciples would launch the wildly successful revival of political Islam in the late twentieth century. In Central Asia, however, the Khalidi order did not become as widespread, the Husayni branch of the order instead remaining prominent.[26]

---

24 Butrus Abu-Manneh, "The Naksibendiyya– Mujaddidiyya in the Ottoman Lands in the Early Nineteenth Century," *Die Welt des Islams*, vol. 22, 1982, p. 14.
25 Hamid Algar, "Shaykh Zaynullah Rasulev: the Last Grand Naqshbandi Shaykh of the Volga-Urals Region," in Jo-Ann Gross, ed., *Muslims in Central Asia: Expression of Identity and Change*, Duke University Press, 1992, p. 118.
26 Mairamkan Isabaeva, "Bağımsızlık öncesi ve sonrası Orta Asya'da Nakşibendilik: Hüseyniyye kolu örneğinde," Osh State University, Theological Faculty Journal, no. 22, 2017, p. 145. It also traces its chain to Sirhindi, though through a separate, Central Asian

Sufism, thus, can cut both ways. The broader Sufi movement had an important impact upon the folk Islam of Central Asia, particularly its nomadic peoples, where institutionalized, orthodox religion never quite achieved a strong influence on the population. There, folk traditions mingle with Islamic belief, and religious practice for most of the population centers on rites of passage, veneration of holy men, and visits to their tombs, and popular religion has little if any link to textual traditions and institutional religion.[27] This "folk Islam" is infused with strong Sufi influences. But there is also another side to Sufism: the Naqshbandi version, which upholds rather than undermines orthodoxy, and has proven to be a powerful force of resistance against secular government, law, and education.

Between Two Empires: Russian Rule, Ottoman Reforms, and Emergence of Secular Intelligentsia

By the late eighteenth century, Central Asia and the Caucasus were in a deep slump. The empires of yore had disintegrated, leaving political power in the hands of relatively small principalities – *khanates* – that were often bickering with each other and commanded little enthusiasm among the population, whom they taxed heavily. The region had suffered considerably from the shift in global trade. The rise of sea transport routes combined with the instability of Eurasia following the decline of the Mongol empire

---

chain whose most prominent Shaykh was Muhammad Husayn Bukhari (d 1833). After independence, however, Turkish Khalidi orders began to establish their presence in Central Asia, and are likely to influence the revival of Sufism in Central Asia itself.
27 Adrienne L. Edgar, *Tribal Nation: The Making of Soviet Turkmenistan*, Princeton University Press, 2004, p. 26; Victoria Clement, *Religion and the Secular State in Turkmenistan*, Silk Road Paper, Central Asia-Caucasus Institute & Silk Road Studies Program, June 2020. http://silkroadstudies.org/publications/silkroad-papers-and-monographs/item/13372.

made the region, once a hub of continental trade, an increasingly isolated backwater.

In other words, Central Asia was in a downward spiral. For centuries, power had emanated out of Central Asia to rule faraway lands: the Seljuks, Timurids, Mughals, Safavids and Ottomans were all Turkic dynasties with roots in Central Asia. Now, the opposite was happening: from the north, Russia was expanding southward. From the south, British rule in India was spreading northward. Meanwhile, the Ottoman Empire had been forced to retreat from its European holdings.

Domestically, Central Asian societies were in decline as well. Ismail Bey Gaspirali, a leading Crimean Tatar intellectual of the late nineteenth century, summarized the condition of the Muslims of the Russian empire as follows: "In short, whatever may have been the circumstance of the civilized world 400 years ago, we Muslims find ourselves today in exactly the same circumstances; that is, we are 400 years behind!"[28] Munawwar Qori, a leading reformer in present-day Uzbekistan, concurred: "all our acts and actions, our ways, our words, our schools and seminaries, our methods of teaching, and our morals are corrupt. If we continue in this way for another five or ten years, we are in danger of being dispersed and effaced under the oppression of developed nations."[29] In Azerbaijan, publicist Ahmed Aghaoghlu hailed the achievements of early Islamic civilization, but lamented how it "fell into the hands of people who were ignorant and savage, who turned it into an instrument of evil."[30]

---

28 Ismail Bey Gasprinski, "First Steps Toward Civilizing the Russian Muslims," in Charles Kurzman. Ed., *Modernist Islam, 1840-1940 : A Sourcebook*, Oxford University Press, 2002, p. 224.
29 Munawwar Qari, "What is Reform?" in Charles Kurzman. Ed., *Modernist Islam, 1840-1940 : A Sourcebook*, Oxford University Press, 2002, p. 228.
30 Ahmed Aghayev, "Islam and Democracy," in Charles Kurzman. Ed., *Modernist Islam, 1840-1940 : A Sourcebook*, Oxford University Press, 2002, p. 231.

In the Ottoman Empire, similarly, military defeats to European powers drove home the same point: Muslim civilization had been superior to its Christian counterparts both in military terms, as well as in scientific and cultural development. Now, it was falling behind. As historian Roderic Davidson remarks with regard to the Ottoman education system, the *mektebs* or schools "could hardly pass for proper education in the world of the nineteenth century ... the learning of Islam was forgotten, the learning of the modern West not yet acquired."[31]

As we have seen in Chapter one, in many parts of the Muslim world, the reaction to this gradual shift was to find remedy in a stricter observance of Islam, an effort to try to emulate an imagined golden age of the first century following Muhammad's death. The striking point about Central Asian and Ottoman reactions to their growing backwardness was that they drew the opposite conclusion: rather than finding answers in the distant past, their answer was to raise their own level of development, including emulating their European adversaries. To win back control over their own homelands, they needed to change their ways: as Qori put it, "reform begins with a rapid start in cultivating sciences conforming to our times."[32] As Bukharan reformer Abdurauf Fitrat put it, Central Asians should "try to have what the Christians possessed to make them victorious over [Muslims]."[33]

This is not to say that these reformers were universally accepted. Their deep and pointed criticism of their own societies and institutions created considerable friction with the forces that

---

31 Roderic H. Davidson, "Westernized Education in Ottoman Turkey," *Middle East Journal*, vol. 15 no. 3, 1961, p. 290.
32 Qari, "What is Reform?", p. 228.
33 Abdurrauf Fitrat, "Debate between a Teacher from Bukhara and a European," in Charles Kurzman. Ed., *Modernist Islam, 1840-1940 : A Sourcebook*, Oxford University Press, 2002, p. 245.

upheld and benefited from the *status quo*. And there was, everywhere, a minority that believed the solution lay solely in deeper commitment to orthodox religion. But those forces were on the retreat, and the leading intellectual force in both Ottoman, Azerbaijani and Central Asian society was the reformist movement, which has come to be known as the *Jadids*, from the term usul-i jadid, the "new method" of education they developed.

The old system of education was based largely on rote learning of Arabic for Quran recitation, with schools providing no training in mathematics and science, little understanding of the outside world, and even poor training in religious matters – the education relying mainly on studying the commentary of Central Asian *ulama* on the Quran and hadith, rather than original texts. The problems were similar in the Ottoman empire and among Russian Muslims, and in the half-century before the Bolshevik revolution, a dynamic interaction between Muslim reformist thinkers in Turkey and the Russian empire would ensue.[34]

Ottoman military defeats in the eighteenth century had forced the empire to introduce specialized high schools teaching mathematics and engineering, first only for military officers but later also in the civilian realm. By the 1860s, secular elementary and middle schools were being instituted, and these schools soon began to produce many of the emerging Ottoman leaders.[35] In Crimea, Tatar publisher Gaspirali (also known by his Russianized name Gasprinsky) developed a new method of education based on phonetic learning, and a focus on the vernacular language rather than, as previously, literary Arabic and Persian. In sum, Gaspirali developed a European-style curriculum for schools. Such schools

---

34 Adeeb Khalid, *The Politics of Muslim Cultural Reform: Jadidism in Central Asia*, Berkeley: University of California Press, 1998.
35 Davidson, "Westernized Education in Ottoman Turkey," p. 295.

would spread rapidly, first among the Crimean and Volga Tatars and in Azerbaijan, and subsequently also in Central Asia. There, however, it faced more entrenched opposition both from Russian colonial authorities as well as from the upholders of the old order.

The Jadids were a lay movement, although many of its leading voices in Central Asia were children of ulama. They were the carriers of the ideas of the Enlightenment in Central Asia; but they were not necessarily secular, and certainly not atheists. They viewed only Islam *as practiced* in Central Asia to be backward because of the poor education and corruption of its ulama and the mixing of local superstitions with Islamic beliefs. Among them, there was considerable debate on the role of religion in society and the states. Many of them saw no contradiction between a greater Islamization of society and its modernization. But they also saw their communities as nascent nations, and encouraged the development of national consciousness, that is, the development of identities that did not rely exclusively on religion but on common bonds of geography and language.

Azerbaijani writer Ali Huseynzade sought to unify three principles of "Turkicization, Islamization, and Europanization" while his more well-known Ottoman counterpart Ziya Gökalp preferred the trinity of "Turkicization, Islamization and Modernization."[36] To these thinkers, there was no contradiction between seeking to make their societies more Islamic and to make them more modern and European. That, of course, mirrors an understanding of religion's role in society very different from the one that has developed in the twentieth century. While this may appear curious today, it was part and parcel of the development of rationalistic Islamic modernism, and similar to the thinking

---

36 Carter V. Findlay, *The Turks in World History*, Oxford University Press, 2005, p. 174.

of contemporary proponents like Jamal al-din Afghani and Muhammad Abduh.

Such thinking was always controversial in the core Middle East. Among the Turkic and Persian peoples of Central Asia and Azerbaijan, however, it became the dominant strain of thought on the eve of the Russian revolution. When the Russian empire began to collapse, a development the Muslim leaders had neither sought nor expected, they began to develop movements for national independence. In Azerbaijan, they managed to form an actual independent state; but even where they did not, as in Kazakhstan, Bukhara and Tashkent, these movements developed along similar lines.

Political movements in Azerbaijan were, with few exceptions, moderate and progressive by outlook. As Brenda Shaffer observes, "in almost all movements they joined, the Azerbaijanis continued to be at the forefront of Muslims advocating for the adoption of liberal values and enlightenment. One example of this is the insistence on the emancipation of women advocated by political parties in both north and south Azerbaijan."[37] The Azerbaijan People's Republic, set up in 1918, predated the Turkish republic by five years, making it the first republic ever created in the Muslim world. The remarkably progressive spirit and moderation of the Azerbaijani elite did not remain on paper: these traits were reflected in the behavior of the political elite during this brief period of independence. The National Charter of the Republic proclaimed the state a democratic, parliamentary republic. Its fourth article stated that the republic "guarantees to all its citizens within its borders full civil and political rights, regardless

---

37 Brenda Shaffer, *Borders and Brethren: Iran and the Challenge of Azerbaijani Identity*, Boston, MA: MIT Press, 2002, pp. 32–33.

of ethnic origin, religion, class, profession, or sex."[38] The leaders of the republic foresaw a constituent assembly elected on the basis of proportional representation and universal suffrage – giving women the right to vote long before many Western European countries did. The chaos and warfare in the region meant that the planned elections were never held. Yet the Parliament sought to expand its membership by including new groups and giving representation to minority representatives.[39] This experiment was short-lived: by early 1920, Bolshevik forces entered Baku, ending the first republic in the Muslim world.

In Kazakhstan, secular intellectuals developed a historical narrative of Kazakhs as a distinct nation that had a distinct territory as their national homeland. Here emerged the Alash Orda movement, which would seek to establish a modern Kazakh state in the aftermath of the 1917 revolution. Kazakh secular intellectuals concluded that the interests of the Kazakhs could not be represented by the Muslim faction to the Duma: the concerns of the Kazakhs were different and of another order than those of Tatars or Azerbaijanis.[40] While they were challenged by Islamic intellectuals, the Islamic-minded intellectuals – chiefly natives of southern regions of Kazakhstan – lost this intra-Kazakh dispute.[41] The Kazakh secular intellectuals held a first All-Kazakh Congress in July 1917, and resolved to create a Kazakh political party, named Alash Orda. The Party favored a democratic, federal

---

38 Quoted in Tadeusz Swietochowski, *Russian Azerbaijan, 1905-1920: The Shaping of National Community in a Muslim Community,* New York: Cambridge University Press, 1985, p. 129.
39 Swietochowski, 145.
40 Pete Rottier, *Creating the Kazakh Nation: The Intelligentsia's Quest for Acceptance in the Russian Empire, 1905-1920,* Ph.D. Dissertation, University of Wisconsin, 2005, p. 135.
41 Tomohiko Uyama, "The Geography of Civilizations: a Spatial Analysis of the Kazakh Intelligentsia's Activities, from the Mid-Nineteenth to the Early Twentieth Century," in Kimitaka Matsuzato, ed., *Regions: A Prism to View the Slavic-Eurasian World,* Sapporo: Slavic Research Center, 2000, p. 84..

Russian state, with a Duma elected by universal adult suffrage. Kazakh provinces would be autonomous, have their own army, and be able to put an end to immigration of Russian peasants until land had been distributed among the Kazakhs. Importantly, the program provided for the separation of religion and politics, restricting the role of Islamic clergy to life-cycle rituals.[42]

Alash leader Alikhan Bokeikhanov did not have much time for Islamism: as he put it, "the Sharia is a fixed, written law common to all countries and peoples. It is incapable of change and inflexible."[43] He was not much impressed by Russia either, declaring that "the culture of our Russia is low. Russia has no factories and plants capable of producing valuable things. Culture is in Western Europe: in France, England, Belgium and Germany."[44] Alash tried to maintain its autonomy among the struggle between the Bolsheviks and White armies during the Russian civil war.[45] But the Bolshevik leadership determined that the Alash government was a "bourgeois constitutional-democratic organization", and sought to arrest Bokeikhanov. Alash then reached out to the Provisional Siberian Government, under the control of the White armies, which helped them temporarily keep Bolshevik forces at bay, but by mid-1919, they were forced once again to strike a deal with the Bolsheviks.[46] Eventually, the victorious Bolsheviks took over and marginalized the Alash leaders, most of whom were shot

---

42 Gulnar Kendirbay, "The National Liberation Movement of the Kazakh Intelligentsia at the Beginning of the 20th Century", *Central Asian Survey*, vol. 16 no. 4, 1997, p. 502.
43 Gulnar Kendirbaeva, "'We are Children of Alash...' The Kazakh Intelligentsia at the Beginning of the 20th Century in Search of National Identity and Prospects of the Cultural Survival of the Kazakh People," *Central Asian Survey*, vol. 18 no. 1, 1999, quoting 'Tagy da bi kham bilik' [Once again about judge and judgement'], *Qazaq*, no. 50, 1914.
44 Kendirbaeva, "'We are Children of Alash...'", quoting 'Zhauap khat' [The Letter of Response'], *Qazaq*, no. 122, 1915.
45 Ian W. Campbell, *Knowledge and Power on the Russian Steppe, 1845-1917*, Ann Arbor: Ph.D Dissertation, University of Michigan, p. 347.
46 Martha Olcott, *The Kazakhs*, Hoover Institution Press, 1987, pp. 145-59.

in the 1937 purges. This shows that at the time of Sovietization, just as in Azerbaijan, the Kazakhs had begun to develop a nascent national elite, which was in the process of building the fundaments of a secular nation-state.

In southern Central Asia – today's Uzbekistan and Tajikistan – the situation was more complicated. The incorporation into Russia happened almost forty years after the South Caucasus had become part of the empire, and three centuries after present-day Tatarstan on the Volga was incorporated. The impact of European thinking was therefore lower, and modernist forces were weaker to begin with – a more recent phenomenon than in Tatarstan and Azerbaijan. The resistance to change was stronger, too: the Ulama retained great influence on society. In Bukhara, the situation was compounded by the fact that Bukhara was never formally incorporated into the Russian empire: it was a protectorate, allowing the Emir great leeway in internal affairs. This worked against the interests of the modernists, as the Emir saw no benefit coming out of their efforts to nudge him toward reforming the traditional order on which his power rested. As a result, across Central Asia, the power relationship involved three parties – the jadids, the Ulama, and the Russians, in an intricate dance that produced more than its share of unholy alliances. The main line of conflict ran between the jadids and the ulama. In fact, the ulama's authority had benefited from the Russian conquest: Russian authorities left their authority in religious and social matters intact, but weakened or eliminated the temporal authorities that had existed prior to conquest.[47]

In spite of geographic distance, the Ottoman empire served as an important inspiration to Central Asia's modernizers. This

---

47 Adeeb Khalid, *Making Uzbekistan: Nation, Empire, and Revolution in the Early USSR*, Ithaca: Cornell University Press, 2015, p. 32.

3. Religion In Central Asia And Azerbaijan

was particularly the case in Bukhara, were the efforts to introduce a constitutional monarchy in Istanbul was directly relevant to the emirate, and modernizers adopted this Young Turk model as their own, becoming known as the Young Bukharans.[48] Linguistic proximity implied that Uzbek-speakers could read Ottoman Turkish and Azerbaijani publications, allowing ideas in the western part of the Turkic world to spread rapidly into Central Asia. This also had important implications for the identity of Central Asian reformers. As they increasingly framed their struggle in national terms, they also adopted much of the Turkist ideology coming out of Istanbul and Baku. While Persian had been the language of the learned people in Bukhara, the reformists embraced an understanding of their nation as Turkic, leading to a shift to Uzbek as their language of communication. When the Young Bukharans took power in 1920, they shifted Bukhara's official language from Persian to Uzbek.

The 1917 February revolution led the Jadids in Tashkent to mobilize, and they organized a First Turkistan Muslim Congress in April and establish a Turkistan Muslim Central Council. Through this, they laid out a vision of a federal Russia with considerable territorial autonomy for Turkistan. But when matters came to the election of a city Duma of Tashkent, the Jadids were railroaded by the Ulama, who first refused to cooperate with them, and then won a landslide, getting six times the votes the Jadids did.[49] The main conflict line laid in the role of religion in politics, and the position of women. The Ulama explicitly resolved that "the affairs of religion and of this world should not be separated, i.e., everything from schools to questions of land and justice should

---
48 Khalid, *Making Uzbekistan*.
49 Khalid, *The Politics of Reform*, p. 259.

be solved according to the shariat," and explicitly decried any idea that women should have the same rights as men.[50]

After Soviet power was declared in Tashkent, the Jadids moved to Kokand in the Ferghana valley, where they established a Provisional Government in November 1917. Only three months later, Soviet troops supported by Armenian Dashnaktsutyun militias crushed the budding government in a massacre that led to the death of at least 14,000 people.[51] Following this violence, the Jadids gradually made accommodations to the growing Soviet power. Having been repressed in Bukhara by the Emir, and struggling in Tashkent with the traditional sources of power, the Jadids rationalized an alliance with the revolutionary forces as a tactical move to gain power and influence. Allying with the Bolsheviks in Tashkent, they supported the incarceration of many of the Ulama leaders that had worked to stifle their agenda.

In Bukhara, the Jadids had been severely repressed by the Bukharan emir, leading them to accept an alliance with the smaller Bukharan Communist Party and allowing themselves to be swept to power by a Soviet military expedition in the late summer of 1920. They then tried to set up a state – the Bukharan People's Republic – in which they sought to maintain maximum autonomy from Moscow, while working to implement modernist policies strongly influenced by the Ottoman reformers of the era. As historian Adeeb Khalid concludes, the Bukharan republic "sought to establish a centralized, modern nation-state with full sovereignty and membership in the then nascent world order of nation-states ... It also had a clear mission to civilize its citizens, and fighting

---

50 Khalid, *The Politics of Reform*, p. 261.
51 Paul Bergne, "The Kokand Autonomy, 1917-18: Political Background, Aims and Reasons for Failure," in Tom Everett-Heath, ed., *Central Asia: Aspects of Transition*, London: RoutledgeCurzon, 2003.

ignorance and fanaticism set the agenda for the Ministry of Education. The government also sought to reform Islam by bringing Muslim institutions and large swathes of Islamic activity under the state's bureaucratic control."[52] By 1923, the Bolsheviks were powerful enough to rein in the Young Bukharans and reshuffle leading personnel to their liking. By 1924, Stalin decided to do away with the Bukharan republic entirely, and instead create the republic of Uzbekistan in the process of the territorial delimitation of Central Asia.[53]

In sum, the Muslim areas of the Russian empire saw a dynamic development of reformist thought in the late nineteenth and early twentieth century. Modern ideas inspired by developments in Turkey and Europe were leading inspirations, which led to the emergence of secular national-building projects. The intellectual leaders of the time never had the chance to fully implement their vision, however, and the full reckoning with the role of religion in society in independent states of the region had to be postponed for the post-Soviet era.

Soviet Rule and its Unexpected Consequences

Russian colonization and the subsequent Soviet experience had a significant impact on the intellectual traditions of the region. But its impact is much more complex than what is widely assumed. The Soviet assault against religion was very real, as only a handful of mosques remained in Central Asia by the mid-1920s, and religion was effectively curbed from public life.[54] As a result, it is

---

52 Khalid, *Making of Uzbekistan*, p. 128.
53 Arne Haugen, *The Establishment of National Republics in Soviet Central Asia*, New York: Palgrave, 2003; Steven Sabol, "The Creation of Soviet Central Asia: The 1924 National Delimitation," *Central Asian Survey*, vol. 14 no. 2, 1995, pp. 225-241.
54 Shoshana Keller, *To Moscow, Not Mecca: The Soviet Campaign against Islam in Central Asia, 1917–1941*, Westport: Praeger, 2001.

often assumed that the Soviet experience led to a comprehensive secularization not only of the state and its institutions, but to the public lives of Central Asians themselves.[55]

Until 1925, the Soviet power was relatively conciliatory toward Islamic practices. Lenin had issued strict instructions to this effect, both in order to curry favor with the local population and distinguish the Soviet leadership from the Czarist rulers. There was initially considerable religious freedom, and even the persistence of Sharia courts adjudicating family law. But all that changed in 1927, when the Soviet government introduced the *Hujum* campaign, literally meaning assault, which was a large-scale campaign to promote gender equality by seeking to eradicate "backward" cultural and religious practices including the veiling and seclusion of women. The Soviets expected this campaign to receive the strong backing of Muslim women, but it misfired. Rather than throwing off their veils, many women saw the campaign as an effort to force Russian cultural practices on Muslim societies, and according to some scholars, it led to an increase in veiling. Still, the program continued, and included the closure of mosques and madrasas, the confiscation of Islamic endowments, and the elimination of Islamic-minded elites.

The Second World War led the Soviet state to seek a truce with Islam, as the government needed the participation of the population in the anti-Nazi war effort. Religious persecution was halted, and the Soviet leadership created Spiritual Authorities for Soviet Muslims that would survive until the collapse of the USSR. Following the war there were ebbs and flows in Soviet religious policy, but overall, the atheist campaigns continued in the rhetorical realm, and were backed up by a continued removal

---

55 Eg. Yaacov Ro'i, *Islam in the Soviet Union*, London: Hurst, 2000.

3. Religion In Central Asia And Azerbaijan

of religion from the public sphere. The main exception was rites of passage that remained Islamic in nature, and were observed by an overwhelming majority of Soviet Muslims, often including Communist Party functionaries. Religion continued to exist in the private realm, however, as the Soviet effort to create new, common Soviet identity only succeeded in small part. In fact, the Soviet government actively contributed to the creation of modern nations in Central Asia and the Caucasus through the delimitation of national boundaries and the affirmative action processes, known as *korenizatsiia*, that led natives to take up positions of authority in the Communist system. While the Soviet leadership may not have intended for this outcome, the national republics built new national identities that included significant religious elements as cultural markers.[56]

On one hand, thus, the Soviet government removed religion from the public sphere and presided over half a century during which laws, courts and education system were thoroughly secular. Yet in fact, while Central Asians may not have been conversant in theological matters, Muslim *identity* may even have been strengthened during the Soviet period. In a 1979 study, Rasma Karklins showed that Central Asians maintained strong elements of Islamic identity that differentiated them from the Slavic majority of the Union.[57]

Less known is that while Soviet authorities targeted Sufi practices and "folk Islam," which they considered to be potentially

---

[56] Bayram Balci, *Islam in Central Asia and the Caucasus Since the Fall of the Soviet Union*, London: Hurst, 2018; Shoshana Keller, *To Moscow, Not Mecca: The Soviet Campaign against Islam in Central Asia, 1917-1941*; Yaacov Ro'i, *Islam in the Soviet Union from World War II to Perestroika*, London: Hurst, 2000.

[57] Rasma Karklins," Islam: How Strong Is It in the Soviet Union? Inquiry Based on Oral Interviews with Soviet Germans Repatriated from Central Asia in 1979", *Cahiers du Monde Russe et Soviétique*, vol. 21 no. 1, 1980, p. 65-81. (http://www.persee.fr/doc/cmr_0008-0160_1980_num_21_1_1374)

subversive, they appear to have encouraged the flow of orthodox theological currents inspired by Salafism and the stricter Shafi'i and Hanbali *madhabs*. This conformed with the Soviet penchant for sowing division: just as Moscow encouraged the splintering of the Muslim and overwhelmingly Turkic peoples of Central Asia and Western Siberia into nine different territorial entities,[58] it sought to splinter the Muslim community along religious lines as well, weakening the region's Hanafi-Maturidi traditions by supporting more orthodox and anti-Sufi practices.

A key figure in this development was the Lebanese-born al-Shami al-Tarabulsi, who came to Central Asia in 1919 from Kashgar.[59] This Salafi-inspired graduate of Al-Azhar in Cairo forcefully endorsed the Bolshevik destruction of Sufi saints' tombs.[60] As one regional scholar notes, "[Al-Shami] completely rejected the inheritance of the medieval ulama, called for the development of new judgments returning to the roots of Islam— the Qur'an and the authentic hadiths of the Prophet."[61]

Al-Shami made a strong mark on the theological establishment that came to dominate Soviet Central Asia. Significantly, and unlike the Jadids, most of his disciples survived the 1937 terror, and were freed from prison during the Second World War. Those included Ishan Babakhan, who was appointed to head the newly formed Soviet Spiritual Administration of Muslims of

---

58 These were the Soviet Republics of Kazakhstan, Kyrgyzstan, Tajikistan, Turkmenistan, and Uzbekistan; the Autonomous Republics of Karakalpakstan in Uzbekistan; Gorno-Badakhshan in Tajikistan; and Bashkortostan and Tatarstan in Russia.
59 Ashirbek Muminov, "Fundamentalist Challenges to Local Islamic Traditions in Soviet and post-Soviet Central Asia", in Tomohiko Uyama, ed., Empire, Islam and Politics in Central Eurasia, Sapporo: Slavic Research Center, 2007. Sébastien Peyrouse, "The Rise of Political Islam in Soviet Central Asia", *Current Trends in Islamist Ideology*, vol. 5, 2007, p. 41; Martha Brill Olcott, *In the Whirlwind of Jihad*, Washington: Carnegie Endowment for International Peace, 2012, p. 81.
60 Vitaly Naumkin, *Radical Islam in Central Asia: Between Pen and Rifle*, Lanham, MD: Rowman & Littlefield, 2005, p. 40.
61 Muminov, "Fundamentalist Challenges," p. 255.

Central Asia and Kazakhstan (SADUM). In 1947, he and his son were allowed to perform the Hajj and to travel to Al-Azhar; three generations of the Babakhan family would remain at the helm of SADUM for a half century, until 1989.[62]

Thus, the very institution Moscow created to regulate and control religion was handed to figures deeply steeped in Salafi theology, and who were hostile both to the folk Sufi Islam and to the indigenous Hanafi-Maturidi tradition of Central Asia. In 1952, they issued a fatwa denouncing Sufism.[63] From the 1960s onward, they benefited from repeated travels to the Middle East, bringing back religious literature from there that conflicted with Hanafi traditions of Central Asia.[64]

This helped spur an Islamist revival in Central Asia. From the 1970s onward, independent theologians of a Salafi bent became even more outspoken critics of indigenous religious traditions. These included Abduvali Qori Mirzoyev and Obidxon Qori Nazarov, who would have great influence in the rise of extremist Islamism in the Ferghana valley during the transition to independence.[65] Research has confirmed that Soviet covert support for Salafi tendencies continued into the 1980s.[66]

During the 1980s, a younger generation of Salafi imams and activists began to organize in Tajikistan, as well as in the Uzbek part of the Ferghana valley, particularly the towns of Andijan, Namangan and Margilan. Not surprisingly, this led to conflict

---

62 Olcott, *In the Whirlwind*, p. 81-90.
63 Pawel Jassa," Religious Renewal in Kazakhstan", in Chris Hann, ed., *The Postsocialist Religious Question: Faith and Power in Central Asia and East-Central Europe*, Münster: LIT Verlag, 2006, p. 177.
64 Peyrouse, "The Rise of Political Islam," p. 43.
65 For a valuable rendering of the ideas of these theologians, see Allen J. Frank and Jahangir Mamatov, *Uzbek Islamic Debates: Texts, Translations, and Commentary*, Springfield, VA: Dunwoody Press, 2006.
66 Naumkin, *Radical Islam*, p. 52.

between the Salafi-minded reformers and the remaining Hanafi traditionalists of Central Asia. The latter were led by Muhammadjon Hindustani, based in Dushanbe, who spent the last decades of his life providing Islamic education to select students in his home and devoting his life to maintaining the region's Hanafi tradition and its respect of Sufi currents. His balancing act required an ear acutely tuned to the political realities of the Soviet Union. Yet this caution also led a number of his more impatient disciples to defect to the more radical factions.[67]

This curious game of shadows among atheist communists, Hanafi traditionalists, and assertive Salafis set the tone for Islamic activity in Central Asia in the late Soviet era and the early years of independence. All major actors on the Islamic scene in the first decade of independence were formed in this environment, which prevailed to the end of Soviet rule. What occurred in Soviet Central Asia was thus not just the attempted destruction of religion, but a purposefully orchestrated competition between traditionalist Hanafi Islam and a Salafi-inclined tendency with growing ties to the Middle Eastern heartland. As will be seen in the next chapter, this set the stage for a new confrontation at independence: between the supporters of the weakened indigenous traditions and the proponents of purportedly more authentic imported doctrines from the Middle East.

---

67 Olcott, *In the Whirlwind*, p. 93-97

4. INDEPENDENCE AND THE RELIGIOUS QUESTION

ALL OVER CENTRAL ASIA, policies toward religion were conditioned by the sudden arrival of independence. Few had expected independence, let alone fought for it. The lone exception was Azerbaijan, where Moscow's manipulation of the conflict with Armenia had spurred a strong nationalist movement that sought separation from the USSR. In Central Asia, while there were outbursts of nationalism – such as the *Zheltoqsan* riots in Almaty in 1986 – no concerted struggle for independence developed, and the new states continued to be run by their Soviet-era elites. The exception, as seen below, was Tajikistan.

The collapse of the USSR also meant the collapse of state atheism, and the ushering in of new freedoms, including in the religious realm. But religion had been suppressed for a good seventy years, meaning that the region's population had only superficial knowledge of their own religious traditions. This vacuum was not lost on religious ideologues outside the region: a hodgepodge of religious missionaries from the Muslim heartland and from the West saw former Soviet states as a wonderful place to recruit followers. More acutely, the region bordered both Iran and Afghanistan, hotbeds of Islamic radicalism whose potential appeal in the region was impossible to determine. Such radicals gained a foothold in Tajikistan and played a key role in that country's civil war, leading elites across Central Asia to view religious ideologues as an acute threat to their statehood.

The region's states faced unique circumstances. Tajikistan dealt with the fallout of a civil war that had strengthened Islamic radicalism. Uzbekistan had its own Islamist uprising in the Ferghana valley. By comparison, the religious challenge in Kazakhstan and Kyrgyzstan was less acute, but these states also had considerably greater non-Muslim populations. Most complicated was the situation in Azerbaijan, which is linguistically close to Sunni Turkey but is majority-Shi'a and borders both Iran and the Russian North Caucasus, yet another hotbed of radicalism.

The Challenge of Statehood: Central Asia at Independence

Were the Central Asian republics and Azerbaijan actually *states* at independence? On a superficial level, they were. World maps showed their borders; and they had governments, flags, parliaments, and rudimentary institutions. Under the surface, however, reality was quite different, as these were acutely weak entities. Western observers of the 1990s, who tended to view all post-Communist countries as somewhat similar, largely failed to capture this. This led to the idea that all these countries, from Poland to Tajikistan, were in "transition" from Communism to liberal democracy. This missed an important point: East European countries like Poland had been under Soviet influence, but not formally part of the Soviet Union. Central Asian republics, by contrast, had not even been independent states on paper – they had been fully incorporated in the Soviet Union. While they formally had large autonomy, the Communist Party, which controlled all the fifteen union republics, was highly centralized. Therefore, these states were immeasurably less prepared for independent nationhood than their Eastern European counterparts. This severely complicated the building of statehood.

For starters, the states of the region had never existed with the names or borders that they inherited in 1991. The lone exception was again Azerbaijan, which had briefly known statehood from 1918 to 1920. Central Asian republics were created by the Soviet leadership in the 1920s, and they bore little if any resemblance to the many and often powerful states that had existed in the region. Unlike many African colonies and Middle Eastern states, they were not entirely artificial. Soviet planners created each republic around a titular majority nation – Uzbeks in Uzbekistan, etc. But they *were* created in an arbitrary fashion by faraway rulers who gave them boundaries that often defied settlement patterns on the ground. This handicapped the states at independence, because their national development had not been organic, it had been manipulated by Moscow.

Challenges to the building of effective state institutions were even more profound. Because they formed part of the Soviet Union, Central Asian states lacked many of the key institutions that define statehood. The most glaring problem was the absence of governing institutions. In the Soviet era, key political decisions were taken in Moscow. While the administrative structure of the union delegated authority to the republics, the Communist Party – where real power lay – was never decentralized. Meanwhile, responsibility for most economic affairs rested at the provincial level. In other words, the Soviet republics were undermined from both above and below. Thankfully, republican institutions had been allowed to grow stronger in the 1980s, but in the USSR's last years, Gorbachev worked hard to weaken them and concentrate power in Moscow. Independence therefore came at a time when republican institutions were deliberately being emasculated.

After independence, the central executive, legislative and judiciary institutions continued to be plagued by Soviet ailments and needed to undergo fundamental reform in order to function in an independent state. Some institutions did not exist at all: the states had no military or border guards. When they set out to create these key bodies, personnel proved a major challenge because of the authoritarian mentality and corrupt ways that had dominated the Soviet government. In the late Soviet era, public office was gained through bribery or nepotism and held for the benefit not of the public but of the officeholder, his family, and his network. While even well-meaning political leaders could institute reforms, they still had to deal with staffs that were unwilling or unable to adapt to new ways. It is no coincidence that the most well-functioning and progressive institutions across the region are those that were created from scratch after independence.

The economy and infrastructure posed further challenges. The economies of Soviet republics were far more closely tied to Moscow than were the "satellite" countries in Eastern Europe. Central Asian states were commanded to produce raw materials for industrial centers that were elsewhere in the union. Similarly, transportation and communication infrastructure connected these republics to Moscow, but denied them connections to neighboring countries that historically had been their major trading partners. Therefore, Uzbekistan continued to market most of its cotton crop through the Baltic port of Riga, not the harbors on the Indian

Ocean, though these are a thousand miles closer. Worse, the command economy produced goods that could not compete on the world market, and in any case Central Asia and Azerbaijan were landlocked, and had no way to get their goods efficiently to global markets. It is no surprise that their Soviet-era factories soon became known as "Large Abandoned Objects" – simply left to rot until Chinese demand for metals caused them to be sold for scrap.[1]

Soviet-era economics and transport infrastructure also completely ignored the borders between Central Asian states. Travel by road or rail between two points in a given country often required transit through a neighbor's territory. This suddenly mattered when these borders became national boundaries. And energy infrastructure was not republican but regional in nature, leading to complicated problems between states with oil and gas, and those that had hydropower resources.

Thus, at independence the challenges confronted by states in Central Asia and Azerbaijan were of a different order of magnitude compared to their counterparts in Eastern and Central Europe. It was therefore entirely predictable that the transition to independence would be extremely painful across the region. The new governments had to deal simultaneously with building new state institutions, managing the fallout of the collapse of the Soviet economic system, and handling challenges to their newfound sovereignty. In most states, gross domestic product fell by half in the first three years of independence, and in countries affected by armed conflict like Azerbaijan and Tajikistan, much more. Poverty levels rose rapidly, and social, educational and health services verged on collapse. This prompted high levels of emigration, with lasting consequences for the population that remained.

---
1 Wendell Steavenson, *Stories I Stole*, Grover Press, 2004.

Rural areas were particularly hard hit, especially company towns where the large single employer had gone out of business. In the absence of a functioning economy and efficient state institutions, there emerged semi-feudal types of social organization. Important sectors of the economies and entire branches of government came under the influence of persons who were akin to medieval barons – heads of informal networks of power held together by common familial or regional identities or simple economic interest. These networks established themselves so strongly that in many countries they gained the ability to check the power of central governments.

All this had important implications for identity, and thus for the state's relationship to religion. Soviet state ideology had had a measurable impact on the region's population. Republics like Estonia or Georgia had never accepted a Soviet identity, largely because of the strength of their pre-existing national consciousness. In Central Asia, however, there had been only limited national consciousness: identity rested either at the sub-national level – in the city, region, clan or tribe the individual belonged to; or at the supra-national level – in the form of Muslim identity. But seventy years of Soviet rule weakened both, through the systematic targeting of religious identity, the promotion of economic and social development, as well as the creation of national republics and the promotion of Communist, Soviet community. The collapse of the Soviet bond therefore left a void, which leaders of the new states all sought to fill with carefully crafted appeals to solidarity with the newly independent nation.

This still left unanswered the question what role religion played in the people's identity. After all, Central Asians had viewed themselves as Uzbeks or Kazakhs for several decades; but they had been Muslims for centuries, in some areas a millennium or more. And timing matters: Central Asia did not gain independence at a time when secular ideologies were running strong in the Muslim world – as they had from the 1920s to the 1950s, an era dominated by Arab socialism, Kemalist Turkish nationalism, and the Shah's secular Iranian nationalism. Quite to the contrary, the 1990s saw the largely uninterrupted rise of Islamism, and its growth to hegemonic position across southwest Asia – from Pakistan in the east to Turkey in the West. This weighed heavily on the minds of the leaders of the new states.

In sum, Central Asia and the Caucasus faced an uphill battle at independence. The region's leaders were steeped in their Soviet upbringing, but faced huge political, economic and social challenges to guide their nations into the world community. To an extent that is poorly understood in the West, the question how to deal with religion played a key role in their calculations.

The Challenge of Radical Islam

The challenge of radical Islam predates the collapse of the Soviet Union. As viewed in chapter three, a series of conditions had emerged in the 1980s to allow the emergence of radical Islam across the region. At the basis was the gradual hollowing out of any hold the Communist ideology had on the population, and the central authorities' loss of control. Another was the Soviet tolerance of Salafi ideas in Soviet religious institutions with a purpose to weaken traditional, Hanafi Islam; yet a third was Central Asia's exposure to the Afghanistan conflict. As a result, Islamic radical forces moved rapidly to fill the ideological vacuum in the transition to independence. This was a classic transnational challenge:

the ideology was foreign in origin, and had outside support, but the forces in Central Asia were home-grown, indigenous groups often working hand in hand with foreign ideologues.

The Geopolitical Context: Afghanistan, Pakistan, and Iran

The transition to independence took place at a time of significant turmoil in the region's southern borderlands. As mentioned, radical forms of political Islam were on the ascendant in Iran, Pakistan and Afghanistan, and even in Turkey.

The Iranian revolution was only a decade old, and the Iran-Iraq war had just concluded. Iran's ability to survive the Iraqi onslaught was a victory of sorts, and at a minimum guaranteed the survival of its revolutionary regime. Because of Iran's peculiar form of Shi'a theocracy, its model is often thought to have limited relevance for Central Asia. The exception is Azerbaijan, also majority Shi'a, whose conflict with Armenia would seem to create grievances that might have made it a leading candidate for the export of Iranian revolutionary ideas. But in a twist, Iran's fear of separatist sentiments among its own large Azerbaijani population led it to adopt a clear hostility toward Azerbaijan, and an ill-concealed sympathy for Armenia. In Central Asia, by contrast, the Iranian model had little appeal, even in Persian-speaking Tajikistan, where it offered only lukewarm support for the Tajik opposition. Iran's main objective was to prevent Turkish and Western inroads into its northern neighborhood, and this led to a tacit alignment with Russia, something that could have been jeopardized by greater intervention in Tajikistan or anywhere in the region.

But this does not mean Iran's role was irrelevant. Quite to the contrary, it had the same impact in Central Asia as it did elsewhere in the Muslim world: by showing that an Islamic revolution was possible and no pipe dream, the revolution began to change the way Iran's Shi'a were viewed by Islamists around the world. Previously, they had largely been viewed as heretics. Salafi Muslims continued to view them in this way; but the mainstream Sunni radicals of the Muslim Brotherhood variety did not. Instead, a form of respect and admiration for the Iranian regime began to develop among Islamist activists in the Sunni world, which led them to seek to emulate the success of their Iranian counterparts. This was true for Turkish Islamists, and certainly also the case for Islamists in Central Asia, for whom the Iranian example meant that the replacement of Communist rule with Islamic rule was not beyond the realm of the possible.

The impact of Afghanistan and Pakistan was much more direct. And because of the influence of Pakistan on the politics of Afghanistan, the two cannot be separated. Afghanistan was much more directly relevant because of its proximity to Central Asia, the close ethnolinguistic ties across the border, and the close family ties that remained: Stalin's collectivization in the late 1920s, for example, had led over half a million people to flee southern Tajikistan for refuge in northern Afghanistan.[2] But from a political point of view, Pakistan's role was crucial, because Pakistan had played a key role in pushing the ideology of the Afghan Mujahideen in an increasingly radical direction.

In the 1980s, Pakistan went through a process of Islamization under the rule of military leader Zia ul-Haque. Zia, and Pakistan's Inter-Services Intelligence, had insisted on supporting

---

2 Tim Epkenhans, *The Origins of the Civil War in Tajikistan*, Lanham, MD: Lexington Books, 2018, p. 5.

the most radical Islamist forces in the Afghan resistance to the Soviet invasion. This was as much for pragmatic as for ideological reasons: just as in Kashmir, Pakistani planners believed they could exercise much more control over Islamist rebels than nationalist ones. In both Kashmir and Afghanistan, nationalists had their own contentions with Pakistan: Kashmiri nationalists wanted independence from India, *not* accession to Pakistan; and Pashtun nationalists in Afghanistan had designs on Pakistan's own Pashtun-populated Northwest Frontier Province, the separation of which from Afghanistan they never accepted. Islamists, by contrast, were much more willing to accept Pakistan's guidance and leadership.[3]

While largely ethnically Tajik, the Jamiat-e Islami of Burhanuddin Rabbani and Ahmad Shah Masoud drew its ideological inspiration from the Pakistani movement of the same name, which also provided it with initial support. This changed only when the more orthodox Gulbuddin Hekmatyar split from the Jamiat, because he advocated an immediate uprising rather than a gradual infiltration of society and the state. This led Pakistan to direct the bulk of its support to Hekmatyar's forces. Hekmatyar, an ethnic Pashtun from Kunduz in northern Afghanistan, saw a significant boost in 1992, when Pashtun officials in the collapsing Afghan government defected *en masse* to his faction. This led to the Afghan civil war, which played out just as Central Asia transitioned to independence. Masoud and Hekmatyar were the two main protagonists, a third being the ethnic Uzbek warlord Abdul Rashid Dostum. At independence, while fighting for power in Kabul, Dostum's forces controlled the border areas with

---

[3] Svante E. Cornell, "Pakistan's Foreign Policy: Islamic or Pragmatic?", in Brenda Shaffer, ed., *The Limits of Culture: Foreign Policy, Islam and the Caspian*, Cambridge, MA: MIT Press, 2006.

4. Independence And The Religious Question

Uzbekistan, while Masoud held the bulk of Afghanistan territory bordering Tajikistan.

Had the power-sharing agreement that the UN negotiated in April 1992 held, Afghanistan would have had a coalition government of varying Islamist factions, some of which with strong ethnic and cultural connections to Central Asia. That would have seemed a logical conclusion of the war in Afghanistan, with a Soviet-supported government giving way to an Islamist one led by the Mujahideen forces that had effectively defeated the USSR with Pakistani and American support. That would have had important implications for Central Asian states, but it was not to be. Islamabad had other ideas: Pakistani leaders viewed the independence of Central Asia as a historic chance to gain what they called "strategic depth." The idea was to secure a friendly backyard to the north in Afghanistan, and expand Pakistani influence into Central Asia – including by spreading Islamist ideology as well as opening up the trade routes to the ocean that Central Asians so desperately needed. The first step in that direction was to ensure a pliant, pro-Pakistan government in Kabul, which Pakistan's intelligence services sought to do by backing Hekmatyar's bid for power in Kabul. Had it succeeded, it would have led to an even more radical Islamist regime in Kabul with designs on Central Asia. But it failed miserably, leading instead to an all-out war among the rebel factions, which essentially leveled Afghanistan's capital. Hekmatyar's failure also led Pakistan, by 1995, to drop its support for him, shifting it instead to a newly formed Taliban movement. The Taliban conquered Kabul in 1996 and expanded control northward until, on the eve of 9/11, only the mountainous areas of northeast Afghanistan wre outside their control. As a result, for several years the Taliban controlled Afghanistan's borders with Turkmenistan and Uzbekistan.

From Central Asia's perspective, one thing was clear: Islamic radicalism reigned supreme in Afghanistan, with Pakistan's backing, and provided a geopolitical context where the fear of a spread of the turmoil into the region did not seem far-fetched at all. Furthermore, the Islamist groups inside Central Asia rapidly established connections to their counterparts in Afghanistan. These connections were both ideological and commercial, with involvement in the booming narcotics trade from Afghanistan proving an important common denominator. As will be seen, this created a transnational threat in particular to Tajikistan and Uzbekistan, with very different results.

Uzbekistan's Ferghana Valley

Radical Islamists rose to prominence in Uzbekistan's section of the Ferghana Valley in the chaotic period of the Soviet Union's collapse. This was a period of increasing lawlessness, including ethnic riots particularly between Kyrgyz and Uzbeks in the Osh region of Kyrgyzstan in 1990. Uzbekistan as a whole experienced a period of turmoil as Soviet central authorities had sought to assert greater direct control in the Gorbachev era. By the time Islam Karimov was selected to head the republic in mid-1989, Tashkent's ability to exert power over Uzbekistan's territory had declined considerably. Meanwhile, Soviet attempts at economic reform had aimed at economic liberalization, but in fact led to widespread racketeering, as corrupt local officials were able to control and supervise the conduct of business activity.[4]

---

4 Vladimir Brovkin, "Fragmentation of Authority and Privatization of the State: from Gorbachev to Yeltsin", *Demokratizatsiya*, vol. 6 no. 3, 1998, pp. 504-17. (https://www2.gwu.edu/~ieresgwu/assets/docs/demokratizatsiya%20archive/06-03_brovkin.pdf)

4. Independence And The Religious Question

In the Ferghana valley, this lawless atmosphere contributed to the rise of Salafi-inspired radical groups, who variously referred to themselves as *mujaddidiylar* (reformers) or *vohhobiylar* (Wahhabis). These groups were the product of alien influences and the Soviet policies discussed in the previous chapter: they rejected the local folk Islamic practices and sought to impose a literalist practice of Islam, and developed paramilitary formations that challenged – or competed with – racketeering practices that local authorities were involved in.[5] The city of Namangan was the epicenter of the growing confrontation between these forces and the increasingly inept local authorities. By January 1990, a group calling itself *Islam Adolati* (Islamic Justice) gradually began to usurp the functions of law enforcement. The group patrolled markets and apprehended thieves, but also violently closed down stores that sold alcohol and enforced Islamic dress for women. The outspoken aim was to impose a Sharia-based order first in the city, and gradually to the entire territory of the republic and beyond.[6] The bulk of these vigilantes were recruited from heavily criminalized martial arts circles.[7] Subsequently, the Uzbek militants became heavily involved in the trafficking of drugs from Afghanistan; and the motivations of at least parts of the movement appear to have been strongly affected by this involvement.[8]

The Ferghana valley had also become a haven for foreign

---

5 Bahtiyar Babajanov, "Le jihad comme idéologie de l'"autre' et de 'l'éxile' à travers l'étude de documents du Mouvement islamique d'Ouzbékistan", *Cahiers d'Asie Centrale*, 15/16, 2007. (www.asiecentrale.revues.org/84)
6 Olcott, *In the Whirlwind of Jihad;* Naumkin, *Radical Islam in Central Asia.*
7 Bakhtiyar Babajanov, Kamil Malikov, and Aloviddin Nazarov, "Islam in the Ferghana Valley: Between National Identity and Islamic Alternative," in Ferghana Valley, The Heart of Central Asia, ed. S. Frederick Starr (Armonk, NY: M.E. Sharpe, 2011); Naumkin, *Radical Islam in Central Asia*, p. 262.
8 Svante E. Cornell, "The Islamic Movement of Uzbekistan", in Svante E. Cornell and Michael Jonsson, eds., *Conflict, Crime and the State in Postcommunist Eurasia*, Philadelphia: University of Pennsylvania Press, 2014, pp. 68-81.

Islamic missionaries from the Gulf, Afghanistan, and Pakistan.[9] This encouraged Tahir Yuldashev, the local Islamist leader, to set himself up as a *de facto* ruler of the Ferghana valley.[10] The government of Uzbekistan was very nearly overwhelmed by this challenge. With Soviet power collapsing, the republican administration needed to consolidate its control over the functions of government. In this power vacuum, Uzbekistan's new leader, Islam Karimov, went so far as to travel to Namangan in December 1991 to meet with the Salafis, who demanded the declaration of Uzbekistan as an Islamic state. In a dramatic episode that has been preserved for posterity on the internet, Yuldashev forced Karimov, in a very hostile environment, to listen to his lecture on proper Islamic governance.[11]

This experience proved formative both for Karimov and for the leadership of the country as a whole. Over the next few months, the government managed to consolidate enough power to restore control over the restive Ferghana, and engaged in a broad effort to suppress Islamist forces, Salafi and non-Salafi alike.[12] President Karimov's apprehensions concerning political Islam were exacerbated by events in Tajikistan, discussed below, where Islamists played a key role in the emerging civil war. The Uzbek militants exiled from the Ferghana valley became an important component of that war. Tajikistan's descent into chaos strengthened the conviction of the Uzbek leadership that stability had to

---

9 Naumkin, *Radical Islam*, 66-70; Michael Fredholm, *Uzbekistan and the Threat from Islamic Extremism*, Sandhurst: United Kingdom Royal Military Academy, Conflict Studies Research Centre, Report no. K39, March 2003, p. 4.
10 Naumkin, *Radical Islam*, pp. 52-60.
11 Babajanov, Malikov, and Nazarov, "Islam in the Ferghana Valley" pp. 319-320. The video is available at https://www.youtube.com/watch?v=xwVS8CQg2s4
12 Naumkin, *Radical Islam in Central Asia*, p.70; Ahmed Rashid, "The Fires of Faith in Central Asia", *World Policy Journal*, vol. 18 no. 1, 2001, pp. 45-55.

4. Independence And The Religious Question

be maintained at any cost, and Islamic extremism fought with all available means.

Following the 1997 peace agreement in Tajikistan, the Uzbek militants moved to Afghanistan, established close ties with the Taliban and Al Qaeda, and officially reconstituted themselves as the Islamic Movement of Uzbekistan. This organization then planned and executed a series of attacks on the homeland. In early 1999, a series of bomb explosions in Tashkent presumed to be the work of the IMU nearly killed President Karimov. In August 1999, the IMU conducted a military incursion into the Batken region of Kyrgyzstan, close to Uzbekistan's borders. The IMU was repelled but returned the next summer, better armed, and this time managed to reach several areas of Uzbekistan, where they engaged government forces. It was only after the U.S. intervention in Afghanistan in the fall of 2001 that the IMU was forced back into the Tribal Areas of Pakistan, where it merged with other foreign fighters loyal to Al Qaeda.

The government managed to largely remove violent Islamist extremists from the republic's territory. But purportedly non-violent foreign groups sought to fill the vacuum, including Hizb-ut-Tahrir al-Islami (HTI) and Jamaat al-Tabligh. HTI, a global Islamist movement, eschews violence, but aims to build a Caliphate uniting all Muslims in which there would be no place for non-believers.[13] HTI spread rapidly in Central Asia in the 1990s,[14]

---

13 Zeyno Baran, *Hizb-ut-Tahrir*, p. 48.
14 This is documented in Baran, *Hizb-ut-Tahrir*; Emmanuel Karagiannis *Political Islam in Central Asia: The Challenge of Hizb Ut-Tahrir,* London: Routledge, 2010; and Naumkin, *Radical Islam in Central Asia,* pp. 127-200. Further studies include International Crisis Group, "Radical Islam in Central Asia: Responding to Hizb ut-Tahrir," Asia Report no. 58, June 30, 2003; Emmanuel Karagiannis and C. McCauley "Hizb ut-Tahrir al-Islami: Evaluating the Threat Posed by a Radical Islamic Group That Remains Nonviolent" *Terrorism and Political Violence*, Vol. 18, 2006; Alisher Khamidov, "Countering the Call: The U.S., Hizb-ut-Tahrir and Religious Extremism in Central Asia", Brookings Institution, 2003; Didier Chaudet, "Hizb-ut-Tahrir: An Islamist Threat to Central Asia", *Journal of*

and by the mid-2000s, there was much alarm raised about the organization's proliferation. Post-2010, however, HTI appears to no longer be functioning in Uzbekistan, while it continues to exist in Kyrgyzstan and Tajikistan. The Tabligh movement is outlawed in most of the region, but has gained prominence in more liberal Kyrgyzstan.

The Tajik Civil War

If Uzbekistan's leadership managed to retain control, their Tajik counterparts' failure to do so resulted in a prolonged civil war. This conflict had strong regional undertones, fueled by Soviet policies as well as the republic's geography. In fact, the territory allocated to Tajikistan by Soviet planners was largely mountainous and rural; it did not include centers of Tajik culture like Samarkand and Bukhara, which remained part of Uzbekistan. Nor did it include the kindred populations in Afghanistan, where there were and remain more Tajiks than in Tajikistan itself. The republic itself was divided into at least three distinct geographic and cultural zones divided by mountain ranges. The sparsely populated eastern half in the Pamir mountains, populated largely by Ismaili Shia minority groups, was cut off from the rest of the territory. But even in western Tajikistan, the more urban and industrialized northern areas around Leninabad, which geographically were part of the Ferghana valley, were separated from central Tajikistan by another mountain range. And while Soviet planners located the capital in the central town of Dushanbe, they largely handed political and economic power to elites from Leninabad.

Soviet planners also played with the demography of the

Muslim Minority Affairs, vol. 26 no. 1, 2006, pp. 113-125; Svante E. Cornell and Regine Spector, "Central Asia: More than Islamic Extremists", *Washington Quarterly*, vol. 25 no. 1, 2002, pp. 193-206.

republic. Aside from causing the emigration of thousands, on several subsequent occasions, authorities forcibly resettled large numbers of people within Tajikistan, moving them from remote areas to central places where labor was needed. Most came from the Karategin valley in east-central Tajikistan, and were moved to the cotton fields in the Vakhsh river valley in the Southwest. As the population grew while the Soviet economy slowed in a republic whose arable land is estimated at only five percent of the total land area, this generated considerable tensions between communities, something that would have enormous implications for independence.

Karategin – the erstwhile Gharm province – was known to be among the most religiously conservative areas of Tajikistan, and it had been a hotbed of the anti-Soviet Basmachi rebellion already in the 1920s.[15] Forced resettlement had the effect of strengthening both the regional and religious identity of the settlers, and as a result religious ideology came to frame the grievances the resettled Gharmis held against both the central government and the local elites they competed with, primarily from Kulyab. Conversely, opposition to radical Islam became a rallying cry for the mainly Leninabadi and Kulyabi supporters of the neo-Communist government of Tajikistan.

The Soviet war in Afghanistan played an important role in driving a wedge between the official Soviet Islamic clergy, which was compelled to support the war, and the underground religious movements discussed in the previous chapter, who grew in stature as a result of popular dissatisfaction with the Soviet clergy. Meanwhile, Gorbachev's reforms had reduced the dominant position of the Communist Party in Tajikistan, and a series of political parties

---

15 William S. Ritter, "Revolt in the Mountains: Fuzail Maksum and the Occupation of Garm, Spring 1929," *Journal of Contemporary History*, vol. 25, 1990, p. 537-80.

emerged to contest its position of power. The Tajik Communist leadership's decision to back the 1991 Moscow coup further weakened its position, and in the fall of 1991 and spring of 1992, a tug-of-war emerged in Dushanbe between supporters of the post-Communist government and an opposition force in which Islamists provided the muscle and the manpower. Rivaling sets of demonstrators took over two large squares in Dushanbe, and in April 1992 the leader of the country's official clergy – who had long maintained neutrality and sought to mediate between the two sides – announced his support for the opposition. Meanwhile, by May Islamist opposition leaders began chanting demands for an Islamic state, and the two sides began to acquire large quantities of weapons – which at least one Islamist leader claimed had been delivered through the Islamists' connections to the Afghan *Mujahideen*.[16] Indeed, even before the Soviet Union's collapse, Afghan warlords such as Ahmad Shah Masoud had begun to establish their presence in Tajikistan, developing both commercial and ideological relations with their counterparts there, as well as acquiring homes there for their families.[17]

The weakness of the Tajik state could have led to an Islamist victory, but that was not to happen. Russia and Uzbekistan both intervened, and by December 1992 had helped the Leninabad-Kulyab grouping rout the opposition forces and to establish a new government led by the Kulyabi Emomali Rakhmon, who remains president of Tajikistan at the time of writing. This led to the flight of up to 100,000 civilians to Afghanistan, where the Islamist opposition had set up camp in Taloqan, a city close to the

---

16 Kiril Nourzhanov and Christian Bleuer, *Tajikistan: A Social and Political History*, Canberra: Australian National University Press, 2013, p. 317.
17 Scott W. Tousley, *Afghan Sources of the Tajikistan Civil War*, Ft. Leavenworth, KS: U.S. Army Command and General Staff College, 1995, p. 20.

border controlled by the Jamiat-e-Islami. Having thus regrouped, the Islamist-led opposition managed to fight their way back into the war, leading eventually to a UN-mediated power-sharing deal in 1997.

The former opposition commanders maintained their militias and continued to have dominant influence in their core areas of support, particularly the Rasht valley. Their connections to foreign radicals did not stop because of the peace agreement: in spring 1999, hundreds of Uzbek Islamists moved back into Tajikistan from Afghanistan, taking up positions in the Tavildara valley on the border between Tajikistan and Kyrgyzstan. In August, they launched the above-mentioned military incursion into Kyrgyzstan. When they retreated back into Tajikistan and Afghanistan, they received support from Tajikistan's Minister of Emergencies, the former opposition warlord Mirzo Zioyev.[18] The same operation was repeated on a more sophisticated scale the next year; again, it was helicopters from Tajikistan's Emergency Ministry that airlifted Uzbek Islamists back to their camps in Afghanistan.[19] It was only with the U.S. invasion of Afghanistan after 9/11 that the militant Islamist threat to Central Asia was effectively neutralized.

The North Caucasus

Islamic radicalism also developed a strong foothold in the North Caucasus, particularly in Chechnya and Dagestan – also the two territories that had most strenuously fought Russian expansion in the nineteenth century. It is notable that this part of the North

---

18 Ahmed Rashid, "They're Only Sleeping – Why Militant Islamicists in Central Asia Aren't Going to Go Away," The New Yorker, January 14 2002.
19 Rashid, Jihad, 176-178.

Caucasus is the only part of the former Soviet Union where the more orthodox Shafi'i school of law was predominant – elsewhere in the North Caucasus, just as among Muslims in the Volga region or Central Asia, the Hanafi school predominates. This more Orthodox form of Islam proved difficult for the Soviet leadership to eradicate. An Islamic revival began to be seen in Dagestan in the 1970s, concentrated to the mountainous northwest parts of the republic. Salafi ideas also began to spread at the time, facilitated perhaps by the predominance of Dagestanis, who often numbered close to half of the small contingent of Soviet Muslims allowed to perform the pilgrimage to Mecca.[20]

The war in Chechnya, which raged from 1994-96 and again from 1999 until 2003, with low-intensity conflict continuing after that, has come to be closely associated with Islamic radicalism. However, this was not always the case: the Chechen movement for independence was an almost entirely secular affair. This is not to say that Islamist elements were not present: they did develop among the Chechen leadership, but initially remained marginal, asserting themselves only tepidly, and there is significant evidence suggesting that leading advocates initially embraced Islamism in a mainly instrumental way.[21]

Islamism did not cause the war in Chechnya, but it was the war that led Islamism to develop. The first jihadi elements appeared in Chechnya *after* Russia's brutal invasion of late 1994. There is ample evidence that there was little love lost between the Chechen leadership and the foreign jihadis that flocked to the region —but beggars cannot be choosers, and the Chechens

---

20 Mikhail Alexseev and Sufian Zhemukhov, *Mass Religious Ritual and Intergroup Tolerance: The Muslim Pilgrims' Paradox*, New York: Cambridge University Press, 2017, p. 25.
21 Julie Wilhelmsen, "Between a Rock and a Hard Place: The Islamisation of the Chechen Separatist Movement," *Europe-Asia Studies*, Vol. 57, No. 1, January 2005, pp. 38-39.

needed all the help that they could get, all the more since they were exceptionally effective in combat. The number of foreign fighters in the first war was small, perhaps a few hundred at most. These were mainly roving "Arab Afghans" who had fought in Kashmir, Tajikistan, and Bosnia-Herzegovina after the end of the Afghan war. Islamic radicalism then spread after the 1996 peace agreement, which left Chechnya in limbo – Russian troops withdrew, but the territory's status remained undetermined, preventing an international presence there.

The unresolved situation led to a disastrous economic situation, and to the slipping of the authority of Chechnya's secular president Aslan Maskhadov. Various criminal groups emerged that engaged in smuggling and kidnapping, and the government showed its inability to deal with this problem. Most alarmingly, warlords like Shamil Basayev and the Jordanian-born Samir Saleh Abdullah al-Khattab began planning for the unification of Chechnya with the neighboring republic of Dagestan. Maskhadov was either unwilling or unable to rein in these warlords, fearing an intra-Chechen war. As a result, Basayev and Khattab were able to recruit hundreds of Dagestanis and other North Caucasians, including Chechens, into what they termed an Islamic Brigade based in Southeastern Chechnya. This brigade – which appears to have been infiltrated by Russian security services looking for an excuse to start a new war – would eventually launch the incursion into Dagestan in August 1999 that precipitated the second war.

Looking back, Chechnya was similar to Bosnia in terms of the level and character of the jihadi presence. Where it differed was in the absence of a Dayton-type internationalized conflict management mechanism. The leadership of the Bosnian Muslims in many ways leaned more toward Islamism than the Chechens:

Alija Izetbegovic, the Bosnian Muslim leader, had a long history of Islamist inclinations, as did his closest advisor, Haris Silajdzic. By contrast, the only Islamist to have a leadership position in the Chechen resistance was Zelimkhan Yandarbiyev, who served as interim president for several months after the Chechen President Jokhar Dudayev was killed in 1996. But in Bosnia, the foreign jihadis were evicted shortly following the Dayton Accords, after several altercations with NATO forces. Nothing of the sort happened in Chechnya, and their role instead grew during the course of the second Chechen war, when the Chechen resistance acquired a much stronger Islamist character. The use of Islamic vocabulary such as jihad or mujahedin increased markedly, as did active support for the Chechen cause by radical Islamic groups in the Middle East, at least until the U.S. invasion of Iraq led jihadis to flock to that conflict.

Russian policies contributed directly to turning the Chechen war from nationalist to an Islamist insurgency. Moscow consistently portrayed the conflict as one between civilization and Islamic extremism, even when it was actually about ethnic nationalism; it also actively worked to make the reality of the conflict conform to this vision. There is a clear pattern whereby Moscow prioritized targeting the nationalist Chechen leadership over the jihadi elements, most likely because the former had some international legitimacy. Both on the battlefield and on the diplomatic front, Russia targeted the more nationalist leaders of the resistance first, thereby ensuring the conflict would turn into one between Moscow's local strongman, Ramzan Kadyrov, and the Jihadis. Incidentally, this is a strategy Moscow used in Syria later on: it did not primarily target the Islamic State forces in Syria but the more moderate fighters, thereby forcing the west to choose between the only two remaining forces: the Assad regime and Islamic State, thus practically forcing the West to accept Moscow's client regime.[22] Moscow's policies were actually previewed in the Chechen war: the evidence is ample that Russian security services infiltrated large sections of the Islamist insurgency, and were able to manipulate it for its own purposes. When the Syrian war broke out, the same services organized a virtual pipeline for North Caucasian jihadis to leave the country and join the ranks of Islamic State and the Al Qaeda-aligned Nusra Front.[23] This allowed Moscow to hit two birds with one stone: first, it reduced the risk of terror attacks ahead of the 2014 Sochi Olympic games; and second, it accelerated the transformation of the Syrian conflict to a binary one between Assad and the jihadis.

The rise of radicalism in the North Caucasus had serious implications for Azerbaijan, Georgia and Kazakhstan: it created a hotbed of radical ideology very close to their border, which developed connections into their territory. In northern Georgia, Chechen civilian rebels fled the violence of the war, and benefited from the weakness of the Georgian state to establish a miniature caliphate that drew in Salafists from the Middle East as well. Salafi-inspired groups started spreading into Northern Azerbaijan as well, seeking to gain a foothold among the Sunni Muslim populations with ethnic ties to Dagestan.[24] And in Kazakhstan,

---

22 Andrew Foxall, "To See Syria's Future, Look at Chechnya", *American Interest*, December 4, 2015.. (http://www.the-american-interest.com/2015/12/04/to-see-syrias-future-look-at-chechnya/)

23 Elena Milashina, "'Халифат? Приманка для дураков!'", *Novaya Gazeta*, July 29, 2015. (https://novayagazeta.ru/articles/2015/07/29/65056-171-halifat-primanka-dlya-durakov-187)

Maria Tsvetkova, " How Russia allowed homegrown radicals to go and fight in Syria", Reuters, May 13, 2016. (https://www.reuters.com/investigates/special-report/russia-militants/)

24 Emil Souleimanov and Maya Ehrmann, "The Rise of Militant Salafism in Azerbaijan and

the main external source of radicalism in the country's western parts is not Afghanistan but nearby Dagestan.[25]

Challenges and Responses

The short overview above can hardly do justice to the tumultuous challenges faced by new states emerging of the ashes of the Soviet Union, and the unpredictability of the situation they faced. But it is important in providing an idea of the frame of mind that dominated among regional elites as they faced the task of developing state approaches to religious matters. The next chapter will delve into the specifics of the six regional states, and seek to track the commonalities and differences between them.

Its Regional Implications," *Middle East Policy*, vol 20. no. 3, 2013. (https://mepc.org/rise-militant-salafism-azerbaijan-and-its-regional-implications)
25 Svante E. Cornell, S. Frederick Starr and Julian Tucker, *Religion and the Secular State in Kazakhstan*, Washington/Stockholm: Silk Road Paper, p. 53. (https://silkroadstudies.org/resources/pdf/SilkRoadPapers/2018-04-Kazakhstan-Secularism.pdf)

5. DEVIL IN THE DETAIL:
Specific Challenges and Responses

SINCE INDEPENDENCE, former Communist leaders in new, weak states have had to grapple with the challenge of transition not only in the political and economic realms, but also in the spiritual one. Dealing with religious affairs was a task they were, as a class, poorly equipped to do: they had spent their lives as far removed from organized religion as possible, and in fact many of them had spearheaded Soviet atheist campaigns against religion. As they adjusted to a new reality, the abolition of state-imposed atheism was a given. But what would replace it? And how would new states approach religious affairs? As will be seen, while their circumstances varied greatly, they all moved toward a similar approach to religious matters.

This chapter discusses the experience of Central Asian states and Azerbaijan, beginning with the most critical case: Tajikistan, which had to grapple with the fallout of a civil war with Islamist elements. We then move to Uzbekistan, the largest state of Central Asia, whose policies were formed by the Tajik experience and its own extremist scare in the transition period. That is followed by the example of Azerbaijan, whose population makeup with a Shi'a majority and a Sunni minority called for a slightly different approach. Then, we view the examples of Kazakhstan and Kyrgyzstan, which both initially took a more liberal and permissive route, only to gradually gravitate toward greater restrictions. The final case is the more isolated Turkmenistan.

Tajikistan:
From Power-Sharing to Growing Restrictions

Tajikistan faced the most serious challenge to its statehood of all countries in this survey, as the outbreak of civil war in 1992 in practice amounted to state failure. But thanks to external support, the government and its affiliated militias were able to regain control over the country, though at a high human and material cost. The country's leadership was too weak to halt widespread abuses by militias aligned with it, and President Imomali Rakhmon initially led a government that was effectively dependent on warlords. This put Tajikistan apart from the rest of Central Asia, where there had been continuity of government from Soviet times and no similar disruption.

President Rakhmon had been considered a protégé of one of the warlords, Sangak Safarov. But Safarov was killed in a shootout with another warlord in 1993, leaving Rakhmon's position weakened. As if his own warlords were not enough, Rakhmon's authority was initially limited also by a power-sharing agreement with the United Tajik Opposition (UTO), whose strongest component was Islamist in nature.

Buoyed by Russian and Uzbek support, the government had been able to negotiate from a position of strength, and managed to keep the UTO's share in government posts to 30%. Furthermore,

5. Devil In The Detail: Specific Challenges And Responses

in subordinate positions, only a small number of UTO representatives were appointed to administrative positions.[1] Still, Rakhmon had to agree to appoint the Islamist commander Mirzo Ziyoyev as Minister of Emergencies, a position that allowed him to maintain his private militia. The opposition had insisted on Ziyoyev being appointed Defense Minister, a position that would have put Islamists at the core of the state, but the government had managed to defuse that demand.[2]

During peace negotiations, one key opposition demand was to scrap the constitution's provision that the state be secular. President Rakhmon adamantly rejected this demand, however, and the opposition did not have the strength to force the issue. That said, the 1999 amendment to the constitution stood out in Central Asia as it allowed political parties with a religious basis, something prohibited in the rest of the region.[3] As a result, the Islamic Renaissance Party continued to be represented in parliament for several years, but had only a small contingent there.

Two parallel processes took place in Tajikistan during the early 2000s. First, Rakhmon's ultimately successful effort toward authoritarian consolidation. Second, the growth of religious activity in the country. These two tendencies came to ultimately collide.

Rakhmon proved astute at using the office of the presidency to gradually outmaneuver the various warlords that had acquired positions in his government – be they aligned with the government or the opposition. In fact, at times he directed greater efforts at ridding himself of the influence of the very warlords that had

---

[1] Sumie Nakaya, "Aid and transition from a war economy to an oligarchy in post-war Tajikistan," *Central Asian Survey*, vol. 28 no. 3, 2009.
[2] Liz Fuller, "Tajikistan between Islam and democracy?" RFE/RL, September 24, 1999. (https://reliefweb.int/report/tajikistan/tajikistan-between-islam-and-democracy)
[3] Muriel Atkin, "Token Constitutionalism and Islamic Opposition in Tajikistan," *Journal of Persianate Studies*, vol. 5, 2012, 244-72.

helped his side win the war. One example was Gaffur Mirzoyev, who had been made Head of the Presidential Guards, but whom Rakhmon arrested in 2004. By the late 2000s, the government was in a stronger position: Rakhmon fired Ziyoyev and disbanded the Emergency Ministry, leading the former commander to return to the Rasht valley and set up a fiefdom there. He was eventually killed by government forces in 2009. But warlordism continued to plague Tajikistan. In 2015, the country was rocked by the defection of Gulmurad Khalimov, head of the Interior Ministry's special forces, to the Islamic State terrorist organization. Later the same year, the country's deputy Defense Minister Abdulhalim Nazarzoda, a former UTO commander, staged an abortive rebellion.[4]

Meanwhile, the relative weakness of the government – compared to the continuity of government elsewhere in Central Asia – led to a considerable pluralism in the religious realm. What happened was what one analyst termed the "proliferation of various forms of Islamic media and literature,"[5] including domestically produced and foreign books, the rise of an Islamic internet, and not least, the rapid spread of recordings of sermons by various religious figures. Besides being distributed at mosques, these sermons would be spread by drivers of taxis and routed minibuses in Dushanbe and other cities, and became ubiquitous by the end of the 2000s.[6]

While some may have viewed this as a sign of growing religious freedom, the Tajik government saw it otherwise, as a sign of growing efforts of religious indoctrination and recruitment by

---

4 Catherine Putz, "Tajikistan's Recent Violence: What We Know (and Don't Know)", *Diplomat*, September 8, 2015. (https://thediplomat.com/2015/09/tajikistans-recent-violence-what-we-know-and-dont-know/)
5 Shahnoza Nozimova and Tim Epkenhans, "The Transformation of Tajikistan's Religious Field", *Central Asian Affairs*, vol. 6 no. 2-3, 2019, p. 133-165.
6 Tim Epkenhans, "Islam, Religious Elites and the State in Post-Civil War Tajikistan, in Pauline Jones, ed., Islam,

5. Devil In The Detail: Specific Challenges And Responses

a variety of religious groups over which it had little or no control. In particular, the government's concern focused on the growth of foreign-inspired religious practices, which were clearly visible through the spread of dress codes not traditionally seen in Tajikistan. This started with the rapid growth of women wearing the *hijab* rather than a headscarf in traditional Central Asian style; but it was soon followed, particularly in the capital, by the growth of specific Salafi forms of dress – the long beards and ankle-length pants worn by men, and the full *niqab* showing only women's eyes.[7]

The government decided to crack down on this in the late 2000s, a crackdown that accelerated following the emergence of the Islamic State in Syria in 2011 and served to reassert control over religious practice in the country. This included an effort to build state-controlled religious institutions, coupled with restrictive measures to discourage unsanctioned religious practices and beliefs, as well as the construction of an official narrative on Tajik Islam.

During the Soviet era, Muslims in Tajikistan had been subordinated to the Tashkent-based Spiritual Administration of Muslims covering all of Central Asia. This was nevertheless broken down into the constituent republics in the late Soviet era, and Tajikistan developed its own institution, known as the *qoziyot*. It was led by the influential Islamic scholar Akbar Turajonzoda, who played a key role in the runup to the civil war. But Turajonzoda, while nominally the highest religious authority in the country, sided with the opposition as the civil war broke out. This influenced government perspectives on religious institutions writ large, and caused the government to close down the spiritual

---

7 Farangis Najibullah, "Niqab Adds New Wrinkle To Tajikistan's Head-Scarf Ban", *RFERL*, May 4, 2010. (https://www.rferl.org/a/Niqab_Adds_New_Wrinkle_To_Tajikistans_HeadScarf_Ban/2032293.html)

administration in 1994. Some years later, it created two new institutions: a Council of Ulema, nominally independent from the government, as well as a state committee for religious affairs. Through these institutions, the government sought to standardize Islamic practice, not least by issuing – on the model of Turkey's *Diyanet* – a single Friday sermon that imams in the country' mosques were to use following Friday prayers.

The government also introduced increasingly restrictive regulations regarding the registration of religious communities and the publication of religious literature. A new Law on Religion, passed in 2009, kick-started this process, though the law was amended on several occasions. Hijabs had been banned in schools already in 2005, a decision followed by a 2007 law that prohibited "provocative" clothing in schools, a term understood to include both the hijab and highly revealing clothes.[8] This was followed in 2017 by state policies that aggressively urged citizens to abstain from alien clothing traditions, and instead to wear "national" clothes. More specifically, the government sought to force women to abandon the hijab in favor of a headscarf tied loosely under their neck. There were numerous reports of state officials forcing women to remove *hijabs*, as well as to forcibly shave beards of men thought to sport Islamic-style facial hair.[9] Amendments in 2018, furthermore, put tight restrictions on foreign religious education, requiring anyone seeking to engage in foreign ventures to first receive religious education in the country and obtain state permission to

---

8 "Tajik Government Issue Hijab Ban", *Al Jazeera*, October 21, 2005; "Tajikistan bans miniskirts and head scarves", *Independent*, April 18, 2007.
9 "Tajikistan police shave beards of 13,000 men 'to tackle radicalism,'" *Independent*, January 21, 2016. (https://www.independent.co.uk/news/world/asia/tajikistan-police-shave-beards-of-13000-men-to-tackle-radicalism-a6825581.html)

leave. These amendments also banned minors' involvement in the "activity of religious organizations."[10]

Alongside these efforts, the government also changed its official approach to religion. While he had always remained committed to the notion of state secularism, in the early years of independence Rakhmon had sought to build a national idea heavily focused on Persianate imagery. It chose the Sunni, Persian-speaking Samanid dynasty of the ninth and tenth centuries as its reference point, but also emphasized continuity with the pre-Islamic Zoroastrian past of the Persianate people of Central Asia.[11] By the late 2000s, however, this narrative had shifted: the government now moved to promote, instead, a specific, traditional Tajik form of Islam in the Sunni Hanafi tradition. Thus, the 2009 law on religion continued to emphasize secularism, but simultaneously noted that the role of the Hanafi branch of Sunni Islam in the life of Tajiks must be taken into account.

Uzbekistan:
From Defensive to Proactive

Uzbekistan is in many ways the lynchpin of Central Asia. its population of 32 million is equal to the other four post-Soviet Central Asian states combined. Uzbekistan borders all Central Asian states including Afghanistan, and there are substantial ethnic Uzbek populations on the territory of all its neighbors. Moreover, the great majority of historical religious and political centers of Central Asia are located on Uzbekistan's territory. As

---

10 Felix Corley, "Tajikistan: 'Religious Activity is only banned up to the age of 18'", F18 News, July 21, 2011. https://wwrn.org/articles/35792/
11 Marlène Laruelle, "The Return of the Aryan Myth: Tajikistan in Search of a Secularized National Ideology," *Nationalities Papers*, vol. 35 no. 1, 2007; Matthias Battis, "The Aryan Myth and Tajikistan: From a Myth of Empire to One National Identity," *Ab Imperio*, no. 4, 2016.

already discussed, present-day Uzbekistan played an important role as host to the development of Islamic doctrine a millennium ago, while also being the birthplace of several of the world's most renowned Sufi orders. Equally importantly, since independence Uzbekistan developed the most professional military force in Central Asia, while its political leadership remained strongly committed to the country's sovereignty and independence. The country also has a balanced economy, with a respectable extractive sector as well as a developed industrial base.

Uzbekistan's approach to religious affairs is important in a regional perspective, because it set the tone for policies that most regional states came to embrace. The approach was deeply colored by the extremism scare during the country's transition to independence, described in detail in the previous chapter. President Karimov appears to have been deeply colored by his December 1991 encounter with the Salafi extremists in Namangan.[12] This experience combined with Tashkent's acute awareness of the descent into chaos in neighboring Tajikistan and Afghanistan, and helped shape the government's approach to religious affairs. Karimov made it a top priority for his government to counter the spread of radical religious ideology. It would not be an exaggeration to state that this was seen as an existential issue for the Uzbek state. Partly because the Uzbek leadership at the time was not particularly well-versed in Islamic theology, it adopted a very broad definition of what it considered extremism – at times including pretty much anything that was outside traditional Uzbek religious observance.

Uzbekistan's policies led to sometimes draconian punishments

---

12 Babajanov, Malikov, and Nazarov, "Islam in the Ferghana Valley" pp. 319-320. The video is available at https://www.youtube.com/watch?v=xwVS8CQg2s4

5. Devil In The Detail: Specific Challenges And Responses

for individuals and groups deemed extremist in nature. Many individuals were convicted to lengthy prison sentences. These policies became among the most contentious issues in Uzbekistan's relationship with Western countries and certain international organizations, as both Western officials and representatives of advocacy groups issued frequent condemnations of Uzbekistan. Critics of Uzbekistan's policies took offense for at least three distinct reasons. First, they voiced allegations of abuse against the individuals affected by these policies and accused Uzbekistan's government of failing to live up to international human rights commitments. Second, they opposed the very notion of restricting or punishing individuals for exercising or voicing their beliefs in a non-violent manner, even when the beliefs in question were manifestly extremist, and incompatible with either secularism, the equal rights of citizens, or democracy. Third, they predicted that Uzbekistan's policies would be counter-productive: it was (and remains in some circles) widely assumed that efforts to restrict religiously based ideologies would only strengthen the appeal of such ideologies.[13]

At the bottom of this controversy lay an important distinction between the Western and the Uzbek (and emerging Central Asian) approach to extremism. Western laws on freedom of expression tend to tolerate almost any form of ideas in the abstract, but draw the line at the incitement to or actual use of violence.

---

[13] Prominent examples of this criticism include Ahmed Rashid "The Fires of Faith in Central Asia." *World Policy Journal* Vol. 18, No. 1, 2001; Rashid, *Jihad: The Rise of Militant Islam in Central Asia*, Yale University Press, 2002; Eric McGlinchey, "The Making of Militants: The State and Islam in Central Asia," *Comparative Studies of South Asia, Africa and the Middle East* Vol. 25, No. 3, 2005; McGlinchey, "Autocrats, Islamists and the Rise of Radicalism in Central Asia", *Current History*, October 2005; International Crisis Group, "Radical Islam in Central Asia: Responding to Hizb ut-Tahrir," Asia Report no. 58, June 30, 2003; Alisher Khamidov, "Countering the Call: The U.S., Hizb-ut-Tahrir and Religious Extremism in Central Asia", Brookings Institution, 2003;

Uzbek officials, by contrast, were not content to target only the violent manifestations of extremist ideology. They considered that the problem lay not simply in violent acts but in the nature of the ideology itself, which they considered particularly dangerous in view of the vulnerable nature of a young nation in the process of consolidating it national identity. Further, Uzbek authorities rejected out of hand the notion that restricting extremist groups would only fuel their appeal. As it happens, western scholars of radicalization have failed to establish a direct link between repression and radicalization. Rigorous scholarly studies of the drivers of extremism elsewhere have failed to prove this widely touted hypothesis, pointing instead to a complicated array of other factors as the main drivers of extremism.[14]

When Shavkat Mirziyoyev succeeded Islam Karimov as president in late 2016, the general sense in Uzbekistan was that the country had largely succeeded in containing the spread of extremism. No terrorist attacks or religiously motivated violence had taken place in Uzbekistan in fifteen years. Building on policies that restricted the operations of religious groups considered non-traditional, Uzbekistan's government now complemented this essentially defensive policy with an effort to restore the traditionally dominant Hanafi form of Islam in the country. President Mirziyoyev, whose Prime Ministership coincided with the implementation of this approach, now moved to put greater emphasis

---

14 Royal United Services Institute, *Drivers of Violent Extremism: Hypotheses and Literature Review*. London: Royal United Services Institute, 2015; Matthew Francis, "What Causes Radicalisation? Main Lines of Consensus in Recent Research", January 24, 2012. (http://www.radicalisationresearch.org/guides/francis-2012-causes-2/) Katerina Dalacoura, *Islamist Terrorism and Democracy in the Middle East*. New York: Cambridge University Press, 2011; Michael Freeman, "Democracy, Al Qaeda, and the Causes of Terrorism: A Strategic Analysis of US Policy." *Studies in Conflict & Terrorism*, vol. 31 no. 1, 2008, pp. 40–59.

5. Devil In The Detail: Specific Challenges And Responses

on this aspect of governmental policy, while easing restrictions on religious life overall.

President Mirziyoyev has maintained the emphasis on secularism in the field of education, while he has advocated explicitly for "traditional" Islam. Soon after Mirziyoyev took office in 2016, the Cabinet of Ministers passed three decrees related to secular education, while also emphasizing the importance of religious tolerance in a secular society. The government emphasized that students needed to exhibit understanding of "religious relations in a secular country,"[15] and reaffirmed that the curriculum of both government and non-government preschool institutions and programs "shall be secular."[16]

In parallel, in July 2017, Mirziyoyev issued a decree on "Establishing the Imam Bukhari International Scientific Research Center,"[17] whose mission would be to "study the rich cultural and spiritual heritage" as well as "secular and religious knowledge."[18] In addition, Mirziyoyev also announced the establishment of other new Islamic academies and centers. This included the Islamic Academy of Uzbekistan, dedicated to "learn through scholarly research and to promote the true essence of Islam, which is kindness and humanity."[19] The president explained the rationale in the following terms: "We cherish our sacred religion as the focus of time-honored values. We strongly condemn and we will

---

15 Decree No 187 of the Cabinet of Ministers of the Republic of Uzbekistan on Approving Education Standards for Secondary Schools and Vocational Training Institutions, April 6, 2017; Annex 2, Paragraph 5 (History); Paragraph 22 (Philosophy).
16 Decree No 528 of the Cabinet of Ministers of the Republic of Uzbekistan on Improving the operations of preschool education institutions, dated July 19, 2017; Annex 1, Article 10.
17 Decree No. 483 of July 10, 2017 on "Establishing Imam Bukhari International Scientific Research Center. The law is available at (http://lex.uz/pages/getpage.aspx?lact_id=3263382&query=%D0%B4%D1%83%D0%BD%D1%91%D0%B2%D0%B8%D0%B9).
18 Ibid.
19 "Ўзбекистон Ислом академиясини ташкил этиш чора-тадбирлари тўғрисида," president.uz, December 15, 2017 (http://president.uz/uz/lists/view/1350).

never reconcile with those who rank our great faith together with violence and bloodshed."[20]

Mirziyoyev also inaugurated the Islamic Culture Center in Tashkent, to take over the running of Islamic educational establishments in Uzbekistan from the Directorate of Muslims of Uzbekistan, including Tashkent Islamic University and the Mir Arab higher education madrasah in Bukhara, as well as eight Islamic secondary educational institutions.

While the decrees on secularism and educational institutions reflect a continuation of earlier policies, state policies since 2017 indicate a shifting emphasis toward the promotion of traditional Uzbek forms of Islam. In a separate vein, Mirziyoyev has sought to remedy Uzbekistan's reputation for violating religious freedoms by reducing restrictions on religion. Initiatives in this area included plans to build "numerous small mosques,"[21] the organization of Qur'an recital competitions, and the elimination of 16,000 of the 17,000 individuals that had been registered as "religious radicals" from a state watchlist.[22] Further, the government released several individuals imprisoned on extremism charges, and extended invitations to religious dissidents to return to the country.

The Uzbek government has also argued its case on the international scene. It successfully campaigned to have Uzbekistan removed from the U.S. list of "Countries of Particular Concern" for violating religious freedoms.[23] Uzbek officials also invited the

---

[20] "President Shavkat Mirziyoyev addressed the 72nd Session of the United Nations General Assembly," uza.uz, September 20, 2017 (http://uza.uz/en/politics/president-shavkat-mirziyoyev-addressed-the-72nd-session-of-t-20-09-2017?sphrase_id=2638544).
[21] "Uzbekistan Plans 'Mini-Mosques' To Help Muslims Pray," rferl.org, January 16, 2018 (https://www.rferl.org/a/uzbekistan-mini-mosques-muslims-pray/28978754.html).
[22] "Leader Says Most Of Uzbeks Listed As Extremists Rehabilitated,"
[23] "U.S. Removes Uzbekistan From Nations With Worst Religious Tolerance," *RFE/RL*, June 21, 2019. (https://www.rferl.org/a/us-removes-uzbekistan-nations-worst-religious-tolerance-russia-pakistan-iran/30013281.html)

5. Devil In The Detail: Specific Challenges And Responses

UN Human Rights Council's Special Rapporteur on Freedom of Religion of Belief to showcase the changes taking place in the country,[24] and welcomed human rights organizations, including Human Rights Watch, to return to the country.[25]

To sum up, Uzbekistan's early scare with violent Islamic extremism led it to adopt harsh, restrictive policies in the religious field, and to champion the secularism of the state. This effectively helped the country purge extremist ideology from its territory, by steeply raising the cost for extremist networks of operating in the country. An example of this is Hizb-ut Tahrir, which made considerable inroads among ethnic Uzbeks all over Central Asia in the late 1990s. But over time, the group appears to have become unable to operate in Uzbekistan, and focused its energies instead on ethnic Uzbeks in neighboring countries. Uzbek extremists, however, did not disappear: they were pushed abroad, first to Salafi-Jihadi groups in Afghanistan and Pakistan, and subsequently to Syria and Iraq.

Having ensured that extremist ideology did not gain a foothold within the country' borders, Uzbek authorities gained some confidence they lacked in the first decades of independence, and have more recently sought to transition from a defensive to a more proactive model of secular governance. While loosening religious restrictions, the government is also now advancing a positive model, encapsulated in Mirziyoyev's concept of "Enlightened Islam," to promote a tolerant Islam both at home and abroad.

---

24 "President of the Republic of Uzbekistan received the UN Special Rapporteur on freedom of religion or belief," ombudsman.uz/, October 13, 2017 (http://ombudsman.uz/en/press_center/news/uzbekistan/president-of-the-republic-of-uzbekistan-received-the-un-special-rapporteur-on-freedom-of-religion-or/).
25 Ibid.

Azerbaijan:
Sunni-Shia Relations and "Multiculturalism"

Azerbaijan differs from Central Asian states by being, historically, roughly two thirds Shi'a and almost one third Sunni. Culturally, it is drawn in two directions: ethno-linguistically, it is most closely connected to Turkey. But by historical and religious ties, Iran has had an equally strong impact. In recent decades however, the Shia-Sunni balance has undergone a shift. The emergence of an Azerbaijani nation-state has made ethno-linguistic community a stronger marker of identity than sectarian and religious identity. Furthermore, and aided by Iran's hostility to Azerbaijan since independence, the influence of Shi'a Iran has declined while Sunni Turkey's cultural impact has skyrocketed. This has led to a shift also in the religious area, as Turkish Islam has come to appeal to many Azerbaijanis, whose sectarian identity had in any case been weakened by the Soviet experience. As a result, many Azerbaijanis who were Shi'a by birth have adopted Sunni ritual as they became religiously observant. The opposite – a shift from Sunni to Shi'a – is a rarity. Unofficial estimates therefore suggest that the real proportion of Shia to Sunni believers is actually heading from a two-third-one third division in the direction of a rough parity.[26]

Azerbaijan's policies in the religious field have been strongly affected by this part Shi'a, part Sunni reality. It should be mentioned that Azerbaijan is among only four Shi'a-majority countries in the world alongside Iran, Iraq and Bahrain. The consequence is that Azerbaijan is exposed to the sectarian divisions of the Middle East to a much greater extent than any Central Asian state. The Turkish-Iranian rivalry was already a considerable concern for

---

26 Sofie Bedford and Emil Aslan Souleimanov, "Under construction and highly contested: Islam in the post-Soviet Caucasus", *Third World Quarterly*, April 2016, p. 8.

5. Devil In The Detail: Specific Challenges And Responses

Azerbaijan, and its exposure worsened with the growth of sectarian strife in the Middle East in the early twenty-first century. Few countries have perceived an urgency in avoiding the spread of sectarian conflict from the neighboring Levant quite like Azerbaijan has. Remarkably, the effect in Azerbaijan has been to reinforce the government's commitment to secularism.

Two state institutions regulate religious organizations in Azerbaijan. The 1992 Law on Freedom of Religion states that clerics and mosques in Azerbaijan are under the jurisdiction of the Caucasus Muslims Board (CMB), led by Sheikh-ul-Islam Allashukur Pashazade since before independence. All Islamic associations are subordinated to the CMB in terms of "organizational matters", while non-Islamic associations can choose to be subordinated to religious organizations both in Azerbaijan and outside it.

The CMB is not technically a state-controlled institution or subordinated to the political leadership of the country. In practice, however, Azerbaijan's centralized political system ensures that the CMB must pay close attention to the priorities of President Aliyev. That said, it is an interest group of its own, and to that one that is dominated by representatives of the southern areas of Azerbaijan, which are traditionally strongly Shi'a and more religiously observant. As an institution with Soviet roots, the CMB faces challenges to its trust in society. As in other post-Soviet Muslim republics, former Soviet clerics face criticism for their close allegiance to political authority. Furthermore, the CMB only has authority over Muslim groups, and *de facto* only over official religious structures – it therefore has little authority over independent Islamic communities. That said, it has played a role in the government's efforts to promote a moderate and inclusive form of Islam domestically and abroad, as well as in showcasing the close and harmonious relations between members of the Muslim, Christian, and Jewish communities in the country.

Until 2001, the only institution that regulated all aspects of religious life in the country was the Ministry of National Security, whose instruments of power were mainly coercive. This void led to the establishment of the State Committee for Work with Religious Organizations (SCWRO) in 2001. The committee was made responsible for oversight and registration of religious structures and non-governmental religious organizations and their activities. Not surprisingly, the CMB and the Committee did not initially agree on their distribution of duties, and relations between Pashazade and the first Head of the SCWRO, Rafiq Aliyev, were best described as acrimonious. Pashazade remains Head of the CMB at this time of writing, and personal and institutional tensions have diminished under subsequent leaders of the SCWRO.[27]

The SCWRO has, in practice, been forced to share some powers with the CMB. Islamic organizations and mosques remain under the CMB's mandate, and must therefore receive letters of approval from it in order to register with the SCWRO. In fact, the CMB itself is registered with the SCWRO. The creation of the SCWRO was a response to a sense that the state was risking losing control over the religious field following the growing role of foreign-sponsored religious groups in the country, with origins in the Gulf states, the North Caucasus, Turkey and Iran, who were benefiting from the post-Soviet ideological vacuum to establishing a presence in Azerbaijani society. A former SCWRO official estimated that around 15 "Arab" religious organizations and around 20 "sects" were active in Azerbaijan between 1991-1997,

---

27 Interview with political analyst, Baku, June 2016.

before the 1997 amendment on "religious propaganda by foreigners" was put in place.[28]

Continued concerns over radicalization led to a 2009 amendment to the Law on Freedom of Religion, which called for a re-registration of religious associations with the committee. The SCWRO has over 650 religious associations registered, including 25 non-Muslim associations including various Christian and Jewish denominations, as well as Krishna and Bahai communities. The incentives offered for registering with the SCWRO include a subsidized (effectively free) supply of natural gas from the State Oil Company of the Azerbaijan Republic (SOCAR) provided to buildings registered with the association and the allocation of state funding for projects.[29]

The SCWRO is tasked both with promoting religious tolerance and preventing radicalization. This work takes place through institutional cooperation with local religious associations and the Ministry of National Security to track potential or suspected "foreign fighters" going or having gone to fight abroad, as well as making sure that they are intercepted by border police or security services if they return. The SCWRO is also tasked with monitoring and vetting religious literature, especially literature imported from abroad. The committee prohibits importing literature it deems to be incompatible with its mission to ensure the secular nature of the state; approved books available for sale must carry a SCWRO stamp.

Amendments to the Law on Religion in 2014-2015 prevented clerics educated abroad (with the exception of those educated in state-approved educational institutions) from working

---

28 Svante E. Cornell, Halil Karaveli and Boris Ajeganov, *Azerbaijan's Formula: Secular Governance andCivic Nationhood*, Central Asia-Caucasus Institute & Silk Road Studies Program, Silk Road Paper, November 2016, p. 48.
29 Cornell, Karaveli, Ajeganov, *Azerbaijan's Formula*, p. 84.

in Azerbaijan, while also allowing the SCWRO to monopolize religious education for the conduct of rites. To fill the need for training clerics, the SCWRO expanded its own role and conducted thousands of trainings. While clerics can be attested by the committee, they cannot be appointed by it to positions within religious associations. The amendments were not applied retroactively, implying that any previous training that existing clerics may have received has not been invalidated.[30] Whereas the official state estimate is that 1,800 individuals have already received religious education abroad, the real number may be closer to 3,000.[31] Nonetheless, observers maintain that even those educated abroad tend to support a secular model of governance, and that the long-standing fear of foreign clerics importing the Shia-Sunni conflict into Azerbaijan has not been realized.[32]

Similarly to Uzbekistan, Azerbaijan has moved from defense to offense in religious affairs. It has done so by launching the notion of multiculturalism as a part of state ideology. This notion builds on the ideology of "Azerbaijanism," a civic nationalism designed to embrace all citizens irrespective of ethnic or religious identity. Government representatives explain that Azerbaijanism foresees a civic state model where only citizenship is of consequence to the state, while religious affiliation, ethnicity and native language is not. Akif Alizade, the former President of the National Academy of Sciences of Azerbaijan, has argued that Azerbaijanism is an answer to global challenges, an integral part of the country's democratic development process, and an important paradigm for its

---

30 Interview with Nijat Mammadov, Head of International Relations Department, State Committee for Work with Religious Organizations, Baku, June 22, 2016.
31 Interviewee with expert in Baku, Azerbaijan, 2016.
32 Interview with Elchin Askarov, Eurasian Regional Forum Director, Islamic Conference Youth Forum for Dialogue and Cooperation, June 22, 2016.

national security.³³ He argues that multiculturalism is crucial to Azerbaijan's very national security: "every country must provide for its own energy and economic security, national security, and 'multicultural security.'" "Multicultural security" implies the maintenance of the cultural values of all peoples and ethnic groups, regardless of their ethnic, religious, racial or cultural affiliation.³⁴ Azerbaijan has made it its endeavor to promote its multicultural model through international events such as the World Forum on Intercultural Dialogue in Baku (hosted every two years since 2011), the hosting of the 7th Global Forum of the United Nations Alliance of Civilizations in April 2016, and the Baku Process launched in 2008 on the initiative of the President of Azerbaijan. It also finances half – a disproportionately large share – of the Eurasian activities of the Islamic Conference Youth Forum for Dialogue and Cooperation (ICYF-DC).³⁵

Given the growing criticism of the concept of "multiculturalism" in recent years, it is noteworthy that Baku has chosen to embrace this term. But the Azerbaijani understanding differs from the predominant western one, where it has come to mean an approach to strengthen and perpetuate separate ethnic and racial subcultures rather than work toward integration into a single society.³⁶ That is not what Azerbaijani leaders advocate: they are promoting what would traditionally be known as a "civic nation." As a majority Shi'a and minority Sunni country in a region where

---

33 Akif Əlizadə, "Dəqiq ideoloji hədəf", Azərbaycan Milli Elmlər Akademiyası, April 8, 2016, http://www.science.gov.az/news/open/3455. Also published as "Точная идеологическая цель – мультикультурализм", *Multikulturalizm jurnalı*, no. 1, 2016, pp. 28-36.
34 Əlizadə, "Dəqiq ideoloji hədəf".
35 Interview with Elchin Askarov, Eurasian Regional Forum Director, Islamic Conference Youth Forum for Dialogue and Cooperation, June 22, 2016.
36 Arthur M. Schlesinger, Jr., *The Disuniting of America – Reflections on a Multicultural Society,* New York: W.W. Norton & Co, 1991; William Pfaff, "Canada's Lesson in Multiculturalism" *St. Louis Dispatch*, November 2, 1995.

territorial claims are very much alive and the Middle East has seen growing sectarian conflict, Azerbaijan seeks to advance an inclusive conception of the nation that maintains social peace and reduces openings for foreign powers seeking to use ethnic or religious fissures as a lever to exert pressure.

In sum, Azerbaijan's approach has been to double down on state secularism in the face of growing sectarian tensions in its neighborhood, and to promote a civic national identity to maintain social harmony.

Kazakhstan and Kyrgyzstan: The Limits of Openness

Kazakhstan and Kyrgyzstan differ from their neighbors to the south in important regards. They are traditionally nomadic societies, something that has important implications for their population's historic relationship with organized religion. Whereas Islamic institutions like mosques and madrasahs planted deep roots in the settled agricultural societies of southern Central Asia, they could not and did not do so in the same manner among the nomads. Several scholars have observed that Islam is in many ways an urban religion, with its authority resting on collective worship and educational institutions.[37] Frequently on the move and living in close proximity to nature, the nomadic peoples were less subservient to any political or religious authority. It is therefore no surprise that while Islam gained a hold of the oases of southern Central Asia only a century or two after the death of Muhammad – and Bukhara became a center of Islamic learning by the ninth century – it would take hundreds of years before the

---

37 Walter J. Fischel, "The City in Islam", *Middle Eastern Affairs*, vol.7, no. 6/7, 1956, pp. 227-232; William Marcais, "L'Islamisme et la vie urbaine," Comptes-Rendus the *l'Académie des Inscriptions et Belles-Lettres,* vol. 72 no. 1, 1928.

5. Devil In The Detail: Specific Challenges And Responses

steppe and mountain areas to the north were Islamized. Kazakhs embraced Islam only by the sixteenth century, some Kyrgyz tribes later than that. Most importantly, the Islamization of the nomads was undertaken almost exclusively by the Sufi brotherhoods, infusing a heterodox form of Islam that fused with many folk beliefs that predated Islam.[38]

The Kazakhs and Kyrgyz also endured a deeper assault on their way of life during the Soviet period. Even before the Bolshevik revolution, the Kyrgyz in particular were badly affected by the brutal 1916 repression of an uprising against conscription into the Russian army, which forced several hundred thousand to leave for China. Soon after came collectivization, which was not harmonious anywhere. Among the nomads, however, it involved forced settlement and therefore thoroughly destroyed the way of life of the people. Up to 40 percent of the Kazakh nation was wiped out by Stalin's collectivization and politically induced famine. Needless to say, many of the "folk Islam" practices of the pre-Soviet period disappeared as well. In addition, during the Soviet period Slavic migration led Kazakh and Kyrgyz societies to become much more multi-ethnic than their neighbors, with considerably larger Russian populations that came to dominate the capital cities of the two republics. As a result, their elites were culturally Russianized to a degree unknown in Uzbekistan and Tajikistan. Moreover, there were regional divisions: in both states the levels of orthodox religious observance were considerably higher in the southern parts of the countries, particularly near Shymkent in Kazakhstan and Osh in Kyrgyzstan, areas with considerable ethnic Uzbek populations.

---

38 Bruce Privratsky, *Muslim Turkistan: Kazak Religion and Collective Memory*, New York: Routledge, 2013; Mehrdad Haghayeghi, *Islam and Politics in Central Asia*, New York: St. Martin's Press, 1996.

Following independence, practices like saint worship were restored and shrines rebuilt; but because many traditions had been lost, the content of religious practice was by necessity largely novel or reimagined. Similarly, the Hanafi ulama of pre-Soviet times had been thoroughly transformed by the Soviet period, and in particular by the alien influences that the Soviet clerical authorities had encouraged. In terms of official Islamic institutions, Kazakhstan and Kyrgyzstan had historically been dominated by Islamic religious authorities based either in Kazan or Tashkent. They now embarked on the building of new, national religious institutions.

A further point of difference is that neither state suffered the traumatic experience of Islamic extremism that Tajikistan and Uzbekistan shared. As a result, they initially adopted a more liberal approach to religious matters than their counterparts in Uzbekistan. They tolerated the spread of foreign religious groups in the country, and in general had a lighter hand in religious affairs.

Independence led to a burst of mosque-building that continued unabated for 20 years. Kazakhstan took the regional lead in the number of mosques built: by 2013, it sported over 3,200 places of worship, of which over 2,300 were mosques – a larger number than Uzbekistan, in spite of that country's population of Muslims being more than twice larger.[39] Kyrgyzstan built a thousand mosques in the first five years of independence, growing to over 2,600 today. That is a number greater than Kazakhstan's, despite that country's population being three times larger.[40] This rapid growth of mosques posed a serious human resource problem:

---

39 "Kazakhstan Leads in Number of Mosques in Central Asia", *Bnews.kz*, May 15, 2013. (https://bnews.kz/en/news/obshchestvo/kazakhstan_leads_in_number_of_mosques_in_central_asia)

40 Johan Engvall, *Religion and the Secular State in Kyrgyzstan*, Washington: Central Asia-Caucasus Institute & Silk Road Studies Program, 2020, p. 15. (https://silkroadstudies.org/publications/silkroad-papers-and-monographs/item/13371)

staffing these mosques required a similar number of trained imams, something that did not exist in either country. While this was theoretically the domain of the newly established religious authorities, the *Muftiats*, in practice many mosques were staffed with Imams with poor training or subjected to foreign religious influences.

This process was possible because unlike in Uzbekistan, the leadership of Kazakhstan and Kyrgyzstan took a hands-off approach to religion. Over time, however, both Kazakhstan and Kyrgyzstan changed their approach to religious affairs, adopting more interventionist policies. This came as a result of shifts in both global and regional affairs. Kazakhstan's shift was the more drastic one: it had a relatively liberal approach into the 2000s, resting on the belief that Kazakh society's more secularized nature would prove an effective antidote to radicalism. But as Kazakh analyst Erlan Karin details, Kazakhstan became a target for extremist organizations in the early 2000s exactly because of its less restrictive policies. In particular, the Islamic Jihad Union, an offshoot of the IMU, in 2002 dispatched two experienced operatives to develop its presence.[41] They were initially based in Taraz, in southern Kazakhstan and near the border with Kyrgyzstan and Uzbekistan. They chose Kazakhstan not only because it was a more liberal and permissive environment than Uzbekistan; but because this enabled the recruitment of both ethnic Kazakhs and Uzbeks residing in southern Kazakhstan. Subsequently, they managed to set up cells also in nearby Shymkent and Semey (Semipalatinsk) in northeast Kazakhstan.

The IJU network was responsible for a spree of suicide bombings in Tashkent in 2004, that among other targeted the U.S.

---

41 Karin, The Soldiers of the Caliphate: The Anatomy of a Terrorist Group, Astana: KazISS, 2016, p. 68.

and Israeli embassies.⁴² This led to a temporary spat in relations between Tashkent and Astana, as Uzbek investigators uncovered the Shymkent cell of the IJU and concluded their Kazakh counterparts did not take the terrorist threat seriously enough. From that point onward, Kazakh officials changed their approach, and rapidly rounded up IJU cells.⁴³ In subsequent years, Kazakhstan was rocked by terrorist attacks in 2011 and again in 2016, both of which led the state to adopt further restrictions in religious affairs.

In late 2011, Kazakhstan adopted legislative amendments that focused on regulating religious associations and groupings, as well as the opening of new places of worship and the dissemination of religious material. Now, only Kazakh citizens were permitted to register religious organizations, and the law endorsed government policies to promote traditional religions and resist the growth of "non-traditional" religious groups.

The government created an Agency of Religious Affairs, subsequently upgraded to a Ministry of Religious Affairs. It tightened requirements for registration of religious groups, and the updated law on religion also focused on controlling the dissemination of spiritual literature and material, including requiring any religious literature to be submitted to the Agency on Religious Affairs for approval.⁴⁴ Further amendments in 2018 limited the ability of minors to attend religious services without parental permission, and tightened restrictions on obtaining religious education abroad. They also imposed new restrictions on public displays of "attributes and outward signs" of what the government

---

42 Guido Steinberg, *German Jihad: On the Internationalization of Islamist Terrorism*, New York: Columbia University Press, 2013, p. 85-89.
43 Karin, p. 80.
44 "Kazakhstan Agency for Religious Affairs is Checking 3,000 Religious Materials", Tengrinews.kz, September 27, 2012. (https://en.tengrinews.kz/religion/Kazakhstan-Agency-for-Religious-Affairs-is-checking-3000-13302/)

5. Devil In The Detail: Specific Challenges And Responses

terms "destructive religious movements," defined as groups that "threaten people's rights and freedoms." Comments by authorities indicated that the main target of these amendments were what the government termed "pseudo-Salafi" groups.[45]

Kyrgyzstan has gone through more flux in its religious policies, as a result of the greater political turnover at the top – the country, uniquely in Central Asia, has gone through six different presidents since independence. Kyrgyzstan produced a first concept paper on religious affairs in 2006, during Kurmanbek Bakiyev's presidency. Two years later, Kyrgyzstan adopted a new law on religion and religious organizations. The law hardened the requirements for registration and banned the distribution of religious materials in public places, something that would be followed by restrictions on and state censorship of imported religious materials.[46] By this time, the Kyrgyz government had come to consider the activities of foreign religious organizations in the country as problematic. The parliament approved several amendments to the law, including a ban on proselytizing and – like in Kazakhstan – higher thresholds for registering religious organizations.[47] During Almazbek Atambayev's presidency, a new State Concept was developed in 2014 with the explicit purpose of streamlining state control over the religious sphere. It defined key directions of state policy regarding three principal issues: cooperation with religious organizations; religious education; and prevention of religious extremism.[48] As Johan Engvall notes, Atambayev "argued that the

---

[45] Svetlana Glushkova and Farangis Najibullah, "Kazakhstan Targets Beards, Pants in Fight Against 'Destructive Religious Movements'", RFE/RL, February 4, 2018. (https://www.rferl.org/a/kazakhstan-targets-islamist-beards-pants-destructive-movements/29017566.html)
[46] Olcott, "Religion and State Policy in Central Asia," p. 6.
[47] U.S. Department of State, "Kyrgyz Republic 2017 International Religious Freedom Report.", 2018. https://www.state.gov/reports/2021-report-on-international-religious-freedom/kyrgyzstan/
[48] Ibid, p. 3.

concept would serve as a counterbalance to the religious laxness enshrined in the constitution, which had 'allowed the religious sphere to take its own course.'"[49]

The key difference between the experiences of Kazakhstan and Kyrgyzstan lie in their political and economic stability. While Kazakhstan has maintained stability and implemented a relatively successful policy of state-led economic development, Kyrgyzstan has limped from crisis to crisis in the past twenty years, with successive governments unable to curb widespread mismanagement and corruption, or to eradicate poverty. This may be the reason for the significant divergence in popular attitudes on religious affairs: in spite of similar cultural and linguistic characteristics, Kyrgyzstan's Muslims show the strongest support for Sharia law in Central Asia, with 35 percent of responding Muslims supporting it. This differs markedly from Kazakhstan, where 10 percent of Muslim respondents do so – the lowest in Central Asia, with only Azerbaijan in the entire Muslim world posting a lower figure at 8 percent.[50] Anecdotal reports suggest that many Kyrgyz citizens associate Islamic law with lower corruption and greater justice and morality. If this is the case, it would stand to reason that the economic downturn in Kazakhstan, and the ensuing public frustration illustrated by the January 2022 protests, could lead to an uptick in Islamic sentiment in that country as well.

Aside from these differences, the approach taken by the two states have been similar: both have imposed restrictions that make them more similar to policies in Uzbekistan and Tajikistan, and both in recent years sought to boost the role of traditional

---

49 Johan Engvall, *Religion and the Secular State in Kyrgyzstan*, p. 39.
50 Pew Research Center, *The World's Muslims: Religion, Politics and Society*, Washington, DC, 2013, p. 15. Neither Turkmenistan nor Uzbekistan were included in the study.

5. Devil In The Detail: Specific Challenges And Responses

Hanafi Sunni Islam. Both have drawn a sharp distinction between domestic and tolerant, versus alien and intolerant religious groups. While they have accelerated their efforts to curtail the latter, they have also embraced and promoted the former.

That said, the two states have proven unable to develop purely domestic sources of Hanafi Islam. Kazakhstan has struck up a partnership with the Al-Azhar Islamic University in Cairo to train its clergy. In 2013, Yerzhan Mayamerov, a graduate of the Department of Shar'ia and Law at Al-Azhar, was appointed Mufti; the Muftiate then began issuing *Fatwas* on the basis of Hanafi jurisprudence. Mayamerov departed from his predecessors' standoffish approach to social issues, and began to advocate women wearing hijabs in public spaces, a practice that is in no sense traditional in Kazakhstan. He was replaced in 2017 by another Al-Azhar graduate, Serikbay Oraz, and the Muftiate developed its partnership with Egypt through the Nur-Mubarak University, inaugurated in 2003.

Kazakhstan's partnership with Al-Azhar is puzzling, given widespread criticism of the institution over its tendency toward extremism,[51] something even Egyptian President Abdelfattah Al-Sisi has commented upon.[52] As such, clergy educated at Al-Azhar could be considered likely to perpetuate the hostility to folk Islamic currents prevalent at the institution. This is a dilemma for the government, because it characterizes both Hanafi Islam

---

51 Maher Gabra, "The Ideological Extremism of Al-Azhar," *Washington Institute for Near Eastern Policy*, March 3, 2016. (https://www.washingtoninstitute.org/policy-analysis/ideological-extremism-al-azhar)

52 Ismael El-Kholy, "Al-Azhar Controversy Leads to Curriculum Updates," *Al-Monitor*, June 15, 2015. (https://www.al-monitor.com/originals/2015/06/egypt-azhar-university-curriculum-updates-extremist-sisi.html); James M. Dorsey, *A Geopolitical Crossfire: Al-Azhar Struggles to Balance Politics and Tradition*, BESA Center, Bar-Ilan University, Mideast Security and Policy Studies no. 163, August 2019. (https://besacenter.org/al-azhar-politics-tradition/)

and the folk Islam of Kazakh traditions as "traditional," but does not account for the possibility of a conflict between the two. Influenced by Al-Azhar, the official Hanafi authorities appear to develop in an increasingly literalist direction, if nothing else as a requirement for issuing *Fatwas* on varieties of subjects. These *Fatwas* are based on Shari'a, which requires making references to a scriptural interpretation, rather than simply accepting the folk practices of the Kazakhs as Islamic. Such literalism, therefore, stands in direct conflict with the esoteric and often syncretistic nature of folk Islam.

In Kyrgyzstan, a different foreign influence has been on the ascendant, this time with origins in South Asia. The Indian subcontinent-based Tablighi Jamaat organization has been spreading fast in the country. Tabligh Jamaat is technically a Hanafi movement, but is an offshoot of the Deobandi movement, which has been strongly influenced by Salafi ideology.[53] Tabligh Jamaat teaches an apolitical approach focused on spreading Islamic belief and practice at the individual level, but has been considered an incubator of radicalism given its creed and the multiple instances of systematic recruitment by violent extremist organizations among its ranks.[54] While it is banned elsewhere in Central Asia, Tabligh Jamaat has made Kyrgyzstan a center of sorts. It is the most active mass Muslim movement in the country, with a particularly strong appeal among young, predominantly ethnically Kyrgyz people.[55] Surveys conducted by international organizations consulted by this author indicate that over 20 percent of the

---

[53] Luv Puri, "The Past and Future of Deobandi Islam," *CTC Sentinel*, vol. 2 no. 11, November 2009. (https://ctc.usma.edu/the-past-and-future-of-deobandi-islam/)

[54] Alex Alexiev, "Tablighi Jamaat: Jihad's Stealthy Legions," *Middle East Quarterly*, vol. 12 no. 1, Winter 2005.

[55] Roza Duisheeva, "Should Tablighi Jamaat be banned in Kyrgyzstan?" *CABAR*, undated. See also Nasritidinov et al., "Vulnerability and Resilience of Young People", p. 24.

5. Devil In The Detail: Specific Challenges And Responses

Kyrgyz population support the movement.[56] In 2014, Maksatbek Toktomushev, who is known for his close association with Tabligh, was appointed Grand Mufti of Kyrgyzstan. Toktomoushev spent a decade at the Madrasa Arabia Raiwind in Lahore, Pakistan – the center of Tablighi Jamaat in Pakistan – where he received a degree in Islamic law. Toktomushev has endorsed Tabligh Jamaat as an organization that supports traditional Hanafi Islam; the Muftiate "has created a special department to support Tablighi Jamaat preachers despite the fact that it is not a registered religious organization", and has worked to produce special attire for its members "to make their appearances less 'foreign' and aligned more with Kyrgyz culture."[57]

In sum, thus, Kazakhstan and Kyrgyzstan provide a contradictory picture. Both countries started off with a relatively liberal approach to religion. Over time, however, their political leadership adopted more restrictive approaches, while simultaneously attempting to build or strengthen traditional Hanafi religious institutions. In so doing, they have accepted external influence from the Middle East and South Asia that appear to potentially undermine the secularist goals of their own policies.

Turkmenistan

Turkmenistan is the most closed of the Central Asian countries, and the one where information is the hardest to obtain. This applies also to religious affairs. Since independence, the country has taken a different route than its neighbors: it has adopted a policy of "permanent neutrality" with strong isolationist

---

[56] Unpublished manuscript viewed by author, 2022.
[57] Engvall, *Religion and the Secular State in Kyrgyzstan*, pp. 24-25; See interview with the Grand Mufti in Asel Shabdanova, "Muftii: V Kyrgyzstane budem rasprostranyat' tol'ko hanafizm," *Vechernii Bishkek*, April 9, 2014, https://www.vb.kg/doc/268326_myftiy:_v_kyrgyzstane_bydem_rasprostraniat_tolko_hanafizm.html.

tendencies, and remained skeptical toward regional cooperation initiatives. Turkmenistan also stands out geographically, being a large country whose main population centers are separated from the rest of Central Asia by large tracts of desert. That said, in the ninth century Merv, in eastern Turkmenistan, was a center of Islamic learning on the level of Bukhara and Samarkand.

Like Kazakhstan and Kyrgyzstan, Turkmens are descendants of a nomadic tradition, and the form of Islam that developed in Turkmenistan was heavily colored by folk practices and Sufi traditions rather than official, orthodox Islam. Religious practices in the country focus on visiting shrines and tombs of holy men, whereas visits to mosques are reserved for significant Islamic holidays.[58]

The Qur'an was not available in the Turkmen language until translations were prepared in the early post-Soviet period, and until 2003, the Mufti of Turkmenistan was an ethnic Uzbek from Dashoghuz on the border with Uzbekistan. This is an indication of the weakness of official Islam in Turkmenistan. But as Victoria Clement has argued, this should not be taken as proof that Islam "'sits lightly'" on Turkmens, but instead that the form of Islam engrained in Turkmen society is of a very different variety than that either in the oasis cultures of southern Central Asia, or in the Middle East.[59]

More than perhaps any Central Asian state, the Turkmen government has emphasized a national form of Islam, tying it to Turkmen nationalism – a "Turkmen Islam" built on the Hanafi

---

58 David Tyson, "Shrine Pilgrimage in Turkmenistan as a Means to Understand Islam among the Turkmen," *Central Asian Monitor* 1 (1997), 15-32. See Victoria Clement, *Religion and the Secular State in Turkmenistan*.
59 Victoria Clement, *Religion and the Secular State in Turkmenistan*, Washington: Central Asia-Caucasus Institute & Silk Road Studies Program, 2020, p. 14. (https://silkroadstudies.org/publications/silkroad-papers-and-monographs/item/13372).

tradition and explicitly on folk Sufi practices. A new constitution in 2016 was followed by a new Law on Religion, which emphasizes secularism but recognizes the specific role of Islam on Turkmen tradition. As Clement puts it, this law is an indication of the state's move to advocate "a Turkmen form of Islam that is tightly linked to the national identity and buttresses the nation-building project."[60]

Like its neighbors, the Turkmen government distinguishes between traditional and novel, alien religious practices, and actively promotes the former at the expense of the latter. Laws and regulations provide strict control over the registration of religious groups, and essentially prohibit the importation of foreign religious materials. By contrast, the government rarely interferes with traditional practices like shrine worship, and has endorsed many folk practices. The state has also appropriated Sufi traditions, including the national dance Küst Depti. Furthermore, the state encourages the population to make domestic pilgrimages rather than perform the Hajj, in an additional effort to stress the validity of domestic practices and counter the sense brought by foreign proselytizers that Middle Eastern Islam is more authentic than traditional Central Asian practices.

Similarities and Differences

This cursory overview of the six states suggests a broad similarity in the general approach taken by the state to religious matters. However, it also identified important nuances and differences. To determine whether they form a distinct model of state approaches to religion, it is necessary to delve deeper into a comparative analysis of their key attributes. The next chapter proposes to do just that,

---
[60] Clement, p.12.

by studying their approaches to secularism, their constitutions, legislation, religious and state institutions, and their state policies in the religious field.

6. IS THERE A MODEL?

THE PREVIOUS CHAPTER SKETCHED the individual trajectories of state interaction with religion in Central Asia and Azerbaijan. This overview indicates a superficial similarity between the regional states. To determine whether there is a Central Asian model of state-religion interaction, however, two questions are in order. The first, subject of the present chapter, is whether there is enough commonality among the states in the region to speak of a common approach. The second, treated in the next chapter, is whether this common approach is sufficiently different from other states in the Muslim world to make the region distinctive. This chapter will delve deeper into several general characteristics of the regional states' approach, before continuing on to an analysis of their laws, institutions, and policies. It will end with a brief discussion of the differences among them. The contention is that there is an emerging model of state-religion relations in the region. This approach includes an effort by the state to maintain its autonomy from religion, thus adopting elements of the French-inspired "skeptical-insulating" model as defined in chapter two. But it also features a determined effort to restore the region's indigenous religious traditions to their place in society, at the expense of novel religious approaches coming from abroad. This adopts elements of the "dominant religion" model, making the Central Asian and Azerbaijani approach a hybrid of these two ideal types.

Each state in this study has faced different circumstances. And as will be seen, their approaches do differ in important ways, particularly on the intensity of restrictions they apply to religious life. Still, the similarities among the six states surveyed here are striking, and have gotten more so over time.

Embracing Secularism

In the Baltics, the Caucasus, and even in Russia, the transition to independence was coupled with a change of elites: Soviet-era elites were removed from power, and new forces took charge of young independent nations. But in Central Asia, no revolution occurred. The new nations were led by the same elites that had taken the helm in the late Soviet era. Only in Azerbaijan did an anti-Soviet nationalist movement – the Popular Front – manage to take over, but it lasted for only a year before the Soviet-era elite under Heydar Aliyev was restored to power. The Azerbaijani popular front, however, was part of the secular, Soviet intelligentsia, as were opposition movements in Central Asia. Only in Tajikistan and in Uzbekistan's Ferghana valley did a religiously minded counter-elite emerge. In Kazakhstan, Turkmenistan and Uzbekistan, the Presidents were all former communist party heads; while new figures came to power in Kyrgyzstan and Tajikistan, they were all products of the Soviet system and part of the Soviet bureaucratic elite.

This posed a problem, because as a class and often personally as well, the leaders of the new states had been closely associated with Soviet Communist ideology, including the assertive propagation of both the unity of Soviet republics and official atheism. Now, they had to transition into champions of the new nations they led, and began denouncing communism and atheism. This about-face may seem appallingly cynical to outsiders. But historians have shown that since the Brezhnev era, regional leaders had become more assertive and played on nationalist sentiments. For a long time, Central Asian and Caucasian leaders had advocated for the interests of their republics in Moscow. Some also privately were observant Muslims: a Tajik Communist Party Head, for example, ensured that his children received underground religious education and shielded mainstream Sunni Muslim clerics from persecution.[1] In this sense, it was understood across the region that much of the leaders' Soviet propaganda was a form of theater for Moscow's consumption, and that their real agenda might be very different.

That being said, most leaders in Central Asia and Azerbaijan were relatively distant from their cultural origins. It is true that some, like Azerbaijan's Heydar Aliyev, grew up in poverty in remote areas. Two even grew up in orphanages: Turkmenistan's Saparmurad Niyazov and Uzbekistan's Islam Karimov. But as a group, these leaders were thoroughly Sovietized by years in the Communist party machine, and years if not decades of study and work in Moscow led many to speak Russian better than their mother tongue. Even among themselves, these elites largely spoke and wrote in Russian. It is an ill-concealed secret that more than one Central Asian leader essentially re-learned the national language on the job after independence. Their exposure to organized religion was, almost by definition, usually close to nil, and many

---

[1] Naumkin, *Radical Islam in Central Asia*.

lacked basic knowledge of religious principles and texts. A Pakistani colleague related to this author how a Central Asian president visited Islamabad in the early 1990s and participated in the groundbreaking for his country's embassy there. As is customary in Pakistan, this ceremony included a prayer. The problem was that the visiting president did not know how to hold his hands during the prayer, generating an awkward situation.

This lack of religious knowledge certainly limited the appetite of regional leaders for introducing religious elements into politics and meant many continued to be suspicious of religion as a societal force. But it did not mean they sought to prevent a resurgence of religion in society. Indeed, already by the late Soviet period, Central Asian and Azerbaijani leaders were tacitly endorsing a national revival, a process that embraced the observance of cultural practices that often had religious roots – such as male circumcision and Islamic funerals, and in southern Central Asia also more limited daily rituals like the holding of brief prayers following a meal. As Adeeb Khalid puts it, "being Muslim had little to do with personal belief or observance of ritual and everything to do with customs and way of life."[2] This embrace of Islamic customs was endorsed by the republican leaders, who proceeded to denounce the restrictions on religious rituals that they had helped impose only recently. Islam Karimov, for example, in 1991 bemoaned the fact that party officials risked dismissal if caught attending the religious burial ceremony of a loved one. Going further, he shared his conviction that "the destruction of age-old moral principles for ideological reasons will be far more difficult to overcome than the chaos in the economy."[3]

---

2 Khalid, *Islam after Communism*, p. 90.
3 Mikhail Berger, "We have to make our own way: a conversation with Islam Karimov, President of Uzbekistan," *Current Digest of the Soviet Press*, Vol 43 no. 4, 1991, p 30.

6. Is There A Model?

Thus, with some credibility, regional leaders could portray themselves as reformers within a decaying Soviet system who, even before the Soviet Union collapsed, embraced a general liberalization of the ideological climate. Therefore, atheism as a state ideology was essentially doomed already before independence. The question was what would replace it, and how the state would approach religion going forward.

Central Asia and Azerbaijan were in a unique position: not only did leaders lack religious legitimacy, but seventy years of atheism had, as already seen, sharply reduced religious observance among the population. While there was a growing interest in exploring national and religious identities, and widespread instances of religious rituals and customs, the content of religious practice had largely been removed. Attending university in Turkey in the early 1990s, this author asked an Azerbaijani classmate whether he was Sunni or Shi'a. The young man looked back perplexed and answered: "I don't know. I will have to ask my father. No! He wouldn't know either. I have to ask my grandfather." While this may be representative mainly of an urban elite, where sovietization was stronger, three generations of Central Asians and Azerbaijanis attended an atheist education system and lived under secular laws, in a society where traditional Islamic practices such as hearing the Muezzin call for prayer or attending Friday prayers largely did not happen.

As a result, leaving aside marginal groups, there was no popular demand for an immediate infusion of religious content into political life. In fact, because the Soviet system had permitted and even institutionalized expressions of national and ethnic identity, nationalism as an ideology had a head start over religious

---

(from *Izvestiya*, January 28, 1991)

ideologies in capturing the minds of the people of the region. What leaders did do was to define religious identity and history as a key cultural element in the definition of their new nations. In this sense, independence brought both continuity and radical change: change, because official atheism was denounced, and continuity because the elites continued to promote an understanding of religion as a cultural marker rather than a set of rituals and beliefs.

This, however, could take many shapes. Across the Muslim world, most nations formally acknowledge their Islamic identity in one form or another, usually through some stipulation in their constitution. Many others, including countries with religiously mixed populations like Indonesia or Nigeria, pledge allegiance to an unidentified higher being. Nothing of the sort happened in Central Asia or Azerbaijan. Regional presidents took steps to indicate their personal respect for religion, including making the pilgrimage to Mecca. But as will be seen in detail below, they all embraced a secular form of government, resolving in their constitutions to not privilege any religion, and in fact to separate religion from politics. This decision was taken in six states without any apparent formal coordination among them. But it reflected their international orientation and identity. They did not take religious identity as a point of reference in foreign policy and did not see themselves exclusively or even primarily as part of the Muslim world. In fact, at least initially, they invested more energy in European cooperative structures. The six states all gained membership in the Organization for Security and Cooperation in Europe, and joined NATO's Partnership for Peace initiative. Azerbaijan, in addition, became a member of the Council of Europe. Only later did these states invest time and energy into the Organization of Islamic Cooperation.

On a broader scale, the elites across Central Asia and the Caucasus sought to maintain the link to European civilization that they had acquired through the intermediary of Russian colonialism. Simply put, they saw European structures – and Western assistance – as far more attractive than their neighbors to the south, such as Afghanistan, Pakistan and Iran. On a deeper level, these elites – and much of the population – also felt closer mentally to the developed societies of the West than to their southern neighbors. Organizationally, most states and international organizations grouped them together with Eastern Europe. Only in the aftermath of 9/11 did the United States move Central Asia out of its governmental departments dealing with Europe and merge the region with South Asia. Although this move allowed more U.S. government attention to the region, regional leaders were not unanimously pleased. A senior Uzbek government official at the time complained to this author that the U.S. now lumped the region together with Afghanistan and Pakistan, and in doing so ignored Central Asia's connection to European civilization.[4]

There was no Islamic model of government that appeared attractive to the leaders of the region, let alone to their population. All the talk of possible Iranian influence proved widely off the mark. Only two models of societal and political organization appeared attractive: East Asia and Turkey. The East Asian model, a model of authoritarian political modernization, appealed to Central Asian leaders that were reluctant to engage in a political liberalization that they feared would both undermine political

---

4 Personal communication, Washington D.C., October 2003.

stability and threaten their hold on power. But the East Asian model does not have much to say about organized religion, which is a much less significant political force there than it is in the Muslim world. Central Asian and Azerbaijani leaders, by contrast, were very much aware of the rising power of political Islam across their southern border as well as globally. This made the Turkish model attractive, because it provided a solution to the management of religious affairs: a formal separation of state and religion, as well as safeguards to ensure state control over religious affairs.

The impact of the Turkish model is difficult to quantify, but it is clear that Central Asian leaders were interested in the Turkish experience, and adapted elements of it into their process of state construction.[5] Uzbekistan's President Karimov even "acknowledged Turkish help in 'our efforts to achieve good relations between the state and religion, conducted in the same ethnic-cultural conditions [as in Turkey].'"[6] The fact that this model was supported by the United States as well did not hurt matters. But inherently, it so happened that the introduction of a secular form of government was appealing both to the elites and the majority of the population of the region, which wanted to jettison the negative aspects of Soviet rule but keep the undeniable advances in social development they had made compared to their southern neighbors. In this regard, fear of the Islamic radicalism spreading in Afghanistan, Iran, and domestically in Central Asia – as discussed in previous chapters – played a key role in driving Central Asian states and Azerbaijan toward a secular model of government.

---

5 Bess Brown, "Central Asia's Diplomatic Debut," *RFE/RL Research Report*, March 6, 1992.
6 As quoted in Dilip Hiro, *Inside Central Asia*, New York: Overlook Duckworth, 2009.p. 150.

The Legal Basis

Across Central Asia and Azerbaijan, the relationship between state and religion is defined by stipulations in the constitutions of these six countries, as well as in specific laws on religion. As will be seen, there are numerous similarities among them.

Constitutions

The constitutions of regional states are all relatively specific on the question of religion, and most countries also in addition have laws on religion that develop on the broader concepts defined in the constitutions. Most importantly, the principle of secularism is enshrined explicitly in the constitutions of five of the six states. Only Uzbekistan does not explicitly mention secularism, but the constitutional amendments introduced in 2022 would change this, as seen below.

Azerbaijan's constitution emphasizes secularism in three separate places: the Preamble speaks of its intention to "to establish a law-governed, secular state," and article 7 defines the country as a "democratic, law-governed, secular, unitary republic." Article 18 is more specific: it establishes that "religion is separated from the State" and that "all religions are equal before the law" while noting also that the "state education system is of secular character." Turkmenistan's constitution is structured similarly: the preamble defines the ambition to establish the country as a "democratic, legal and secular state" and article one repeats this definition verbatim. Article 12 defines the education system as "separate from religious organizations and secular."

As for Kazakhstan, Article 1 of its constitution specifies that the "Republic of Kazakhstan proclaims itself a democratic, secular, legal and social state." Furthermore, the constitution explicitly prohibits "advocating religious superiority," a stipulation that has entailed a prohibition in the country's criminal code against religious proselytizing. Article 5 stipulates that all foreign religious activity in the country shall be undertaken in "coordination with respective state institutions," thus indicating the importance paid to the state's regulation of foreign religious influence.

Kyrgyzstan's constitution similarly in its first article establishes the country as "a sovereign, democratic, secular, unitary and social state governed by the rule of law." Tajikistan only differs on the margins from this formulation: article one establishes the country as "a sovereign, democratic, law-governed, secular, and unitary State." Furthermore, article 100 defines the secular nature of the state as "unchangeable."

Uzbekistan differed during most of its independence by not having an explicit and prominent statement of secularism in its constitution. The first article only established the country as a "sovereign democratic republic." However, article 61 enshrined secularism by commanding that "religious organizations and associations shall be separated from the state and equal before law." So did article 31, which established that "everyone shall have the right to profess or not to profess any religion. Any compulsory imposition of religion shall be impermissible." Article 18, in the same vein, prohibited discrimination on the basis of religion. However, the Constitutional Amendments proposed in the summer of 2022 rectify this by including language in the Preamble that specify that Uzbekistan is "a humane, democratic, social and secular state."[7]

Furthermore, with the exception of Tajikistan, regional states

---

7 Mirafzal Mirakulov, "Constitutional Reform in the New Uzbekistan," in Svante E. Cornell, ed., *Constitutional Reform in Uzbekistan: A Symposium*, Washington, DC: Central Asia-Caucasus Institute & Silk Road Studies Program Joint Center, December 2022, p. 16-17.

ban political parties based on religious or ethnic principles. This ban is enshrined in the constitution of Kazakhstan, where article 5 bans "religious parties." As for Kyrgyzstan, article 4 prohibits "political parties on religious or ethnic basis" and extends this ban to the "pursuit of political goals by religious associations." In Turkmenistan, article 44 bans "political parties with ethnic or religious attributes." In Uzbekistan, article 57 bans any political party "based on national or religious principles." Azerbaijan's constitution lacks such a provision but makes up for it through separate legislation to the same effect. Tajikistan stands out in this regard, as the power-sharing deal of 1997 legalized the country's Islamist party. As a result, article 28 of the constitution specifically mentions the right of citizens to create political parties "including those of a democratic, religious and atheistic character." But its 2009 law on religion banned religious associations from participating in political activities, a provision potentially contradicting the constitution's acceptance of religious parties.

Laws on Religion

Building on the general principles of the constitutions, all regional states have issued specific laws on religion that have stipulated more detailed rules for religious activity. These laws were designed in the 1990s, but close to twenty years after independence, most states engaged in significant revisions of these laws that increased state control over religious affairs. While these laws differ in detail and emphasis, they have a number of striking similarities. These deal specifically with the registration of religious organizations; the role of foreign religious organizations in the country; the importation and publication of religious literature; and religious attire, particularly as it concerns young people.

Provisions for registration of religious organizations existed since the 1990s across the region. But in the 2000s, most states changed the criteria for registration of religious groups, which in turn led to a requirement for re-registration, with more stringent measures than existed previously. This process began in the mid-2000s in Uzbekistan, and was followed by changes in criteria for registration across the region, typically involving an increase in the number of individuals required to register a religious organization, as well as other restrictions, particularly involving the role of foreign citizens. Kyrgyzstan initially did not have a clear legal framework for religious organizations, but a 2008 law on religion required their registration with the State Committee for Religious Affairs. New religion laws in Azerbaijan and Tajikistan in 2009 forced all religious organizations to re-register with the respective State Committees the following year, and in Tajikistan's case doubled the number of members required to obtain registration. In Kazakhstan, a similar law passed in 2011 created a tiered system for re-registration at the local, regional and national levels.

These new laws reflected an ambition by governments to gain greater control over religious activity within their territory. Tellingly, these laws were passed mainly in the countries of the region that had thus far been more permissive toward foreign religious activity, but which now sought to walk that back in the face of growing Islamic and Christian proselytism. In Azerbaijan, the amended law on religious beliefs of 2011 prohibits "to propagandize religions with the appliance of religious violence or sowing discord among the people," while also banning any claim to the "superiority or limitations of one religion in comparison with another," and holds that "religious activities only be conducted at the legal address where a religious organization is officially registered."[8] Kazakhstan's constitution already bans advocating religious superiority, but the 2011 law goes so far as to ban the conduct of religious ceremonies in private homes, as well as in government buildings and educational institutions. Kyrgyzstan's amendments banned "destructive and totalitarian sects."[9] Tajikistan's 2009 law prohibits private religious education, bans proselytism and the involvement of minors in the activities of religious associations, and prohibits religious associations from participating in political activities.[10]

A particular target has been foreign influence in religious affairs, whether in the shape of missionaries or religious literature. Changes to Azerbaijan's Law on Religious Belief forbid "foreigners and persons without citizenship" from conducting "religious propaganda," restricts the distribution or sale of religious materials and literature outside of approved venues and establishes special licensing procedures for religious education. Similarly, Kazakhstan's 2011 law introduced "expert examination" of religious literature before allowing its importation, and provides for steep fines for anyone who "imports, publishes and/or disseminates illegal religious literature or other materials.[11] Kyrgyzstan's 2009 law only allows importation of religious literature following state examination, and prohibits the door-to-door distribution of such literature

---

8 "'Dini etiqad azadlığı haqqında' Azərbaycan Respublikasının Qanununda dəyişikliklər edilməsi barədə Azərbaycan Respublikasının Qanunu", President.az, July 4, 2011, http://www.president.az/articles/2672.
9 Dmitry Kabak, Gulshaiyr Abdirasulova, "About the realization of the right for religious freedom in Kyrgyzstan", *Freedom of Religion or Belief in the Kyrgyz Republic: an overview*, Bishkek: OpenViewPoint Foundation, 2013.
10 U.S. Commission on International Religious Freedom, "Tajikistan", 2012 Annual Report. https://www.uscirf.gov/sites/default/files/resources/2012ARChapters/tajikistan%202012.pdf
11 U.S. Department of State, Bureaus of Democracy, Human Rights and Labor, *International Religious Freedom Report for 2011*. https://2009-2017.state.gov/j/drl/rls/irf/2011religiousfreedom/index.htm#wrapper

as well as handing it out in public places.¹² In Uzbekistan, all religious literature produced in or imported into the country must be approved by the State Religious Affairs Committee in Tashkent. Tajikistan's 2009 law requires state approval for the importation, sale and distribution of religious literature, an activity that only registered religious organizations are authorized to engage in.¹³

A further target of government attention has been the growth of religious attire. As in France and Turkey, the wearing of Islamic headscarves in schools has been the subject of most controversy. Governments have uniformly sought to counter the spread of overt displays of religion in the shape of Middle East-derived Islamic attire, which they have slammed as a foreign phenomenon alien to their traditions. In some countries, the restrictions on religious dress have been coupled also with restrictions on "revealing" clothes, indicating that governments have no issue with conservative dress *per se*, but with attire they deem to deviate from mainstream society and to generate unrest. Restrictions on dress had long existed in Turkmenistan and Uzbekistan, but has been introduced successively elsewhere in the region. Since 1994, Turkmenistan actively discourages the use of the hijab as well attire such as jeans, shorts, and short skirts. In 2004, the government imposed the use of traditional Turkmen dresses for female students and teachers in schools. Since 2019, the government also enforced a ban on the hijab in public places.¹⁴ In Uzbekistan, a law dating to the 1990s permits only clergy to wear religious clothing.

---

12 "Kyrgyzstan: Human Rights Activists Condemn New Religion Law", *Eurasianet*, January 16, 2009; Norwegian Helsinki Committee, "Law on religion in Kyrgyzstan should be amended in an open and inclusive process," April 25, 2012. (https://www.nhc.no/en/law-on-religion-in-kyrgyzstan-should-be-amended-in-an-open-and-inclusive-process/)
13 Martha Brill Olcott, *Tajikistan's Difficult Development Path*, Washington: Carnegie Endowment, 2012, p. 40.
14 Felix Corley, "Turkmenistan: Raids, searches, fines, threats, beatings, headscarf bans," *Forum 18*, January 16, 2020. (http://www.forum18.org/archive.php?article_id=2534)

While this is not fully enforced and left open the question of what exactly constitutes religious clothing, a 1998 law explicitly forbade the wearing of religious symbols in public.[15] As a result, several dozen male students refusing to shave beards and female students refusing to remove headscarves were expelled from universities and schools. More recently, the government has had to address the issue in conjunction with the general liberalization under President Mirziyoyev. But the Uzbek government has made clear it is not compromising on secularism: in August 2018, Prime Minister Abdullo Aripov signed a decree imposing a secular dress code in all educational institutions.[16]

Kyrgyzstan in 2009 passed a law prohibiting headscarves in schools, with Education Minister Damira Kudaibergenova justifying the decision by emphasizing that Kyrgyzstan is a secular state and stating that "children are coming under a massive attack and we will protect them."[17] The government began to implement this law assertively beginning in September 2011.[18] As for Azerbaijan, in 2010 the government introduced a requirement for the wearing of a school uniform, which explicitly prohibits head covering. The regulation was thus introduced more obliquely, largely to avoid provoking a reaction from Islamist-leaning neighbors Iran and Turkey. In Kazakhstan, dress codes were long left to individual schools and universities. But in 2011, President Nazarbayev expressed his categorical opposition to the hijab, particularly for

---

15 "Class Dismissed: Discriminatory Expulsions of Muslim Students," *Human Rights Watch*, October 1999. (https://www.hrw.org/reports/1999/uzbekistan/)
16 Mushfig Bayram, "Uzbekistan: Supreme Court challenge to student hijab ban," *Forum 18*, April 29, 2019.
17 "Kyrgyzstan Bans Head Scarves From Schools," RFERL, March 3, 2009. (https://www.rferl.org/a/Kyrgyzstan_Bans_Head_Scarves_From_Schools/1503459.html)
18 "Kyrgyz Protesters Demand Hijab Be Allowed In Schools," RFERL, September 19, 2011. (https://www.rferl.org/a/kyrgyz_protesters_demand_islamic_head_scarves_be_allowed_in_school/24333454.html)

students, noting it had never been part of "our religious traditions."[19] Kazakhstan's Grand Mufti agreed, urging women not to wear hijabs, stating that "we should not wear Afghanistan's national clothes."[20] This led to strong informal pressure on students to forego headscarves. In 2016, a formal ban on clothing that "directly or indirectly propagates religion" was introduced in schools.[21]

As in many other areas, Tajikistan has taken matters the furthest. In 2007, the Tajik government prohibited both the hijab and "inappropriate" clothes in schools, following President Rahmon's condemnation of such attire.[22] The education minister's decree specifically referred to the need for young women to dress "in accordance with their status and national traditions." In following years, the campaign against the hijab expanded to government offices and then to the public at large, with officials from the President down urging women to dress in national clothes, while they deemed the hijab to be an alien, Arab tradition. Similarly, they urged men to shave their beards. The country's Council of Ulamo did not oppose the decision, recommending women to wear "traditional clothes" that are in conformity with religious requirements. Even the oppositional Islamic Renaissance Party's leader, Muhiddin Kabiri, whose party has embraced the cause of veiled women, spoke out against attire he associated with Salafism and with Tabligh Jamaat.[23] In 2017, President Rahmon made his

---

19 "Hijan now a hot topic in Kazakhstan," RFERL, March 20, 2011. (https://www.rferl.org/a/islamic_hejab_head_scarf_hot_topic_kazakhstan/2344233.html)
20 "Supreme Mufti called Kazakhstan women to not wear hijabs," Tengrinews.kz, November 18, 2011. (https://en.tengrinews.kz/religion/supreme-mufti-called-kazakhstan-women-to-not-wear-hijabs-5680/)
21 "Kazakhstan School Hijab Ban Upheld," *Transitions Online*, October 21, 2016. (https://www.tol.org/client/article/26411-kazakhstan-hijab-ban-religion.html)
22 Hélène Thibault, *Transforming Tajikistan*, Bloomsbury, 2018, p. 124
23 "Islamic Party Leader In Tajikistan Says He Supports Secular System," RFERL, September 15, 2009. (https://www.rferl.org/a/Islamic_Party_Leader_In_Tajikistan_Says_

view clear: "Wearing the hijab and blindly copying a culture that is foreign to us is not a sign of having high moral and ethical standards for women."[24] This statement was associated with a systematic effort to confront women wearing a hijab publicly and urge them instead to wear a traditional, Tajik-style headscarf.

The Muftiates

In the Soviet era, religion in Central Asia and the Caucasus was administered through spiritual directorates established during the second world war. For Central Asia, this was the Spiritual Administration of Muslims of Central Asia, based in Tashkent. The Caucasus, however, fell under the purview of the Spiritual Administration of Muslims of the Caucasus, based in Baku. Since independence, regional states have built on these religious institutions while simultaneously establishing secular state agencies responsible for religious affairs.

The Spiritual Administrations were a unique and novel phenomenon. Historically, there had not been any similar centralized structure for Islamic clergy in the region: the traditional Ulama had been highly decentralized. As scholar Eren Tasar points out, the recognition and authority enjoyed by religious clerics had nothing to do with any such structure, and on top of that, complicated by the "nearly total interpenetration of the 'ulama and the Naqshbandi Sufi tradition."[25]

But its creation paralleled the creation in Turkey of a Directorate of Spiritual Affairs, a clerical institution claiming control of

---

He_Supports_Secular_System_/1823086.html)
24 "Tajikistan to ban hijab as restrictions on religious freedom continue," *Daily Sabah*, September 18, 2017. (https://www.dailysabah.com/asia/2017/09/18/tajikistan-to-ban-hijab-as-restrictions-on-religious-freedom-continues)
25 Eren Tasar, *Soviet and Muslim: The Institutionalization of Islam in Central Asia*, New York: Oxford University Press, 2017, p. 56.

houses of Islamic worship in the country and loyal to the secular power. As such, it was a blueprint that the states kept alive, rather than allowing a return to an unregulated form of Islamic organization. Upon independence, each Central Asian state established its own spiritual administration, and as a result the Tashkent administration, known by the acronym SADUM, transitioned to become a purely national, Uzbek institution. This did not happen in the Caucasus: the Baku-based Caucasus Muslim Board had a unique configuration, as it was led by a Shi'a cleric holding the title of Sheikh-ul-Islam and Grand Mufti of the Caucasus, whose responsibility covered all Shi'a Muslims of the Soviet Union. The board also had a Sunni deputy, who was responsible for Sunni Muslims in both the South Caucasus and several republics of the Russian North Caucasus. This configuration has for the most part remained in place, and has come to be utilized by Azerbaijan as an instrument of its foreign and regional policy.

The Caucasus Muslims Board is formally a non-government entity, which claims jurisdiction over all Islamic congregations in the country. As such, no Muslim organization can obtain state registration without obtaining approval from the Board. Skeikh-ul-Islam Allahshükür Pashazade holds the distinction of being the most long-serving of all post-Soviet clerics. He was appointed in 1980 at the young age of 30, and remains at the helm of the Board at the present time.

Other countries have seen considerable turnover in their religious institutions, and have gravitated in different directions. The first head of the Spiritual Administration of Muslims of Kazakhstan, also the country's first Mufti, was the highest-ranking Kazakh cleric in SADUM, Qazi Ratbek Nysanbaiuly, who served until 2000. He was replaced by the former diplomat and Arabist Absattar Derbisali, who, significantly, did not have the background of a cleric. In 2013, he was replaced by Yerzhan Mayamerov. This appointment signaled the growing influence of a new generation of Kazakh clerics trained at Egypt's famed Al-Azhar University. Indeed, as viewed in the previous chapter, the Kazakh government partnered with Al-Azhar to create the Nur-Mubarak University, which is the main institution of Islamic studies in the country. Mayamerov is a graduate of the Department of Shar'ia and Law at Al-Azhar, where he also worked at the Fatwas Adoption Department for two years. His tenure as mufti lasted for four years, after which he was replaced by Serikbay Oraz, also a graduate of Al-Azhar, who in addition attended the International Islamic University in Islamabad.

As for Kyrgyzstan, it has seen considerable turmoil in its religious institutions. In the period between 2010 and 2014, it went through no less than six different Grand Muftis, who were all quickly replaced due to different controversies, scandals and religious as well as political power struggles. But in 2014, Maksatbek Toktomushev was appointed acting Mufti, and duly elected as such in 2017. Toktomushev hails from Osh province in southern Kyrgyzstan, but spent a decade (beginning in 1996) studying at the Madrasa Arabia Raiwind in Lahore, Pakistan, where he obtained a degree in Islamic law. He subsequently became the kazi of Bishkek city and rose to the position of deputy Mufti.[26] As already mentioned, the Mufti's close association with Tabligh Jamaat has made Kyrgyzstan's policy on this movement stand out in the Central Asian context.

Tajikistan's Islamic institutions have been marked by the country's civil war. As mentioned in the previous chapter, when

---

26 "Maksatbek Toktomushev," *Centrasia.org*, https://centrasia.org/person.php.

Tajikistan established its separate religious structure in 1988 Akbar Turajonzoda was appointed its chief jurist or *Qozi Kalon*. Turajonzoda hailed from a prominent Qadiri Sufi family from Samarkand, and had studied in the Mir-Arab madrasa in Bukhara before pursing studies in Islamic Law at the University of Amman in Jordan. Turajonzoda found himself in the middle of the emerging conflict between the Islamist opposition and the government. He initially sought to maintain his neutrality, while opposing the very idea of an Islamic political party, something he felt was divisive of the Muslim community. Its creation would also, of course, undermine his own power as the head of the country's Muslims. Instead, he used the conflict to advance his own calls for the Islamization of the country, which were rebuffed by the political leadership. By 1991, Turajonzoda abandoned his neutrality and sided with the opposition. When the civil war escalated in 1992, he was dismissed and forced into exile.[27] The next year, the government officially established an independent *Muftiyat*, severing ties with SADUM. President Rakhmonov appointed to the position of Mufti Fetullahkhan Sharifzoda, a traditionalist Sufi Shaykh that had strongly rejected the opposition forces.[28] Sharifzoda was nevertheless assassinated in 1996.[29] After this traumatic event, the government introduced further institutional reforms. It established a High Council of Ulama that united over 20 high clerics, and also created the Islamic Center of the Republic of Tajikistan. The Islamic Center is directly subordinated to

---

27 Nourzhanov etc, p. 273-75.
28 Tim Epkenhans, "Muslim without Learning, Clergy without Faith: Institutions of Islamic Learning in the Republic of Tajikistan," in Michael Kemper, Raoul Motika and Stefan Reichmuth, eds., *Islamic Education in the Soviet Union and Its Successor States*, London: Routledge, 2010, Sophie Roche, *The Faceless Terrorist: A Study of Critical Events in Tajikistan*, Springer, 2019, p. 62.
29 Emily O'Dell, Subersives and Saints, Sufism and the State in Central Asia. In Pauline Jones, ed., *Islam, State and Politics in Central Asia*.

the government, and the Head of the Islamic Center is also the Head of the High Council. Until 2010, Amonulloh Nematzoda held this position, and after his death in 2010, it passed to Saidmukarram Abdulqodirzoda, who hails from a clerical family near Kulyab in southeastern Tajikistan. Abdulqodirzoda, born in 1963, traveled to Pakistan in 1995 to study at the International Islamic University in Islamabad, where he spent eight years studying Quranic exegesis and hadith. Following a few years of teaching in official Islamic institutions in Tajikistan, he served as a head of department in the Government Committee for Religious Affairs.

Turkmenistan's Muftiate was created shortly after independence. It consisted of nine people, including a mufti, representatives of each province, and two representatives of the Shi'a community. The Muftiate is subordinated to the Ministry of Justice. From 1996 until 2003, the country's mufti was Nasrullah ibn-Ibadullah, an ethnic Uzbek from the eastern Dashoguz region who had studied in Uzbekistan, Egypt as well as Syria during the Soviet period. He was nevertheless dismissed in 2003 and sentenced to a lengthy prison term in 2004. This occurred during the time of turmoil following an alleged attempted coup against President Niyazov, which led to a general crackdown on the ethnic Uzbek community after the government accused Uzbekistan of complicity in the coup attempt.[30] Ibadullah had also resisted Niyazov's order to display the president's book on spiritual values, the *Rukhnama*, in mosques alongside the Quran. In 2007, soon after the succession to President Berdimuhamedov, the former mufti was nevertheless pardoned and offered a new state position.[31] Ibadullah was replaced by an ethnic Turkmen,

---
30 Antoine Blua, "Turkmenistan: Former Chief Mufti Sentenced To Prison For Reasons That Remain Unclear," *RFERL*, March 22, 2004.
31 See Victoria Clement, *Religion and the Secular State in Turkmenistan*, Washington:

Kakageldi Vepayev. In subsequent years, there has been considerable turnover in the position of Mufti, a practice common in the Turkmen government, where frequent rotation of officials is a practice intended to counter the emergence of independent power centers. As a result, the imam of Lebap province, Yalkab Hojaguliyev, was appointed Mufti.

Uzbekistan has the most well-known Islamic institutions of Central Asia, effectively the only ones in continuous operation since the Soviet era. As mentioned, it was also the seat of the Soviet-era spiritual administration of Muslims for the entire region. The core of SADUM was transformed into the Muslim Board of Uzbekistan. It was initially led by the internationally respected cleric Muhammad Sadik Muhammad Yusuf, who was the last head of SADUM, and what scholar Martha Olcott termed the "most charismatic" of all religious leaders in Central Asia. Muhammad Yusuf, from a clerical family in Andijan, studied in Libya for four years in the late 1970s before returning and rising in the ranks of SADUM. Once at the helm of SADUM, he worked to bridge the gap between moderate clerics and the more radical forces in his native Ferghana. But the increasingly restrictive political climate in Uzbekistan in the early 1990s led to a restricted role for compromise and his dismissal and departure for Libya in 1993. He was subsequently given a senior position in the Saudi-based Muslim World League, and allowed to return to Uzbekistan and maintain a role as a senior independent voice on religious affairs.[32] Several figures served as mufti until 2006, when the current holder of the position, Usmankhan Alimov, was appointed. Alimov, born

---

Central Asia-Caucasus Institute & Silk Road Studies Program, Silk Road Paper, June 2020, pp. 26-27.
32 Martha Brill Olcott, "A Face of Islam: Muhammad-Sodiq Muhammad-Yusuf", Carnegie Papers, no. 82, March 2007.

in 1950 near Samarkand, received his religious education in Soviet Uzbek religious institutions, but also briefly studied at Morrocco's Al-Qarawiyyin University in the late 1980s.

As this overview suggests, the official religious institutions across the region all connect back to Soviet-era institutions. The strongest continuity has existed in Azerbaijan and Uzbekistan, perhaps not surprisingly, as Baku and Tashkent were the seat of these Soviet-era institutions. A Soviet-era generation of clerics have remained at the helm there, as well as in Tajikistan. In Kazakhstan, and Kyrgyzstan, by contrast, the clerical establishment was considerably weaker. There, a new generation of clerics with connections to the Middle East and South Asia have gained prominence.

The *muftiates* of the region all have similar challenges: their Soviet legacy and their status as semi-official bodies provide both assets and liabilities. Their key asset is their claim to represent, and revive, the indigenous traditional Islamic traditions of the region – at least the formal, orthodox traditions. It should be noted that only Turkmenistan has unequivocally embraced the folk Islam of the region. Elsewhere, governments pay lip service to Sufi traditions, but the religious institutions they have supported are skeptical of these esoteric practices that are, almost by definition, outside of their control. Instead, they promote the region's formal, Hanafi Sunni Islamic traditions, and at best tolerate the syncretistic folk traditions such as saint worship that are prevalent across Central Asia and the Caucasus. This skepticism against heterodoxy is growing as the region's clerics are increasingly influenced by the more orthodox and anti-Sufi theology of the Middle East. The official religious institutions walk a fine line: they seek to discourage practices they term as pure superstition, while also rejecting the challenge of Salafi-leaning theology that emphasizes direct textual sources rather than the study of tradition and Quranic commentary that is central to the Hanafi tradition.[33]

Their main asset, however, is also their main liability. The region's official institutions and most of their members have Soviet roots, and the political control over religion in the Soviet era has continued into independence, with these clerics and institutions largely perceived as an extended arm of the state. The extent of the government supervision of clerics differs from country to country, with Tajikistan and Turkmenistan having the most direct government direction over religious bodies, and Kazakhstan and Kyrgyzstan the least. This link to government, as well as poor training of officially approved clerics especially at the regional and local level, has undermined the religious credibility of the official institutions. This problem is the most significant in Tajikistan, where the country's High Council of Ulama contains 27 members, but leaves out many highly respected religious figures that are unpalatable to the government. As anthropologist Sophie Roche summarizes the council, it consists mostly of "relatively unknown religious figures from the south and from the area around the region's capital."[34] As governments are no longer able to restrict citizen's efforts to obtain information on their own in this age of limitless communications, they are forced to contend with the ability of skeptical citizens to seek religious information from foreign sources. As shall be seen, some states have responded to this by seeking to inject a more assertive and positive agenda into their religious hierarchy, while others have emphasized further restrictions.

State Institutions

[33] Olcott, "A Face of Islam;" Khalid, *Islam after Communism*.
[34] Roche, *The Faceless Terrorist*, p. 63.

6. Is There A Model?

All regional states have adopted, separate from their clerical institutions, some version of a State Committee for religious affairs as a direct instrument of the government for supervision of religious affairs. This institution, too, has Soviet roots: its antecedent is the Council for Religious Affairs, itself a successor to the Council for Affairs of Religious Cults, created during the second world war as the Soviet leadership eased restrictions on religion.[35] This institution had a coordinating role for government policy in the Soviet era, but one that was relatively opaque, and whose relationship with more powerful policy-making institutions was highly non-transparent. All regional states did not immediately institute a similar institution at independence, but they all eventually did so.

Azerbaijan created a "State Committee for Work with Religious Organizations" in 2001, with a mandate including "the creation of appropriate conditions for compliance with laws relating to freedom of religion and for the state registration and oversight of religious institutions."[36] Its purview included supervising religious practice, promoting interfaith dialogue, analyzing religious school programs and religious literature, as well as registering all religious organizations. The Committee initially had acrimonious relations with the Caucasus Muslims Board, involving competition for the supremacy of the decision-making process in religious affairs as well as a personal rivalry between Sheikh Pashazadeh and the first Head of the Committee, Rafik Aliyev, who attempted to impose new restrictions and rules on mullahs, especially financial transparency in the mosques. The Board actually went so far as to

---

35 John Anderson, "The Council for Religious Affairs and the Shaping of Soviet Religious Policy," *Soviet Studies*, vol. 43 no. 4, 1991, pp. 689-710.
36 "Azərbaycan Respublikasının Dini Qurumlarla İş üzrə Dövlət Komitəsinin yaradılması haqqında," [On the Creation of the State Committee for Work with Religious Organizations of the Republic of Azerbaijan], June 21, 2001, http://scwra.gov.az/upload/Files/5.doc

sue the State Committee, while the Committee accused the Board of spreading illegal and dangerous literature in the country.[37]

Personal and institutional tensions have diminished under subsequent leaders of the SCWRO, and the SCWRO has in practice been forced to share some powers with the CMB. Islamic organizations and mosques remain under the CMB's mandate and must therefore receive letters of approval from it in order to register with the SCWRO.[38] The SCWRO lobbied for the 2009 amendment to the Law on Freedom of Religion, which called for a re-registration of religious associations with the committee. The Committee also allocates funds for organizational development of religious organizations. It is also tasked with preventing radicalization, including through institutional cooperation with local religious associations and the Ministry of National Security to track potential "foreign fighters," as well as monitoring and vetting religious literature, especially literature imported from abroad. A 2014 amendment allowed the SCWRO to monopolize religious education for the conduct of rites.

Kazakhstan has gone through considerable organizational turmoil in its state agencies responsible for religion during the past decade. At first, the country took a relatively relaxed stance on religion. Kazakhstan eagerly partnered with Egypt and Kuwait to build universities and accepted a Qatari gift to construct the Nur-Astana mosque in the capital. A representative of the Kazakh spiritual board in 2008 told a German interlocutor that "he finds it perfectly legitimate that they are now relearning Islam with

---

[37] See detailed analysis in Svante E. Cornell, *The Politicization of Islam in Azerbaijan*, Washington: Central Asia-Caucasus Institute, Silk Road Paper, October 2006. (https://www.silkroadstudies.org/resources/pdf/SilkRoadPapers/2006_10_SRP_Cornell_Islam-Azerbaijan.pdf)

[38] Cornell et. al., *Azerbaijan's Formula*, p. 82.

the help of teachers from Saudi Arabia or Egypt."[39] But other parts of the Kazakh government were beginning to get concerned. In 2005, the government created a "Committee on Religious Issues" in order to "guarantee religious freedom and to strengthen mutual understanding and tolerance amongst the various religious groups."[40] By 2010, the Committee was transferred from the Ministry of Justice to the Ministry of Culture. A year later, following the country's first suicide bombing, it was upgraded to a "Religious Affairs Agency," tasked with "the formulation and implementation of state policy in the area of religious freedom," as well as studying and analyzing "the operation of religious organizations and the activities of missionaries."[41]

Established through a reorganization of the Ministry of Culture, this Agency incorporated the Center for Research and Analysis on Religious Issues of the Ministry of Justice. President Nazarbayev had suggested establishing such an agency already in 2009, noting the need to "suppress activities of pseudo-religious organizations."[42] Its first head, diplomat Kairat Lama Sharif, noted that "processes in the sphere of religion have gained strategic importance for public and even national security."[43] Following the adoption of a new law on religion, Sharif noted that "one third of the country's religious organizations will be shut down soon," and that the law would mitigate the "use of religion for

---

39 Edda Schlager, "Islamic Revival in Kazakhstan: A Pragmatic Islam", *qantara.de,* December 4, 2008. (https://en.qantara.de/content/islamic-revival-in-kazakhstan-a-pragmatic-islam)
40 https://www.osce.org/files/f/documents/5/1/38008.pdf
41 United States Department of State, "2011 Report on International Religious Freedom – Kazakhstan."
42 Anuar Aubakirov and Yelden Sarybai, "Religious Affairs Agency Works to Protect Freedoms, Stop Extremist Ideologies," *Astana Times,* July 10, 2013. (https://astanatimes.com/2013/07/religious-affairs-agency-works-to-protect-freedoms-stop-extremist-ideologies/)
43 Ibid.

destructive purposes."⁴⁴ The Agency, among other tasks, was tasked to examine religious literature, contribute to state programming to combat religious extremism, counter extremist propaganda, and assist what it termed "victims of destructive religious movements." Unlike in Azerbaijan, it has no role in religious training.

In 2014, the Agency was turned into a Committee for Religious Affairs under the Ministry of Culture and Sport. Following the terrorist attacks in 2016, the entity was upgraded to full ministerial status, the Ministry of Religious and Civil Society Affairs. Finally, in 2018, it was renamed the Ministry of Social Development and in 2019 again changed to the Ministry of Information and Social Development. The Ministry, according to its first Minister, was created with the purpose of "strengthening our determination to preserve the secular nature of our country and its religious moderation while protecting the rights of religious believers and preventing and countering extremism through well-thought-through and balanced policies."⁴⁵

Kyrgyzstan in 1995 created a State Commission for Religious Affairs, which was turned into a state agency in 2006. This shift occurred as the Kyrgyz government began to pay increasing attention to regulating religious affairs. Kyrgyzstan adopted a Law on Religion in 2008, which gave the SCRA greater authority over religious organizations within the country. Under this law, no religious group is allowed to operate without registration with the Agency, which can reject any application it deems a "threat to national security, social stability, interethnic and

---

44 "One Third Of Kazakh Religious Groups And Organizations To Be Shut Down," *RFERL*, October 12, 2012. (https://www.rferl.org/a/one-third-of-kazakh-religious-groups-shut-down/24737345.html)

45 Nurlan Yermekbayev, "Why Kazakhstan Created the Ministry for Religious and Civil Society Affairs" *Diplomat*, November 10, 2016. (https://thediplomat.com/2016/11/why-kazakhstan-created-the-ministry-for-religious-and-civil-society-affairs/)

interdenominational harmony, public order, health or morality." The law requires 200 founders for an organization to be registered or re-registered, and a failure to register or provide proper reporting can lead the Agency to close down an organization.

Since 2008, there have been several amendments to the Law on Religion. A 2011 amendment vested control over pilgrimages to holy sites with the Muftiate, while a 2012 change broadened the authority of "state bodies for religious affairs, national security and internal affairs" to exercise control over the dissemination of religious messages, with a view to counter the spread of extremist ideology. In 2014, the SCRA prepared draft amendments that would bump the requirement from 200 to 500 founders for an organization to be considered for registration and would require anyone working in any capacity in any religious organization, as well as any organization offering religious education, to have an annually renewed SCRA license. Additionally, it called for increased penalties for violations of laws on religious affairs. These amendments were deliberated upon but were never introduced to parliament.

The State Agency was tasked with developing methodologies for teaching religion in public schools as an antidote to the perceived spread of Salafi ideas.[46] The SCRA has banned 21 religious organizations on account of "destructive, extremist, and terrorist" affiliations that are considered to undermine national security. These include international terrorist groups like al-Qaida, ISIS, and the Taliban, as well as smaller, local jihadi groups. Uyghur separatist groups in Xinjiang are also included in the list, as is Hizb ut-Tahrir.

Tajikistan has experienced a similar institutional evolution

---

46 United States Department of State, *Annual Report on Religious Freedom, 2004*, p. 373.

as its neighbors. Initially, the Ministry of Culture's directorate of religious affairs was tasked with controlling matters of faith in Tajikistan, and its responsibilities included organizing the Tajik participation in the hajj, the registration of houses of worship, and supervising the import of religious literature. By 2010, the Tajik president elevated religious matters to the status of an independent agency, creating the "State Commission on Religious Affairs,"[47] whose title now includes "Regulation of Traditions, Ceremonies and Rituals." This Agency oversees the registration of religious organizations in Tajikistan, and assigns fines to individuals and organizations that do not abide by laws on religion.

Following the adoption of a law "On Freedom of Conscience and Religious Associations" in 2009, and a number of amendments in ensuing years, the SCRA has acquired greater powers of oversight. Most of these came following a government crackdown in 2017, during which the SCRA closed down 2,000 mosques in an attempt to centralize control over houses of worship. Amendments since then have led the SCRA to enforce the government's ban on religious activity and religious education without state permission, as well as additional rules introduced in 2018 concerning religious ceremonies, including weddings, funerals, and circumcision. These rules sought to reduce the size of wedding parties, as well as restricting and regulating rites of passage. As a consequence of these amendments, the SCRA has a larger mandate over religious organizations and the practice of religion in the country overall. This included a special commission set up to monitor 'alien' culture and religion in the country, most notably clothing practices and the wearing of hijabs, which the SCRA

---

[47] "Tajik President Puts State Body In Charge Of Religious Affairs," *RFERL*, May 13, 2010. (https://www.rferl.org/a/Tajik_President_Puts_State_Body_In_Charge_Of_Religious_Affairs/2040655.html)

discourages in favor of Tajik traditional dress.[48] More recently, the SCRA and government security agencies in 2020 cracked down on the Muslim Brotherhood, detaining over two dozen alleged members of the organization, which is outlawed in the country.[49]

Uzbekistan's government established a State Religious Affairs Committee already in March 1992, with a mandate to ensure "mutual cooperation between religious sects and to represent their interests in front of the state." The Committee answers to the Cabinet of Ministers. The committee's main official function is to ensure freedom of conscience and freedom of religion, and it issues permits to religious organizations to operate legally in the country. For registration, organizations are required to prove their level of education in their faith, and disclose their sources of income. The local government (*khokimiyats*) also work with religious organizations to ensure that they are in accordance with the local administrative laws.

In 2006, the Committee moved to restrict the importation of religious literature into the country.[50] It instituted new penalties for the "illegal" production, storage, import, and distribution of religious literature, with penalties of up to three years' imprisonment for repeat offenders. In December 2019, the Committee approved an updated list of banned Islamic texts, which include both ancient works and more modern tracts, such as works of exiled Uzbek ideologues as well as materials of the Gülen and Ahmadiyya movements.

Following the accession of Shavkat Mirziyoyev to the Presidency, a gradual softening of the restrictions on religious life in

48 "Tajikistan To Promote Clothing To Counter 'Alien' Traditions," *RFE/RL,* July 21, 2017.
49 Farangis Najibullah, "Imams, Politicians, Professors: Dozens of Muslim Brotherhood Suspects Detained in Tajikistan," RFE/RL, January 9, 2020.
50 U.S. Commission on International Religious Freedom, "Uzbekistan", 2007. https://www.uscirf.gov/sites/default/files/resources/AR_2007/uzbekistan.pdf

Uzbekistan took place. In May 2018, a Joint Resolution of the Houses of Parliament approved a roadmap to ensure freedom of religion and belief. Results were not immediately visible, as the CRA in 2018 introduced additional requirements for religious organizations seeking to register. But following an incident in August 2019 when police forcibly shaved the beards of an estimated hundred men in Tashkent, the President removed the entire leadership of the CRA, and issued an ordering requiring the CRA to "develop a new policy to ensure freedom of conscience."[51] In summer 2020, Uzbek authorities sent a draft of the law to the Venice Commission of the Council of Europe and to the OSCE's Office of Democratic Institutions and Human Rights for review. These institutions responded with a relatively negative opinion, which faulted Uzbekistan for continuing to ban proselytizing activities, regulate religious literature and religious education, and put forward considerable registration requirements for religious groups, among other.[52] Their recommendations appear to seek nothing less than the full deregulation of religious affairs in the country, which is unlikely to take place anytime soon. In July 2021, a new law on religion was passed, which removed the ban on wearing religious clothing and reduced the number of members required for registering religious organizations. The bulk of the existing law remained in place, however.

Traditional vs Novel Religion

A striking element in the politics of religion in Central Asia and Azerbaijan is the alliance between states and representatives of

---

[51] Umida Hashimova, "Religion, Beards, and Uzbekistan's Secular Government," *Diplomat*, September 9, 2019.

[52] European Commission for Democracy Through Law (Venice Commission) and OSCE Office for Democratic Institutions and Human Rights (OSCE/ODIHR), "Uzbekistan: Joint Opinion on the Draft Law "On Freedom of Conscience and Religious Organizations," Adopted By The Venice Commission At Its 124th Online Plenary Session (8-9 October 2020). (http://venice.coe.int/webforms/documents/?pdf=CDL-AD(2020)002-e)

traditional religion. It is a frequent occurrence across the region to see leaders of Muslim, Christian and Jewish religious communities appearing publicly side by side, expressing their support for religious harmony and tolerance. This happens both within countries and abroad. Azerbaijan's Shaykh-ul-Islam has traveled to numerous international destinations accompanied by the Papal Nuncio, the Orthodox Patriarch, and the heads of Jewish congregations. Baku also hosts international religious meetings, including a 2016 conference on religious tolerance. A summit of world religious leaders was held in November 2019. Kazakhstan, similarly, has focused on its initiative to create a "Congress of Leaders of World and Traditional Religions." Held since 2003, six Congresses have been held assembling Muslim, Christian, Jewish and Buddhist leaders, the most recent held in September 2022. Religious leaders of Uzbekistan also frequently appear at joint events, though mainly for a domestic audience.

What all these initiatives have in common is their focus on traditional religious communities, in opposition to novel faith communities. States in the region have drawn a stark dichotomy between traditional and non-traditional religious groups. In fact, across Central Asia and Azerbaijan, the main religious tensions are not *between* religious denominations but *within* them. While conversions across religious boundaries occur, it is mainly the case that foreign-based Muslim groups proselytize almost exclusively in the Muslim community; foreign Christian denominations do so mainly but not exclusively among the region's Christians.

Against this background, the leaders of traditional Muslim, Jewish and Christian communities have struck an implicit alliance to preserve – indeed, restore – the predominant role of their traditional religious institutions over their respective flocks. They therefore have banded together and encouraged state policies that provide them with some form of recognition, while countering the influence of new, alien religious groupings. The inclusion of the word "traditional" in the title of Kazakhstan's main initiative is an explicit example of this.

This striking development is appalling to many western defenders of religious freedom, because it means that religious communities are not treated equally: the state actively discourages religious beliefs and communities that are not considered traditional. In other words, the state picks and chooses among religious groups, something that critics quite correctly consider at odds with the notion of state neutrality toward religion. But this is an approach that is rooted in the particular conditions of post-communism. At independence, the traditional religious institutions and practices in society had been decimated. Religious life was a *tabula rasa*, something foreign missionaries rapidly realized. As a result, the 1990s saw the rapid influx of a broad variety of Islamic and Christian missionaries into the region, who responded to the natural curiosity about matters of the soul that emerged once state atheism had been abolished. Both governments and large sections of the public perceived the sudden ability of foreign religious groups to recruit new believers as profoundly destabilizing to societies reeling from communism. First and foremost, it triggered a fear of the unknown and the different among the majority of society, which sought to reconnect with the national traditions of the past. It was also polarizing, given the contrast between the confidence and ample resources that foreign religious movements displayed, compared to the dilapidated state of traditional religion.

It should also be noted that this took place at the same time as the Taliban movement emerged from Saudi-funded madrasahs in northwestern Pakistan. This offered a sobering example of the

6. Is There A Model?

possible implications of the spread of foreign-funded religious movements, which, in the right conditions, could rapidly undo a traditional and conservative religious order and introduce a fanatical, violent alternative. It is not surprising, therefore, that both popular majorities and national leaders saw the influx of foreign religious groups as an unwelcome development. It undermined their appeal to a restored national pride, and raised fears about the political and security implications of the massive expansion of new sects.

As a result, leaders in Central Asia and Azerbaijan felt two conflicting impulses: one was to permit the natural return of religion into society, and the other to restrain the religious currents that they saw as destabilizing society. The solution, they concluded, was to lend support to the traditional religious institutions that had deep roots in the region but had been decimated by Soviet rule; while also working to restrict the religious currents understood to be alien.

On one hand, the official promotion of religious harmony means that citizens of Central Asia and Azerbaijan are continuously exposed to the message of religious leaders appearing together and expressing the same message, even seeming to enjoy each other's company. It has a direct bearing on the fact that the states of Central Asia and Azerbaijan all have positive relations with Israel, and have among the Muslim world's lowest incidence of anti-Semitic incidents. American Jewish leaders have expressed, with particular reference to Azerbaijan, that they perceive an "atmosphere of tolerance that we can't see even in most European countries."[53] On the other hand, these policies have cemented an

---

[53] "'Zero Anti-Semitism in Azerbaijan' Says Interfaith Delegation in S.F.", *Jewish Weekly*, May 22, 2018.

intolerance to novel religious impulses that is by its very nature illiberal. As will be seen, novel religious trends have been "securitized:" far from being seen only as a societal phenomenon, they have come to be seen as a threat to stability and security.

Residual Soviet Thinking and the Primacy of Security Structures

A third commonality among the regional states is the primacy of security structures in the state's relationship with religion. This is a function of two separate issues: the dominant role of security services in the state-building process across the region and the securitization of religious affairs.

The primacy of security services is, in great part, a legacy of the Soviet era. Unlike many developing nations, where the military wields considerable influence in politics, in the Soviet Union it was the KGB that played this role. As numerous studies have shown, the KGB emerged as a state within the state, playing a key role in the successions of power in Moscow and developing into a bastion of power that was in most ways autonomous from the formal political leadership.[54] This pattern remained in the new nations that emerged in 1991. The military has not been a political factor in any post-Soviet state except Armenia, but the security services have remained the core of state power everywhere.

These agencies, whether organized as Ministries of National Security or State Security Agencies, have wielded enormous power over government approaches to all forms of independent social

---

54 Jeremy R. Azrael, *The KGB in Kremlin Politics*, Santa Monica: RAND/UCLA Center for the Study of Soviet International Behavior, 1989. (https://apps.dtic.mil/dtic/tr/fulltext/u2/a228341.pdf); Robert W. Pringle, "Andropov's Counterintelligence State," *International Journal of Intelligence and CounterIntelligence*, vol. 13, 2000, pp. 193-203; Aaron Bateman, "The Political Influence of the Russian Security Services," *Journal of Slavic Military Studies*, vol. 27 no. 3, 2014, pp. 380-403.

and political activity, and have accorded considerable attention to religious activity. Because religious extremism in the region's neighborhood was demonstrably a serious security challenge with potentially devastating consequences, it was not far-fetched to identify uncontrolled religious activity as a security issue. This, of course, is the case across the world: western democracies also closely monitor religious groups they deem extremist. Where Central Asia and Azerbaijan diverge is in their broad definition of the groups they target. Most Western security agencies focus only on groups they consider prone to engage in violence, but their Central Asian counterparts define religious activity that departs from tradition and is unsanctioned by the state as inherently problematic.

This approach is not entirely without merit. The Western approach essentially ignores the content of an organization's ideology, and therefore, with few exceptions (Germany, Denmark) Western countries permit organizations like Hizb-ut-Tahrir to operate freely. While this group does not itself engage in violence, its ideology is essentially identical to that of Al Qaeda and ISIS, and its openly stated plan for the construction of a Caliphate can only be achieved through violence.[55] Similarly, Western states were caught unawares when Islamist mobilization in their immigrant suburbs led thousands of young Europeans of Muslim descent to join the Islamic State. Central Asian states, thus, are correct in considering extremist ideology to be problematic and to implement measures to curb extremism as such, whether or not the individuals or groups in question directly engage in violence.

Central Asian states, however, have seemed to approximate

---

[55] Zeyno Baran, *Hizb-ut-Tahrir: Islam's Political Insurgency*, Washington: Nixon Center, 2004, p. 1.

Maslow's proverbial hammer: because their main tools to deal with civic activity they feel uncomfortable with are those of the security apparatus, most unsanctioned religious activity appeared to them to warrant security intervention. Thus, it is not only organizations like Hizb-ut Tahrir that have been the subject of state security interest, but many others, including Jehovah's Witnesses, scientologists, and a host of Muslim groups that authorities do not recognize as traditional, such as the Ahmadi community.

These approaches are not uniform. Kyrgyzstan, as noted, adopted a divergent and more liberal approach. In several states like Azerbaijan, Kazakhstan and Turkmenistan, Turkish organizations such as the Fethullah Gülen community were allowed to operate, at least until the Gülen grouping was implicated in a coup attempt against Turkey's President Erdoğan in 2016. And even in Uzbekistan, President Karimov not only tolerated but publicly praised the Akromiya movement's social accomplishments less than a year before the movement turned violent and captured a state prison in Andijan, leading to the government crackdown of May 2005.[56] Thus, there has always been an element of arbitrariness in the type of movements targeted by state security services in the region.

This heavy-handed approach has included state security efforts to attend religious ceremonies, disrupt services, and frequently infiltrate religious organizations to break them up, or conduct raids against them. Practitioners of unregistered religious groups are frequently subjected to detention, questioning, confiscation of their religious materials, and to prosecution. Such

---

56 Jeffry Hartman, *The May 2005 Andijan Uprising: What We Know*, Washington: Central Asia-Caucasus Institute & Silk Road Studies Program, Silk Road Paper, May 2016, pp. 20-21.

actions are frequently accompanied by allegations of wrongdoing, including the exercise of violence by government authorities against targeted individuals. Indeed, the continued harassment of unregistered religious groups is one of the main factors motivating international criticism of human rights practices in regional countries, and is amply described in reports by the U.S. State Department and human rights watchdog organizations.

It should be noted that the restrictive nature of national legislation, and the considerable room for interpretation afforded to law enforcement bodies, has opened the door for a great deal of arbitrary behavior. Thus, while the aim of central legislation has seldom been to target small innocuous groups like Baptist communities, in practice the conversion of individuals to religions other than that of their birth is typically a highly sensitive and unpopular matter. That in turn allows for local law enforcement to act, often on their own initiative, to curb such behavior. Yet overall, it is missionary Muslim movements that have borne the brunt of efforts of the regional state security services.

As mentioned in chapter five, it is frequently alleged that such targeting of innocuous religious activity, and not least the harassment of otherwise harmless citizens, is profoundly counter-productive. Accordingly, critics argue that these government excesses only have the effect of pushing peaceful citizens in the direction of extremism, their frustration and anger with government abuse leaving them easy prey for the recruitment of *real* extremists. Political scientist Eric McGlinchey argued, for example, "radical Islam in Central Asia manifests a society's response to the accumulated injustices of severely authoritarian rule,"[57] and "the more

---

57 Eric McGlinchey, "Autocrats, Islamists and the Rise of Radicalism in Central Asia", *Current History*, October 2005, p. 340.

authoritarian the state, the more pronounced political Islam will be in society."[58]

On the global level, there is some evidence to this effect, but it is decidedly mixed, with academic studies failing to confirm any causal link between repression and radicalization.[59] As for Central Asia, the ominous predictions that were made two decades ago have failed to materialize. In fact, the region's trajectory has been the opposite; those states that employed the most aggressive measures to combat extremism – namely, Uzbekistan and Turkmenistan – have had comparably fewer problems with violent extremism in recent years. Meanwhile, those that adopted more liberal approaches, such as Kazakhstan and Kyrgyzstan, experienced an increase in religiously-motivated violence. By the early 2010s, therefore, leaders in those countries appear to have deduced, to put it simply, that Tashkent had it right and the West had it wrong; and began to emulate the policies adopted by Uzbekistan. It is hard to escape the conclusion that Central Asian leaders have largely succeeded in the aim of preventing Islamist extremism from expanding its foothold in their societies. It is legitimate to ask, however, whether the price of this success has been too high. Further, it is questionable whether security-focused approaches can work in the longer term in a region that is being rapidly permeated by technological change, which implies that even the most zealous state security officers may be at a loss in preventing extremist ideology from spreading.

There is some difference in the trajectory of regional states.

---

58 Eric McGlinchey, "The Making of Militants: The State and Islam in Central Asia", *Comparative Studies of South Asia, Africa and the Middle East*, vol. 25 no. 3, 2005, p. 559.

59 This issue is discussed in detail in Svante E. Cornell, "Central Asia: Where Did Islamic Radicalization Go?", in *Religion, Conflict and Stability in the Former Soviet Union*, eds. Katya Migacheva and Bryan Frederick, Arlington, VA: RAND Corporation, 2018.

6. Is There A Model?

In the 1990s, Turkmenistan and Uzbekistan enforced the harshest restrictions and most zealously engaged in the prosecution of individuals and groups deemed extremist. Azerbaijan and Kazakhstan took an intermediary position, while Kyrgyzstan developed a considerably more liberal environment for religious freedom than its neighbors. Tajikistan was a special case because its civil war ended in a 1997 power-sharing agreement that gave the United Tajik Opposition, which included Islamist warlords, 30 percent of seats in government. For a number of years, therefore, Tajikistan not only had a legal Islamist party in parliament; it also had Islamist warlords in government.

Thus, conditions for independent religious activity in the various countries of the region differed greatly. Kazakhstan and Kyrgyzstan were at first the most permissive environments, something reflected in missionary activity, whereas it quickly became clear that any such activity in Uzbekistan was associated with considerable danger. Thousands of individuals were jailed there on charges of membership in illegal religious groups, an offense that could carry a fine of five years in prison and as much as 20 if the organization was deemed a terrorist one. Members of Hizb ut-Tahrir were the subject of particular government targeting in the late 1990s in Uzbekistan, even as the organization was able to function relatively comfortably in areas of Kyrgyzstan and Tajikistan with large ethnic Uzbek populations. Likewise, Tablighi Jamaat was allowed to operate freely in Kyrgyzstan, but was actively proscribed in Uzbekistan.

Over time, however, these patterns began to change. Whereas Uzbekistan has not experienced an act of religiously motivated violence since 2005, Kazakhstan, Kyrgyzstan and Tajikistan began to see an uptick in such instability, especially from the early 2010s onward. As a result, they all began to impose ever-growing restrictions on religious organizations, including the increased use of state security structures to surveil, supervise, infiltrate and prosecute groups viewed as a potential extremist threat. In recent years, as already seen, the strengthening of restrictions has been the most palpable in Tajikistan, while Kazakhstan has also adopted increasingly restrictive regulations for religious organizations. Uzbekistan, by contrast, has gone in the opposite direction, and eased restrictions on religious life.

What these shifts reflect is, to a significant extent, the changing role of national security agencies within the state structures. It is telling that President Mirziyoyev in early 2018 implemented a full public purge of the Ministry of National Security, going as far as to label its officers "mad dogs" and quipping that "no other country has given so much power to these unscrupulous people in uniform."[60] In parallel, the Uzbek government's approach to religious activity has softened, although changes at the central level do not immediately alter the behavior of officials at the local level. In Tajikistan, by contrast, the role of state security services has grown stronger rather than weaker. Kazakhstan is a more curious case: here, the political leadership gave security services a stronger mandate to counter extremism following terrorist incidents several years ago. But the country is also engaging in significant political and economic reform, as President Tokayev seeks to counter mismanagement and corruption in government agencies. It remains to be seen if the purges in security services following the January 2022 unrest will lead to change. Azerbaijan, for its part, saw the dismantling of its Ministry of National Security in late 2015 following the Minister's alleged wiretapping of the President's family.

---

60 Sadriddin Ashur and Farangis Najibullah, "President Says Time's Up For 'Mad Dog' Uzbek Security Service," RFE/RL, February 19, 2018.

The successor State Security Service has continued to be directly involved in the supervision of religious groups.

Doubling Down:
Articulating Positive Agendas

As the discussion above makes clear, regional states have taken an approach to religious affairs that is inherently defensive in nature, focusing on preventing the influx of alien and radical religious ideas into their societies. As such, there has been more clarity regarding what the leaders of Central Asia and Azerbaijan *opposed* than what they *supported*. True, it was clear early on that they supported secular governance and inter-religious harmony, but what they supported in terms of the evolution of Islamic practice was less so. In the past decade, however, this has begun to change. As regional states have consolidated their independence and overcome the most acute challenges of the early years, they have also been able to develop more concrete visions of their own.

The centerpiece of this effort has been the promotion across Central Asia (but not, for obvious reasons, in Azerbaijan) of the Hanafi-Maturidi tradition as the officially sanctioned religious tradition of the region. States in the region initially developed nation-building projects that centered on historical and secular themes: Kyrgyzstan selected the ancient Manas epos as a narrative of Kyrgyz greatness, Kazakhstan emphasized the connection to its nomadic roots alongside a civic, inclusive conception of the nation, and Tajikistan connected to the "Aryan" identity of the country, which set it apart from the Turkic republics of Central Asia.[61] It is

---

[61] Rico Isaacs, "Nomads, Warriors and Bureaucrats: Nation-Building and Film in post-Soviet Kazakhstan," *Nationalities Papers*, vol. 43 no. 3, 2015; Erica Marat, "Imagined Past, Uncertain Future The Creation of National Ideologies in Kyrgyzstan and Tajikistan," *Problems of Post-Communism*, vol. 55 no. 1, 2008; Marlene Laruelle, "The Return of the Aryan Myth: Tajikistan in Search of a Secularized National Ideology," *Nationalities Papers*, vol. 35 no. 1, 2007.

striking that these conceptions of national identity entirely ignored the Islamic aspect. But over time, viewing the gradual growth of religious observance in society, regional leaders adapted their conceptions of the nation by emphasizing the Hanafi tradition as an indigenous, tolerant and moderate approach to Islam. Tajikistan went the furthest in this direction, appropriating Abu Hanifa – a Persianate scholar from nearby Khurasan – as a national figure of sorts. (Abu Hanifa's legacy was discussed in detail in Chapter three.) President Rakhmon in 2014-15 held several lengthy public lectures on the subject of this historical figure and his legacy.[62] This emphasis on an indigenous Islam compatible with the secularism of the state had, as discussed previously, been taken up by all other regional states as "our Islam," typically contrasted with the alien and undesirable forms of Islam imported from the Gulf or South Asia.

Several states have gone beyond this, however, and adopted more specific positive agendas. Azerbaijan, for example, has made the notion of "multiculturalism" part of its official ideology. The term is used not in its conventional western meaning, but rather to define civic nationhood and secular governance. The beginning of the country's practice of "Unity Prayers" in 2016 coincided with the official year of multiculturalism in Azerbaijan, which aimed to underline the inclusive and tolerant nature of Azerbaijani society.[63] Going beyond religious affairs, the policy also focuses on ethnic relations in the country, and is based on a foundation that emphasizes civic nationalism and secular statehood. Azerbaijan's decision to double down on its emphasis on secularism can be seen as the direct result of the growing sectarian divide in the Middle

---

62 Carissa M. Landes, *Legitimacy and Islamic Symbols in Contemporary Tajikistan*, Chapel Hill: University of North Carolina, 2016.
63 Cornell, Karaveli and Ajeganov, *Azerbaijan's Formula*.

East, which made strengthened secularism the only viable option for a country split between Shi'a and Sunni communities. While the emphasis on "multiculturalism" risks being misunderstood by a Western audience, it is a clear indication that the Azerbaijani state has sought to take a positive initiative rather than stick to a mainly defensive approach.

In another initiative, Uzbek President Mirziyoyev has launched the notion of "Enlightened Islam," which aims to counteract extremist ideology by emphasizing and promoting the tolerant Islamic tradition indigenous to Central Asia. In a 2018 speech to the United Nations, Uzbek Foreign Minister Abdulaziz Kamilov emphasized that the root causes of extremism lie in "the ideology of extremism and violence itself, which is based on ignorance and lack of tolerance."[64] To counteract this, he argued, Uzbekistan's Enlightened Islam relies on the region's "centuries-old traditions of spiritual and moral enlightenment and upbringing," which make it possible to develop "the truly humanistic essence of Islam, which call for kindness, peace and tolerance."

For this purpose, Mirziyoyev has announced the creation of several new institutions. This includes an Islamic Academy of Uzbekistan, as well as an Islamic Civilization Center designed to "fight religious ignorance and promote Islam's true values."[65] In addition, he announced the creation of the Imam Bukhari International Scientific Research Center, headquartered at the Imam Al-Bukhari Academy in Samarkand. That institution aims to focus equally on religious and secular knowledge, echoing the

---

64 "Statement by the delegation of the Republic of Uzbekistan at the open briefing of the Counter-Terrorism Committee," United Nations Security Council, New York, July 2, 2018, 3, https://www.un.org/sc/ctc/wp-content/uploads/2018/06/Statement-by-the-delegation-of-the-Republic-of-Uzbekistan.pdf.

65 "Leader Says Most of Uzbeks Listed As Extremists Rehabilitated," *Ozbekistan Television*, 1530 GMT, September 1, 2017.

era of what the scholar Frederick Starr calls the "Lost Enlightenment" of Central Asia a millennium ago, when the region was the center of an effervescence of learning that was equally religious and secular in character.[66]

While the initiative is new and has yet to be implemented, it reflects a growing confidence in Uzbekistan not only that the problem of extremism is under control, but that Central Asia's Islamic heritage can be harnessed to counter the ideology of extremism both at home and in the Muslim world as a whole. In this sense, Uzbekistan joins countries like Jordan, Morocco, and the UAE, who similarly use their own Islamic legitimacy to counter extremist ideology.

Do Similarities a Model Make?

This chapter has shown that the six countries that are the subject of this study share obvious similarities in the way the state approaches religion. Aside from all being secular states, they all exhibit a duality between a semi-official or official religious hierarchy formed by *Muftiates* or "Spiritual Administrations" on one hand, and an executive state agency for the administration of religious affairs. All, to one degree or another, combine the official secularism of state institutions, laws, and education with the promotion of traditional indigenous religious traditions at the expense of alien influences. All have to some extent securitized religion, leading to an approach in which state security structures are prominent in the state's approach to religion.

In fact, these similarities have increased rather than decreased over time. Twenty years ago, the six states could be divided on a

---

66 Starr, *Lost Enlightenment: Central Asia's Golden Age from the Arab Invasions to Tamerlane.*

continuum ranging from the more liberal (such as Kazakhstan and Kyrgyzstan) to the most restrictive (Uzbekistan and Turkmenistan). Today, such a continuum would be harder to construct. While Tajikistan is an outlier in terms of its increasingly restrictive approach to religion, and Turkmenistan has hardly changed, Uzbekistan is in the process of loosening restrictions while both Kazakhstan and Kyrgyzstan have adopted stricter approaches, making these countries increasingly similar.

Returning to the five models of state-religion interaction introduced in Chapter Three, a first observation is that the six states do not entirely fit neatly within one category. It is easier to determine what category they do *not* fit into. Most obviously, none of the states espouse the "Fusion" model: they have all chosen a secular system of government. Neither do they fit in the "Hostile" model: although they do intervene directly and regulate and restrict religious practice, they are not *per se* hostile toward religion in the manner that the Soviet Union or revolutionary France were. Furthermore, it is equally clear that the six states have not adopted the American model of "State Neutrality" toward religion: on one hand, government interventions into religious life are considerable; and on the other, the state clearly privileges some forms of religion over others.

This leaves two ideal-types in the model: the "Dominant Religion" and "Skeptical" models. And in fact, all states studied here combine elements of these two models. On one hand, skepticism toward organized religion is enshrined in legal systems that ensure the secular nature of law and education and which prohibit religious figures and organizations from a role in politics – as well as state security policies to restrict unwanted religious movements. But on the other hand, their efforts to promote the restoration in society of indigenous religious traditions, primarily the Hanafi school of Sunni Islam, suggests that elements of the "Dominant Religion" model are present as well. This particular conversion of two models is a distinctive feature of Central Asia and Azerbaijan.

It would appear clear, thus, that Central Asia and Azerbaijan have sufficient internal consistency to be termed a model of interaction of state and religion. This leaves the question whether the region is distinctive enough from other parts of the world to be termed a model. To answer this question, we now turn to a brief examination of other approaches across the Muslim world.

7. CENTRAL ASIAN SECULARISM
In Comparative Perspective

AS THE PREVIOUS CHAPTER CONCLUDED, there is a relatively consistent model of interaction between state and religion in Central Asia and Azerbaijan that seeks to combine modernity with an effort to safeguard traditional and moderate religious traditions. But these six states are far from the only ones to have sought to achieve this goal. In order to put the Central Asian model in context, this chapter will conduct a rapid overview of five frequently touted models in the Muslim world.

The first case is Turkey, which was long a model of secular governance in the Muslim world but has, of late, been under the influence of Islamist ideology. The second is Tunisia, similarly with a long history of secularism, but also the only state that emerged from the Arab upheavals of 2011 with some level of success. A third case consists of liberal Muslim monarchies, exemplified by Jordan, Morocco and the UAE, which have made themselves defenders of a moderate interpretation of Islam. Fourth is the only other cluster of avowedly secular states in the Muslim world: former French colonies in West Africa. Finally, we turn to

Indonesia, the largest democracy in the Muslim world with its peculiar ideology of *Pancasila*.

Beyond a general overview of each model, this chapter will explore several key issues in each case. First, does the country provide for laws, courts, and education systems that are secular and treat its citizens equally, irrespective of their identity? Second, where does the country in question fall on the continuum of state approaches to religion outlined in Chapter Two? Third, has politicized religion been able to influence politics and society? Fourth, what appears to be the sustainability of the model? And finally, what, if any, are the lessons it offers for Central Asia and Azerbaijan?

Turkey's Declining Secularism

The Turkish model is of particular interest for Central Asia and Azerbaijan. In large part, the Turkish model served as an inspiration for these states in the 1990s. But while they adopted large portions of the Turkish model, Turkey itself has departed from it in important ways. This provides potentially useful lessons for Central Asia and Azerbaijan as they chart their way forward.

The Turkish approach to religion was largely the product of Mustafa Kemal Atatürk's revolution, which led to the abolition of the Ottoman Sultanate and Caliphate. But secularizing reforms traced back to the mid-nineteenth century, when the Ottoman leadership implemented significant changes in what was ultimately a losing battle to keep parity with rival European powers. Atatürk viewed religious obscurantism as a key reason for the Empire's decline and implemented reforms that turned out to be more far-reaching than in any Muslim nation that was not subjected to Communist rule. These included the banning of religious lodges and brotherhoods, and the creation of a state body supervising religious affairs, the *Diyanet*, which also issues the weekly Friday prayers to be recited in each mosque in the country. Reforms also included transition from the Arabic to the Latin alphabet and the centralization of all education under the control of the state, thereby putting an end to the existence of separate religious and secular paths to education.

However, following Atatürk's death, many of these far-reaching reforms were gradually rolled back, through the resurgence of a parallel religious education system, the introduction of religious education in state schools, and the considerable growth in the size and influence of religious brotherhoods. A system of *imam-hatip* schools was introduced originally for the sole purpose of training imams for Turkey's mosques. Yet during the 1970s, when the Islamist National Salvation Party formed part of several coalition governments, the schools multiplied to a level far beyond the needs of the religious bureaucracy. In 1976, they began admitting girls. Because women are banned from becoming imams, this signified the transformation of these schools into a parallel education system.

The rise of Islamic tendencies was embraced by the Turkish military in the 1980s, primarily to counter the threat of Communism. This led to the so-called "Turkish-Islamic synthesis", an infusion of greater Islamic values within the prevailing Turkish nationalism. In the 1990s, secular political parties largely failed to maintain political and financial stability, and successive coalition governments were characterized by widespread corruption and mismanagement. This led to high inflation and a severe financial crisis in late 2000, which wiped out 40 percent of Turkish society's purchasing power. In turn, this formed a permissive environment for the rise of Islamist political parties, in spite of state efforts to suppress them. In 1997, the military intervened to force the resignation of the country's first Islamist-led government.[1] But these efforts proved a boon for Turkish Islamism, because they prompted a split within the movement. A younger guard led by Recep Tayyip Erdogan split off to form a less explicitly Islamist party, which sought to appeal to a broader electorate. In late 2002, on the heels of the financial crisis, this party managed to win control of parliament. Though it only secured 36 percent of the vote, the failure of all but one other party to meet the high 10 percent threshold to parliament left Erdogan's party with a large majority of the seats. Based largely on the economic success of the government's early years, Erdogan was able to secure nearly 50 percent of the vote in the 2007 and 2011 elections, in the process consolidating power over the Turkish state.

In parallel, the party's Islamist inclinations returned with a vengeance both in domestic and foreign affairs. But over time, this attempt to Islamize the country was undermined by Erdogan's conflict with another Islamist faction led by exiled preacher Fethullah Gülen, growing mismanagement and corruption, as well a serious economic downturn. This gradually led to a loss of the party's popularity, and has forced it to align with far-right nationalists to remain in power.

Even after almost two decades of Islamist rule, Turkey's legal system remains secular. Erdogan's government has tinkered with it at the margins, for example by proposing to proscribe adultery and restrict abortion rights, while seeking to curb the consumption and sale of alcohol. But Erdogan and his party have remained

---

[1] Svante E. Cornell, "Turkey: Return to Stability," *Middle Eastern Studies*, vol. 35 no. 3, 1999, p. 209-234.

largely silent on the main issue for Islamists the world over: the introduction of Sharia, or religious law. Only very recently has the government promulgated regulations of the Islamic finance industry that follows religious rather than secular principles.² While there is a trend toward top-down Islamization, the legal sphere has remained largely intact. Education is another matter: Erdogan has long pledged to raise "pious generations," and has followed this with action. In 2012, parliament passed an education reform bill that strengthened the presence of Islamic content in the secular education sector, while also boosting the position of the alternative religious *imam-hatip* schools – starting a process of the forcible transformation of secular schools into religious schools. This often happens in the face of strong resistance by parents, including in religiously conservative areas.³

On the continuum of state-religion relations, Turkey has gradually shifted its position. During Atatürk's rule, Turkey would have occupied a place somewhere between "skeptical" and "hostile." From the 1950s onward, the country gradually moved to the "skeptical" position, while simultaneously developing aspects of the "dominant religion" model. From the 1980s to the 2000s, these two models coexisted uneasily in the Turkish system. The military's embrace of the idea of a "Turkish-Islamic synthesis" to counter leftist ideology was a dramatic shift in the direction of the dominant religion model. By contrast, its embrace of hard-line secularism in the mid-1990s in response to the rise of Islamist politics signified a shift back to the "skeptical model." This did not last, however, as the rise of Erdogan's AKP led to a momentous

2 Orhan Kemal Cengiz, "Turkey edges toward Islamic law with new finance rules," *Al-Monitor*, January 14, 2020. (https://www.al-monitor.com/pulse/originals/2020/01/turkey-is-the-country-drifting-towards-sharia-rule.html#ixzz6gaQ2enl7)
3 Svante E. Cornell, "Headed East: Turkey's Education System," *Turkish Policy Quarterly*, March 2018. (http://turkishpolicy.com/article/895/headed-east-turkeys-education-system)

shift back in the direction of the embrace of a dominant religion. The rhetoric of the President at times showed an inclination to move further, and incorporate elements of the "fusion" model – his urge for the country to have "a single religion" comes to mind – but this has not been implemented in practice.[4]

It is clear that the evolution of the Turkish model allowed Islamist organizations to exercise a significant level of influence on politics and society. In fact, from the 1970s onward, Islamist politics emerged as the leading counter-force to a decaying political establishment. Still, even in power, Islamism in Turkey has been forced to adapt to a relatively liberal society. It was only through a process of superficial moderation and as a side-effect of a deep economic and political crisis that Islamists could gain control of government. Once in power they have found the secular elements of society unexpectedly resilient to their messaging. In spite of close two decades of AKP power and consistent pro-Islamic messaging, all indicators suggest that Turkish society is growing *less* rather than *more* Islamic.

This has implications for the sustainability of the Turkish model. At first sight, it appears the Turkish model failed to contain the rise of Islamism. Indeed, the authoritarian aspects of the Turkish model, such as the existence of a state-controlled religious bureaucracy, were designed to do just that. But in fact, once the Islamists took over that bureaucracy, they turned it into an instrument for the propagation of Islamist ideology. Under Erdogan, the *Diyanet* grew into an activist behemoth larger than most government ministries. Still, the jury is out: the political regression of the AKP in recent years and its embrace of a rhetoric that is more

---

4 "'Tek dil değil, tek bayrak, tek din, tek devlet dedik!'" *Habertürk*, May 5, 2012. (https://www.haberturk.com/gundem/haber/739892-tek-dil-degil-tek-bayrak-tek-din-tek-devlet-dedik-)

7. Central Asian Secularism In Comparative Perspective

nationalist than Islamist suggest a necessity to respond to the realities of Turkey's society, and a failure of its efforts to reshape the population in its own image.

There are clear differences between the Turkish model and the Central Asian model, however. The embrace of a multi-party system in Turkey was, in fact, what made possible the rise of Islamism as a political phenomenon. Until the late 1960s, the Islamist movement remained contained within existing political parties, but from the 1970s onward a clearly identifiable Islamist political party was able to grow as a result of the increased fragmentation of Turkish politics. Efforts to use the judicial system to ban Islamist parties succeeded in moderating the movement, but in retrospect this moderation was largely an instrumental step in order to circumvent judicial sanctions and appeal to a larger electoral base. If anything, the hurdles imposed by the Turkish state were not decisive in blocking the Islamist instincts of the AKP; the only real check has been the reaction of the electorate, which the leadership cannot ignore in spite of growing evidence that Turkish elections are far from a level playing field.

To some degree, the Turkish example shows the risks of an approach that combines elements of the skeptical and dominant religion models. Under this combined approach, the state essentially seeks to ride the tiger: it supervises and promotes a dominant religion in the hope of seeking to prevent radicalism. But because it remains skeptical, it seeks continued control over religion, and to impose safeguards to prevent excessive religious influence over state and society. The problem is that the state risks losing control over religious mobilization. This is what happened in Turkey, for three inter-related reasons: first, there was a relatively open political system that allowed religious political entrepreneurs to develop. Second, there was a relatively sclerotic political establishment that failed to provide a positive alternative to Islamism. And third, the regional environment was one of growing Islamist mobilization, which affected Turkey significantly from the outside and undermined state efforts to contain it. For Central Asia, any combination of these three factors may lie in a future where these countries gradually loosen restrictions on political activity.

Tunisia:
The Domestication of Islamism?

Tunisia shares a number of similarities with Turkey. It is arguably the most reformist and progressive country in the Arab world, and one where the Islamist political movement has grown in influence. There are also important differences.

Like Turkey, Tunisia was exposed to considerable European influences earlier than most other parts of the Muslim world. Geographic proximity is a key reason for this, as is the history of European colonialism – in Tunisia primarily through the French Protectorate lasting from 1881 until independence in 1956. Like Turkey, Tunisia was led after independence by a secularizing strongman who had been a leader of the struggle for independence, Habib Bourguiba. Like Atatürk, Bourguiba had decisively negative views of the practice of religion in his country, and was an opponent of what he termed obscurantist practices – a category in which he included not just the veil and the *sharia*, but also the practice of fasting during the month of Ramadan. That made him a revolutionary and the subject of the ire of the country's traditionalists. But while their policies at first glance appear similar, there was one big difference: Atatürk's policies, laws, and institutions all sought to break with religion and drew their legitimacy only from the sovereignty of the people, as opposed to the notion of the sovereignty of God. Thus, Turkey imported wholesale the Swiss family code, alongside other European laws, marking a fresh start in the judicial arena.

While Atatürk's Turkey, at least in formal terms, fully relegated religion to the private sphere, it would be more accurate to term Bourguiba an Islamic modernist. Bourguiba never abandoned Islam as a source of legitimacy for the state he sought to build, or for its laws. Instead, he argued that he engaged in *ijtihad* – the practice of adapting religious tenets in the light of current conditions. He even elaborated on his approach in a 1965 speech, symptomatically held in Ankara. There, he stressed that "we consider [the state and religion] to be complementary, not contradictory, and it appears to us more legitimate to unite them than to separate them."[5] As one scholar puts it, Bourguiba sought to adapt a state-defined Islam "to fit his goal of modernisation, and so he prioritised the role of reason, the need for a modern version of Islam to fit the demands of modern times."[6] Unlike in Turkey, Bourguiba took pains to cajole part of the Islamic *Ulama* into supporting his reforms, by making a credible case that they were an acceptable interpretation of Islamic principles.

Rather than ignoring religion like Atatürk hoped to do, Bourguiba sought to re-interpret Islam. Yet the result was in many ways similar: Bourguiba developed a "Code of Personal Status" in 1956, which did away with most of the elements of Sharia in family law matters. For example, laws concerning marriage, divorce, and women's status in society were thoroughly modernized. The veil

---
5 Quoted in Malika Zeghal, "The Implicit Sharia: Established Religion and Varieties of Secularism in Tunisia," in Winnifred Fallers Sullivan and Lori G. Beaman, eds., *Varieties of Religious Establishment,* London: Ashgate, 2013, 107-130.
6 Rory McCarthy, "Re-thinking Secularism in Post-Independence Tunisia," *Journal of North African Studies*, vol. 19 no. 5, 2014, pp. 733-750.

was banned in official buildings, and fasting was discouraged. Like in Turkey, the State assumed a right to control religious institutions and religious life. But the state hardly showed consistency in its efforts: it developed different and sometimes contradictory strategies to deal with the threat of political Islam.

Faced with growing Islamism in the late 1960s, the Tunisian government – particularly during times of Bourguiba's illness – turned to accommodation. For example, it embraced a more Islamic education curriculum and gave up its opposition to fasting. But this only whetted the appetite of the Islamist movement, which by this time had grown inspired by the ideas of Hassan al-Banna and Sayyid Qutb. By the early 1980s, the regime turned to repression to stop the growth of the Islamist movement. When Bourguiba was succeeded by Zine El Abidin Ben Ali in 1987, the regime again attempted an accommodation policy: it made concessions that included releasing Islamists from prison, and sought a "National Pact" with opposition parties, including the Islamists. Ben Ali, in a move reminiscent of the Turkish-Islamic synthesis, embraced a "specific Arab-Islamic" identity as underlying Tunisia's national identity. However, the government would not budge on Bourguiba's Code of Personal Conduct, which it forced the Islamists to accept. But this accommodation was not to last: by 1991, seeing developments in neighboring Algeria and the spread of externally inspired radical Islamic ideas in society, Ben Ali felt enough popular support to repress the Islamist movement entirely. Beyond suppressing political Islam's organizations, the government extended the ban on the veil to educational institutions, insisting it was "a symbol of a 'political ideology' that had nothing to do with Islamic societies."[7]

Famously, the Arab Upheavals of 2011 began in Tunisia, and

---
7 McCarthy, p. 745.

7. Central Asian Secularism In Comparative Perspective

in the October elections that year, the recently legalized Islamist *Ennahda* party came in first with 37 percent of the vote. Crucially, unlike the AKP in Turkey, it did not secure a majority of the seats in parliament and was therefore forced to compromise and form a coalition government with several secular political forces. Following some political turmoil, the party contested the 2014 elections, and came in second at 27 percent, behind the secular Nidaa Tounes party. It readily accepted the election results. In 2019, Ennahda again came in first, but with a support of only 19 percent, with the rest of the vote fragmented among several parties. In February 2020, it took part of a coalition government with four other parties.

Importantly, Ennahda took part in the contested process of developing a new Tunisian constitution in 2014. The party advanced clear Islamist preferences in this process, including demanding reference to Sharia as the supreme guiding principle for law and the criminalization of blasphemy, among other measures. It also resisted language calling for equality between men and women. But while the party advanced these principles, it failed on each of these counts, and ultimately agreed to a constitution that was more liberal than its predecessor and included no additional bow to Islamic principles.[8] As a result, Tunisia has been termed the success story of the "Arab Spring" – in fact, the only country in which the upheavals have led to a positive political development rather than to conflict and violence. More recent events put this success story in doubt, including the country's

---

8 George Sadek, "The Role of Islamic Law in Tunisia's Constitution post-Arab Spring", The Law Library of Congress Global Research Center, May 2013. (https://www.loc.gov/law/help/role-of-islamic-law/tunisia-constitution.pdf) Also Monica L. Marks, "Convince, Coerce or Compromise? Ennahda's Approach to Tunisia's Constitution," Brookings Doha Center Analysis Paper Number 10, February 2014. (https://www.brookings.edu/wp-content/uploads/2016/06/Ennahda-Approach-Tunisia-Constitution-English.pdf)

President's intervention into the political system in 2021 and unilateral assumption of executive authority.

Tunisia is not a fully secular state. Its constitution affirms that Tunisia is a "free, sovereign and independent state whose religion is Islam," creating a constructive ambiguity on whether it is society or the state that is Islamic. This article, dating to the 1959 constitution, was kept verbatim in the 2014 edition. In practice, Tunisian laws are secular, as is its education system. Still, the area of family law has remained a thorny issue. Neither Bourguiba nor post-2014 governments have succeeded in secularizing inheritance laws. The reason is that the Quran is explicit that daughters should receive half what sons receive. Given the absence of any room for creative interpretation, this particular matter has been one that the Islamic modernism underlying Tunisia's progressive approach has not been able to touch.[9] Similarly, a 1973 directive prohibited Tunisian Muslim women from marrying non-Muslims, a law clearly in violation of secular principles. This was only abrogated in 2017. This suggests that the Tunisian state is secular for most practical purposes, but not fully so. That, in turn, means that secular provisions could theoretically be changed, if the interpretations of Islamic principles diverge from the modernist ones advocated by Bourguiba, Ben Ali, and the secular politicians in the post-Ben Ali era. Indeed, this is exactly what *Ennahda* sought to achieve during the debates on the new constitution in 2011-13.

As for Tunisia's place on the continuum of state approaches to religion, it is clear that the system has always had strong elements of the Dominant Religion model. But while Turkey mixed this model with elements of the Skeptical one, Tunisia's case is

---

9 Akram Belkaïd, "Femmes et Héritage en Tunisie, l'Échec d'une Réforme" *Monde Diplomatique*, August 2019. (https://www.monde-diplomatique.fr/2019/08/BELKAID/60165)

more complicated. If judged against the prevailing understanding of Islamic principles in the region, Tunisia has also been decidedly skeptical. But judged against Bourguiba's modernist understanding of Islam, it has not. Still, it is telling that Tunisia prohibited political parties based on religious principles, a typical provision of Skeptical states. Following 2011, the state has retained elements of the Dominant Religion model, while it has moved increasingly in the direction of State Neutrality. Thus, while Article 1 of the 2014 constitution emphasizes the role of Islam as the nation's religion, Article 2 defines the country as a "civil state," a nod to the state's neutrality in religious affairs. Still, a reading of the 2014 Constitution's language – particularly its preamble – make it painfully obvious that the document is a compromise between Islamists and secularists. Time and again, the document emphasizes the virtues of Islam and citizenship, as well as tradition and enlightenment. This uneasy coexistence of principles may reflect the balances of Tunisian society, but it does not make the country a fully secular state, and implies that the state's nature is all but settled.

There should be little question that Islamist movements have had a considerable influence on Tunisian state and society. They have, in fact, been a key factor determining government policy for decades – leading the state to shift between repression and accommodation before 2011, and playing a direct role influencing policy in the post-2011 period. In the immediate post-revolutionary period, Tunisia came very close to a state takeover by *Ennahda*. Had the party secured a majority in parliament, its trajectory could well have been similar to that of Turkey or Morsi's Egypt: a consolidation of power by Islamists, which in the latter case led to a military intervention. If *Ennahda* had controlled the process of drafting a new constitution, it would have been highly unlikely to make the significant concessions that allowed a widespread consensus solution on the 2014 constitution. Still, *Ennahda* should be commended for being amenable to these concessions, and for accepting its successive electoral defeats in following years. This suggests its leadership was cognizant of the fate of neighboring countries like Algeria, Libya and Egypt and sought to avoid such a debacle. But equally important was the determination of the remainder of Tunisia's political forces to maintain the progress from the Bourguiba and Ben Ali eras, and to prevent *Ennahda* from changing the nature of the country. For example, even in the two governments led by *Ennahda*, the party's coalition partners successfully prevented it from controlling the Ministry of Education.[10]

What is the sustainability of Tunisia's model? The fact that the country succeeded in averting an Islamist takeover in the chaotic years following the 2011 upheavals does inspire confidence. It is clear that it was the relatively strong character of Tunisia's body politic and civil society that thwarted the ambitions of the country's Islamists at that critical juncture. It remains too early to say whether the country's Islamists have truly internalized and accepted this compromise, or whether they are likely to seek to challenge it. *Ennahda's* behavior remains a singular outlier among Islamist forces in the region. But Tunisia is also an outlier in terms of social values. In Pew's 2013 poll, support for Sharia law is at 56 percent, compared to 74 percent in Egypt. Similarly, only 42 percent of Tunisians agree that religious judges should rule on family matters, compared to 94 percent of Egyptians. And whereas only 46 percent of Egyptians agreed that wearing a veil

---

10 Michele Brignone, "L'Islam dans l'Enseignement Public Tunisien Avant et Après la Révolution de 2010-2011 : Continuité ou Rupture?," *IPRA - Ressources*, December 3, 2015. http://ipra.eu/centre-ressources/fr/items/show/222

should be a woman's own decision, 89 percent of Tunisians did.[11] Having managed the Islamist challenge in the post-revolution era, Tunisia is on track to continue its process of modernization. The Islamist forces have accepted a role in this system for now, rather than seeking to overturn it. But as the Turkish example, shows, the risk of an Islamist takeover remains present in the case of a renewed political or economic upheaval.

For Central Asia and Azerbaijan, the Tunisian model holds limited value. It is an indication that in the presence of a strong secular body politic and civil society, it may be possible to integrate – and possibly domesticate – an Islamist challenger within the confines of a largely secular political system. But the price for this, in the Tunisian case, has been an acknowledgment of the confessional nature of the state, as references to Islam permeate the Tunisian constitution. In other words, Tunisia suggests that integrating Islamists into the political system may require stepping back from a fully secular state. That, in turn, may become a slippery slope in times of upheavals or socio-economic instability, when Islamists may well seek to advance their positions. In the final analysis, Tunisia is an outlier in the Arab world, whose replicability may be limited.

The Moderate Monarchies:
Jordan, Morocco, the UAE

Tunisia adheres to a republican form of statehood, and among Arab republics, its relative stability constitutes the exception. In fact, the 2011 upheavals led to a remarkable divide between Arab monarchies and republics. Virtually all Arab republics underwent

---

11 Pew Research Center, "The World's Muslims: Religion, Politics and Society", April 30, 2013, https://www.pewforum.org/2013/04/30/the-worlds-muslims-religion-politics-society-overview/.

serious instability in the past decade – ranging from Libya and Egypt to Sudan, Syria, Lebanon and Yemen. Some, like Algeria and Iraq, were destabilized even before that. By contrast, Arab monarchies have fared much better. No Arab monarchy has experienced a revolutionary situation, or has been engulfed in civil war. This perhaps appears counter-intuitive, as republican forms of government should be more able to adapt to changing circumstances than monarchies. But in the Arab world, the opposite has been true, not least because the republics – most of which were based on a revolutionary ideology to begin with – failed to maintain popular legitimacy as the ideologies on which they were based lost popular support. Monarchies, by contrast, appeal to a traditional and often religious legitimacy that has proven to have much greater staying power than expected.

Among these monarchies, some are more worthy of being considered "models" than others. Some monarchies in the Gulf region, such as Saudi Arabia, Kuwait and Qatar, have a long history of supporting extremist ideology, and have themselves allowed extremist interpretations of Islam to hold sway over their societies. In recent years, Saudi Arabia has attempted to change this, embracing moderation – but there is certainly a long way for Saudi Arabia to go to be called a model of moderation. The three monarchies that stand out as torch-bearers of moderation in the Arab world are Jordan, Morocco and the UAE, which despite being thousands of miles apart share numerous similarities.

Jordan and Morocco stand out by basing their legitimacy on tradition and religion. The Hashemite dynasty in control of Jordan traces its lineage to the grandfather of the Prophet of Islam, and for centuries served as the governors of the Hejaz. They also played a critical role in the uprising against Ottoman rule in the

7. Central Asian Secularism In Comparative Perspective

early twentieth century, thus establishing Arab nationalist credentials as well. The Hashemites were initially in control of both Jordan and Iraq, but lost the latter as a result of a 1958 military coup. In Jordan, however, the monarchy has not only survived but prospered in spite of serious domestic challenges, not least related to the Palestinian question. Under the rule of the legendary King Hussein, who reigned for a half century until his death in 1999 and under his son Abdullah, Jordan has developed into a key partner for the United States in the region, and taken a strong stance against radical ideology.

Morocco's monarchy also claims descent from the Prophet Muhammad, and thus uses the term "Sharifi" to mark this descent while also claiming possession of a divine blessing to rule. The King of Morocco lays claim not only to temporal power but also to spiritual authority, with the title of Amir al-Mumineen, or Commander of the Faithful.[12] The dynasty traces its lineage to the early seventeenth century when the Kingdom of Morocco was formed.

As for the UAE, the ruling Al Nahyan dynasty does not possess the same historical legitimacy, the country's independence dating only to 1971. But with the meteoric rise of the UAE as an energy, banking and business hub, the country – in fact seven Emirates led by Abu Dhabi – has acquired great importance in Middle Eastern affairs and worked to fill the void left by the decline of previously powerful Arab states like Iraq, Syria and Egypt.

Jordan and Morocco's monarchies stand out by being, in contrast to the Gulf states, constitutional monarchies that feature elements of popular political participation. Both have parliamentary forms of government, with popularly elected governments

---
12 Mohamed Daadaoui. *Moroccan Monarchy and the Islamist Challenge: Maintaining Makhzen Power,* New York: Palgrave, 2011.

that share power with the monarchy, as the King in both countries retains ultimate authority. In a sense, the two monarchies seem to follow the evolution of European monarchies, which gradually transitioned to constitutional monarchies in the nineteenth century and devolved power to popularly elected assemblies and independent judiciaries. Of course, the two monarchies have yet to relinquish power to the extent that European monarchs have and should not be expected to do so anytime soon. That said, their model of gradual and measured political change appears to combine a sense of continuity and stability with a growing accommodation of popular participation.

As for the UAE, it has moved only slowly in opening up for political participation. Instead of a parliament, it has a Federal National Council, whose membership is partly appointed by the seven rulers, and partly indirectly elected by electoral colleges. But what it lacks in political openness, the UAE has sought to make up for through wide-ranging social and legal reforms to liberalize and secularize the country. In 2020, the UAE adopted major revisions to laws on Personal Status, Civil Transactions, Penal Code and Criminal Procedural laws. This was followed by further liberalization of laws in Abu Dhabi in 2021, which modernized family law and improved women's rights significantly.

In the religious field, these states have developed relatively sophisticated agendas to counter radical ideology. Building on their own religious authority, the three have advanced assertive agendas advancing a positive alternative to radicalism, instead promoting traditional and moderate understandings of the religion.

In 2004, King Hussein of Jordan took the initiative to bring unity to the Islamic world and come to an agreement on key issues such as who is a Muslim, whether Muslims can be excommunicated, and who has the authority to issue *fatwas*. The King subsequently sought to build religious legitimacy for this initiative, and asked a large number of Islamic authorities to develop written answers to these questions. This was in turn followed by a conference in Amman at which Islamic religious authorities achieved a consensus on these matters. They recognized eight major schools of Islamic jurisprudence as well as Sufism as legitimate, prohibited declarations of apostasy among these Muslims, and set standards for religious authority required to issue fatwas. They thereby essentially declare invalid fatwas issued by extremist leaders that often lack religious authority.[13] While this message was mainly aspirational and had limited practical significance, it did constitute an early and important symbolic message to counter extremism in the immediate aftermath of September 11. Jordan also expanded the state's role to interpret religious texts and discourse, began to educate the clergy in moderate Islamic messaging, and worked to rehabilitate radicals. It has also taken steps to use the state repressive power against radical individuals and groups, and in 2020 disbanded the Muslim Brotherhood in the country.[14]

At around the same time, and particularly following a serious terrorist attack in Casablanca, Morocco embarked on a similar trajectory. This featured efforts to include moderate Islamists in a controlled manner in the political system, while also developing a state-led counter-extremist agenda. The Kingdom has launched its concept of "middle path" Moroccan Islam based on three pillars: the Maliki *madhab*, Ashari theology, and Sufism – to serve as a

---

13 Sarah Markiewicz, "The History of the Amman Message and the Promotion of the Amman Message Project", in Mike Hardy et. al., eds., *Muslim Identity in a Turbulent Age*, London: Jessica Kingsley Publishers, 2017.
14 Shehab al Makahleh, "Jordan Navigates the Intellectual Battlefield," in Ilan Berman, ed., *Wars of Ideas: Theology, Interpretation and Power in the Muslim World*, Lanham, MD: Rowman & Littlefield, 2021.

"foundation of a national religious identity that is grounded in openness, respect, and peaceful interpretations of Islamic texts."[15] The Kingdom also expanded its oversight of mosques and religious schools, conducted a review of teaching materials to remove extremist content, and sought to supervise the religious life of the Moroccan diaspora in Europe. Significantly, it also expanded the role of women in religious leadership, including accepting women into the Supreme Ulama Council. In addition, Morocco has invested significantly in training of imams both for domestic purposes as well as inviting foreign imams to study in its institutions, particularly those from sub-Saharan Africa.[16]

The UAE began to move against political Islam already in the 1980s. The Muslim Brotherhood movement had become strong in the country as it had been brought along with Egyptian and other Arab immigrants who staffed much of the country's agencies as the UAE state-building project went into high gear following the 1973 oil crisis. The ruler, Muhammad bin Zayed, appears to have identified the threat of the Brotherhood already in his youth, taking a leading role from the late 1980s onward in successively shutting down avenues for the brotherhood to operate in the UAE, occasionally at the cost of confrontation with smaller Emirates that did not share his concern or where the Brotherhood had established influence. This opposition to political Islam has proceeded in parallel with the country's positioning as a leading center for economic freedom in the Gulf, while maintaining a centralized political system. Economic openness meant welcoming large numbers of expatriates, ranging from lower-paid job seekers mainly from South Asia all the way to senior

---

15 Ahmed Abbadi, "Understanding Morocco's Approach to Violent Extremism," in Berman, ed., *Wars of Ideas*, p. 57.
16 Abbadi, "Understanding Morocco's Approach," p. 58.

7. Central Asian Secularism In Comparative Perspective

managers and businesspeople from Western and other countries. At present, Emirati citizens constitute less than 12 percent of the population. This reality, and the UAE leadership's growing concern to make the country more welcoming for its diverse population, has been an important factor in ensuring that moderation and secularization have been key facets of government policy in the domestic area. Following the 9/11 attacks, the UAE has also taken a leadership role in spearheading counter-extremism programs in the region and beyond, not least through its Hedayah center for counter-extremism, which partners with several dozen countries, offering an assertive indigenous Arab and Muslim model for countering extremism.[17]

All three countries define Islam as the state religion, and thus neither can lay claim to be a secular state. That said, the three have sought to subordinate Islamic law to the state and particularly to written civil codes and laws of personal status. Indeed, both Morocco and Jordan have legal systems that feature secular laws adopted by parliaments. However, in both countries, family law remains within the realm of religiously defined traditional law. In the UAE, a sharia-based system intended mainly for the indigenous population coexists with a secular system to which individuals can opt-in, mainly designed for expatriates.

Jordan inherited parts of the Ottoman legal system, which allowed each religiously defined community to maintain control over family matters according to their respective religious tradition. Jordan's constitution explicitly rules that Sharia courts have exclusive jurisdiction over personal and family law for Muslims. In other matters, however, Jordan has adopted modern legal norms, including drawing on French and British legislation (as well as

---

[17] Theodore Karasik, "The Emirates and the Struggle Against Islamic Extremism," in Ilan Berman, ed., *Wars of Ideas*, Lanham, MD: Rowman & Littlefield, 2021.

Syrian and Egyptian examples) for the development of the civil code, commercial law, and arbitration law.[18] As such, family law matters remain firmly guided by the Sharia in its Hanafi interpretation, while the country's Law on Personal Status was updated in 1976 and again in 2010.

In Morocco, the Kingdom soon after independence promulgated the Moudawana, a Code of Personal Status that was heavily based on the Sunni Maliki *madhab*, and thus strongly discriminatory toward women. Initially, Sharia courts continued to adjudicate such cases, while the Jewish minority was given the right to adjudicate matters in Rabbinical courts. But in 1965, King Hassan ordered the unification of Moroccan courts. While this did not formally do away with the role of sharia a source of family law, it deprived sharia courts of their independence. Hence, both in Jordan and Morocco, Sharia courts have been turned into institutions under statutory law, and have been compelled to adjudicate disputes under state law rather than through traditional Islamic legal methodology.[19] This does not make their legislation secular but could be termed a first step toward secularization because it breaks the hold of the Islamic scholars on legal matters. Instead of applying it according to their own methods, they are now reduced to applying statutory law, much as secular judges would. The next step would be for the state to gradually alter these laws, thus gaining control over legislation at the expense of the Ulama. In 2004, following efforts by Moroccan women to raise attention to the discriminatory nature of the law, a reformed Moudawana

---

18 Hamzeh Haddad, "Jordan", *Yearbook of Islamic and Middle Eastern Law*, 1994, pp. 178-88.
19 Ari Schriber, "Commentary: The Dissolution of Shari'a in the 1965 Moroccan Court Unification Law", Islamic Law Blog, December 16, 2016. (https://islamiclaw.blog/2016/12/16/the-dissolution-of-shari%CA%BFa-in-the-1965-moroccan-court-unification-law/)

was passed that significantly enhanced women's rights and modernized legal proceedings.[20]

The UAE has more recently moved in the direction of greater secularization of its legal system. In 2020, large reforms were undertaken at the federal level, amending laws on Personal Status, Civil Transactions, as well as the Penal Code. These measures decriminalized cohabitating couples, and removed legal protections for perpetrators of honor killings.[21] It also provided a secular option for inheritance laws, to which residents could opt in, while decriminalizing the consumption of alcohol and consensual sexual relations. The next year, the Emirate of Abu Dhabi went further, providing a fully secular option for all issues of personal status, including marriage and divorce, introducing the concept of civil marriage and providing equal value to women witnesses in court proceedings.[22]

These states, thus, have not done away with Sharia as a source of legislation, but have unequivocally taken steps to subjugate sharia to the state by promulgating modern, statutory laws that have shown an ability to change in a progressive direction over time.

On the continuum of state approaches to religion, the three states clearly fit within the Dominant Religion paradigm. They have a state religion but maintain some levels of religious freedom, though these freedoms apply to recognized religions more than smaller or heterodox communities, which are not recognized. The state promotes a particular interpretation of the Islamic religion

---

20 Katie Zoglin, "Morocco's Family Code: Improving Equality for Women", *Human Rights Quarterly*, vol. 31 no. 4, 2009, pp. 964-984.
21 "UAE Cancels Lenient Penalties for Honor Killings," *Reuters*, Nov. 7, 2020. (https://www.reuters.com/article/emirates-lawmaking-int-idUSKBN27N0C7)
22 "Abu Dhabi's new secular family law steps up Gulf talent competition," Reuters, November 11, 2021. (https://www.reuters.com/business/media-telecom/abu-dhabis-new-secular-family-law-steps-up-gulf-talent-competition-2021-11-11/)

while suppressing versions it deems radical or extremist; the state is neither neutral toward religion nor skeptical. But because the state offers religious freedom and a modicum of secularized laws, even if they are based on Islamic norms in Jordan and Morocco and exist alongside Sharia-based systems in the UAE, they cannot be said to exhibit elements of the "Fusion" model either.

The question whether these countries have been able to thwart radicalism is a contested one. The Jordanian and Moroccan model have not stopped hundreds or even thousands of young Jordanians and Moroccans from joining *jihad* in Syria and Iraq; but then again, that does not make them particularly different from other regional states or European nations. However, it is a fact that after Amman and Rabat adopted similar models in the early 2000s, they managed to negotiate the tumultuous period of the Arab upheavals without serious difficulty. Both saw protests and made concessions to some popular demands, but unlike in neighboring states, there was no significant rise in radical and extremist forces contesting government authority. Similarly, the UAE has aggressively moved to establish itself as the leading force of counter-extremism in the Arab world. It has done so through large investments in counter-radicalization programs, but also through the commitment of military resources, including the deployment of Emirati air power in Syria, Libya and Yemen. At home, the Emirates have assertively moved against all forms of political Islam, including movements tolerated elsewhere, such as Tabligh Jama'at, which the Emirates views as a step on the ladder of radicalization.[23]

This suggests that these countries may not have eliminated extremist elements, but they have managed to contain them and

---
23 Karasik, p. 90.

7. Central Asian Secularism In Comparative Perspective

prevent them from gaining attraction in society. The fact that this has been the case in spite of significant unrest in their immediate neighborhood – Syria and Iraq in the Jordanian case; Algeria, Mali and Libya in the Moroccan case; and Yemen in addition for the UAE – suggests these states may have found ways to limit the appeal of radicalism.

As alluded to above, the moderate monarchies have exhibited a degree of sustainability over the upheavals of the past several decades. They have been subjected to serious challenges of both domestic and regional nature, and appear to have found ways to adapt to changing circumstances while maintaining their popular legitimacy, derived from religious authority and tradition. The odds of upheavals and extremism continues to be considerably higher in Arab republics compares to Arab monarchies, a significant and understudied reality.

For Central Asia and Azerbaijan, their experience is relevant in several ways. Of course, the monarchical legitimacy is not relevant for the secular republics of Central Asia, which are new states with a republican form of government and a Soviet period separating them from any historical precedent. Still, the notion of advancing a tolerant, moderate indigenous tradition, while maintaining restrictions on movements and groups considered extremist, is one that is highly relevant for Central Asia, and one that Uzbekistan, in particular, has already taken up. The Jordanian and Moroccans model also suggests that it is possible to gradually open up political systems without necessarily causing an upswing in radicalism – something that will be relevant as Central Asian states and Azerbaijan inevitably move toward opening up their political systems.

Incomplete Secularism:
Laïcité in West Africa

Outside Central Asia and Azerbaijan, the only other cluster of Muslim-majority states that formally adhere to a secular foundation is found in francophone West Africa. States that mention *laïcité* in their constitutions include Senegal, Mali, Chad, Burkina Faso, Guinea, Côte d'Ivoire, Benin and Togo. This is a legacy of French influence on political and legal thought in West Africa. But just as Central Asian states have not simply copied Soviet practices, West African states have all developed their own conceptions of laïcité, which do not correspond exactly to the French model. Nor is the practice of secularism uniform across the region. Most importantly, while they derive the concept from the French legacy dating to the 1905 law, West African secularism lacks the anti-clericalism that, as we saw in Chapter Two, dominated in France and other Catholic countries in the early twentieth century. In fact, while the West African constitutions speak of the non-confessional nature of the state and the equality of all citizens irrespective of religion, they also emphasize the right to worship and present the state as a protector of religious communities.

A key element in the practice of secularism in West Africa is the limited reach and authority of the state. The African post-colonial state is, in international comparison, relatively weak – so much so that it has very little relevance to daily life in a number of African countries. This has given birth to the term "shadow state" in political science, signifying a privatization of state institutions that has led to states gradually ceasing to exercise critical functions. The ideal type of such a shadow state is one that no longer delivers mail and in which security structures are loyal to the personality of the leader rather than the state.[24] As two French scholars put it, leaders in these states "instrumentalize" political disorder because it serves their narrow purposes.[25] In this region, the term has mainly been applied to states like Liberia and Sierra Leone, and most countries in Francophone West Africa do not exhibit this degree of weakness. Yet the chaos unleashed in Mali since 2012, including several military coups and a civil war requiring foreign military intervention, is an indication of the vulnerability of the region's states. Because of the state's inability to enforce laws uniformly across its territory, the relative weakness of African post-colonial states is important to this analysis.

The immediate post-colonial era was marked primarily by left-wing ideologies, with many post-independence leaders embracing versions of African socialism. This embrace of left-wing secular ideology made it natural to retain the *laïcité* inherited from French colonial rule. On paper, all states developed constitutions that followed the practice of western democracies, emphasizing the equality of all before the law and prohibiting discrimination on the basis of ethnicity, religion, and gender. The political systems of the region have remained largely secular: calls to abolish secularism have been voiced by Islamist elements from time to time, but have not thus far gained sufficient traction to seriously threaten the secular order. West Africa is, however, squeezed between Islamist militancy to both the north and south. North of the Sahara is the militancy of Algeria and Libya, which played a key role in triggering the crisis in Mali. To the south is Boko Haram, the Nigerian jihadi group whose influence in the

---

24 William Reno "Clandestine Economies, Violence and States in Africa," *Journal of International Affairs*, vol. 3 no. 2, 2000, p. 433-49
25 Patrick Chabal and Jean-Pascal Daloz, *Africa Works: Disorder as Political Instrument*, Bloomington: Indiana University Press, 1999.

north of Nigeria has spillover effects on both Burkina Faso, Chad and Niger. Chad is further challenged by the proximity of the Central African Republic, where religiously motivated violence has pitted Christians and Muslims against each other.

The political systems of the West African states have largely remained secular in spite of recurring efforts by Islamist groups to challenge the secularism enshrined in their constitutions. The most serious crisis so far developed in Chad, where the 2018 Constitution maintained the principle of secularism but in parallel, introduced an oath of office for high officials that explicitly mentioned loyalty to "Allah," thus indicating a fundamentally confessional nature that would appear unconstitutional. This is indeed what representatives of the country's Christian minority, amounting to 40 percent of the population, have argued.[26] As for Senegal, the issue of secularism arose during the revisions of the constitution in 2001, but the forces seeking the removal of secularism were eventually defeated. Likewise, in Mali the tumultuous shifts of government following the 2012 coup have not led to a formal removal of secularism from the country's constitution. Still, the new President elected in 2013 began his term by citing an extensive portion of the Quran, indicating the growing deference to religion in the region.[27]

West African states do not in practice observe a complete separation of religion and the state. In most regional states, the state participates in religious holidays and provides support for religious events, including religious schools. Conversely, religious

---

26 Guy Bucumi, "Quelques Paradoxes Contemporains de la Laïcité de l'État au Tchad," *Revue du Droit des Religions*, no. 8, 2019.
27 Fatou Sow, "La laïcité à l'épreuve dans les États laïques d'Afrique au Sud du Sahara : Les défis pour le Sénégal et le Mali," Open Democracy, October 10, 2014. (https://www.opendemocracy.net/en/5050/la-laicite-a-lepreuve-dans-les-etats-laiques-dafrique-au-sud-du-sahara-les-defis-po/)

7. Central Asian Secularism In Comparative Perspective

authorities play important roles as brokers in the politics of West Africa, particularly in Senegal, where several large Sufi brotherhoods – particularly the Mouridiya and Tijaniya – count a majority of the country's population as members. Since the country's independence, a political balance developed in which the state remained secular, while the brotherhoods had considerable informal influence on politics. Their ability to strongly influence voters have made them kingmakers of Senegalese politics, but a balance long prevailed in which religious leaders, maintaining a certain ambiguity, did not want to be seen as either too distant from or too close to politics. While this remained the case under Senegal's two first presidents, the Catholic Léopold Sédar Senghor and the Muslim Abdou Diouf, in more recent years, the political linkages between politicians and religious leaders have been more open, and also more controversial as individual politicians have been linked to one or another brotherhood.[28]

The most glaring issue from the perspective of secular government lies in the issue of family and personal law. During the colonial era, family matters, including marriage, divorce, property, and inheritance, were regulated depending on a person's religious identity. Christians fell under the French Civil Code, and Muslims and animists were permitted to adjudicate matters according to their own customs – a system not dissimilar from the Millet system in the Ottoman Empire. The challenge for the post-colonial state was whether, and if so how, to seek to apply a uniform code for such matters in their new state orders. And in general, they have not done so. Senegal stands out by adopting a family law in 1972, which sought a synthesis of sorts between

---

28 See collection of essays in Mamadou Diouf, ed., *Tolerance, Democracy and Sufis in Senegal*, Columbia University Press, 2013.

local customs, Islamic law and the French civil code.[29] But the law has remained highly controversial, and in practice is not observed outside urban areas, with traditional and Islamic institutions sometimes openly flaunting its provisions.[30] Mali adopted a very conservative family code in 1962, and recent efforts to reform it were set back after public protests by Islamic activists.[31] Burkina Faso managed to promulgate a universal family code only in 1989.[32] Niger and Chad still do not have family codes, and instead allow "customary" institutions to handle family matters in the state's place.[33] As a result, across West Africa, the application of secular laws by secular courts is decisively patchy to non-existent, undermining the secular character of these states. As a result, the promise in their constitutions to prohibit discrimination against women, for example, is not implemented in practice.

On the continuum of state approaches to religion, the West African states incorporate elements of the "State Neutrality" model. In a sense, their approaches to secularism derive their term from the French *laïcité* but are in reality more reminiscent of the more positive American approach to secularism, which aspires to state neutrality toward religion while seeing a symbiosis between the state and organized religious life. But they also incorporate elements of a "Dominant Religion," given the strength of

---

29 Marie Brossier, "Les Débats sur le Droit de Famille au Sénégal," *Politique Africaine*, no. 4, 2004, pp. 78-98.
30 Barbara M. Cooper, "Secular States, Muslim Law and Islamic Religious Culture: Gender Implications of Legal Struggles in Hybrid Legal Systems in Contemporary West Africa," *Droit et Cultures*, no. 1, 2010, pp. 97-120.
31 See details in Daphtone Lekebe Omouali, "Les Reformes du Droit de la Famille dans les Etats D'Afrique Noire Francophone: Tendances Maliennes", *Annales Africaines*, vol. 1 no. 6, April 2017.
32 Filiga Sawadago, "Le nouveau code burkinabè de la famille: principes essentiels et perspectives d'application," *Revue Juridique et Politique: Indépendance et Coopération*, vol. 44 no. 3, 1990, 373- 406.
33 Cooper, "Secular States..."; Blaise Dariustone, "Les Tchadiens divisés sur le code de la famille," *DW*, November 16, 2020.

traditional Islamic law in their legal systems and the tight interactions between political and religious institutions.

Religious movements have certainly exhibited a considerable influence over political life in West Africa. In Senegal, they have thus far failed in their attempts to overturn the formally secular nature of the state, or in abolishing the secular family code. But they have succeeded in putting the secular establishment on the defensive, and in undermining implementation of the law. Similarly, in Mali Islamic forces have put the brakes on efforts to modernize family law, and injected a growing element of Islamic rhetoric in the country's politics. Things have gone even further in Chad, where constitutional amendments favoring religion have continued to exist in spite of their apparent defiance of the principle of secularism. Overall, the combined effect of Gulf funding for Islamic movements, and the pressure of Islamist forces in North Africa and Nigeria, has led West African politicians to respond by increasing deference to Islam, in ways reminiscent of the developments in Turkey in the 1980s and 1990s.

As a result, the sustainability of secular rule in West Africa cannot be taken for granted. It should be noted that the proponents of secular constitutions have thus far prevailed, and there appears to be a strong constituency defending secular government in West Africa. Still, it is equally clear that these forces are on the defensive, and that the initiative belongs to those forces that seek to challenge secularism.

Indonesia:
Democracy in a Religious State
Indonesia is the world's largest Muslim-majority country. It has a total population of 270 million, of which an estimated 87 percent

are Muslims, followed by protestants (7 percent), Catholics (3 percent) and Hindus (2 percent). The Indonesian state's approach to religion was, from the outset of independence in 1945, a compromise between secularism and Islamism. While strong forces sought to base the nascent state on Islam, those seeking to build it on a common national basis, led by the country's first president Sukarno, eventually prevailed. The original wording of the constitution would have compelled Muslims to follow Islamic law, but this wording was eventually removed.[34] Still, this did not make Indonesia a secular state. The first of the five principles of the *Pancasila*, the foundational philosophy of the country, is "belief in the one and only God."

A remarkable aspect of this foundational philosophy is its religious pluralism. Although Muslims constituted nearly nine in ten Indonesians, even those who advocated for a state based on Islamic principles recognized the need for religious pluralism, and respect for minority religions. Indonesian Islamic organizations pride themselves on their tolerance, and have on many occasions cooperated with Christian organizations. Thus, the Indonesian state is explicitly observant of religion, but not specifically of any particular creed. However, while the state in theory provides for religious freedom, it has taken upon itself the prerogative to define what religions are considered orthodox. The list has varied over time, but always included Sunni Islam, Protestantism, Catholicism, Hinduism and Buddhism. Confucianism has been added to this, and a 2017 constitutional court ruling also recognized the validity of traditional, customary religions. As such, the state considers Shi'ism and the relatively sizable Ahmadiyya movement

---

34 R. E. Elson, "Two Failed Attempts to Islamize the Indonesian Constitution," *Sojourn: Journal of Social Issues in Southeast Asia,* vol. 28 no. 3, 2013, pp. 379-437

7. Central Asian Secularism In Comparative Perspective

to be deviant, and their followers have been subjected to considerable discrimination. In a situation reminiscent to that of Central Asia, representatives of both the Islamic and Christian mainstream communities have a joint interest in opposing novel, proselytizing religions, and have joined forces to push the state toward curtailing their activities.

Indonesian Islam has itself gone through considerable change in the past century. It has traditionally been strongly influenced by Sufi mysticism and been layered on top of existing traditions rather than replacing them, accounting for its tolerant and pluralistic approach.[35] But over the past half century, as in the rest of Southeast Asia, Indonesian Islam has been increasingly influenced by religious ideologies emanating from the Arabian Peninsula. Paradoxically, the politicization of religion has increased after the transition to democracy in 1998, which opened the door for political mobilization in the name of Islam. In truth, the role of Islamist ideas had begun to grow in the latter portion of the rule of Indonesia's second president, Suharto, who sought to appeal to Islamic sentiment in the 1990s to maintain his rule.

These forces nevertheless ran up against the strength of Indonesia's Islamic mass movements, primarily the *Muhammadiyah* and *Nahdlatul Ulama*. The former, modeled on the reformist movements in early twentieth century Egypt, counts at least 50 million members; the latter is more traditionalist in nature and has a membership exceeding 75 million.[36] These organizations support the foundational ideology of Indonesia, while also claiming considerable influence over society. In the past two decades, they have

---

[35] Azyumardi Azra, "Understanding Indonesia's 'Third Way' Islam," in Ilan Berman, *Wars of Ideas: Theology, Interpretation and Power in the Muslim World*, Lanham, MD: Rowman & Littlefield, 2020 p. 75
[36] Azra, "Understanding Indonesia's 'Third Way' Islam," p. 78.

formed an alliance of sorts with the Indonesian government to counter alien radical ideologies, and their depth of support in society has worked to limit the appeal of radical ideology in the country. However, they should not be mistaken for liberal institutions: in fact, they explicitly reject the liberal ideology that seeks full individual freedoms, and instead are a force promoting the dominance of traditional religious structures in society.[37]

As should be obvious from the above, Indonesia makes no claim to be a secular state. The state is based on a "belief in almighty God," while the constitution guarantees freedom of worship "each according to their own beliefs." The state explicitly aims to ensure that Indonesia remains a religious society, thus leaving no place for any kind of freedom *from* religion. Subsidiary laws, as noted, differentiate between religious groups, protecting some while explicitly rejecting others as illegitimate, thereby essentially voiding the constitution's emphasis on freedom of worship. Furthermore, Indonesia has blasphemy laws that prohibit "dishonoring" religion, and there has been a rapid increase in the prosecution of Indonesians under this law since the transition to democracy. Most infamously, it was used in 2017 to prosecute the Christian mayor of Jakarta for taking issue with the ulama's interpretation of a particular Quranic verse.[38]

There is a strong overlap between the state and religion, and the state actively involves itself in religious matters. This is clear in the legal field, where Indonesia is reminiscent of West African states in the existence of legal pluralism. The Dutch colonial government introduced a Dutch-based civil law in Indonesia, but it

---

37 Jeremy Menchik, *Islam and Democracy in Indonesia: Tolerance without Liberalism*, Cambridge University Press, 2016.
38 Aria Bendix, "Jakarta's Christian Governor Imprisoned for Blasphemy", *Atlantic*, May 9, 2017. (https://www.theatlantic.com/news/archive/2017/05/jakartas-christian-governor-imprisoned-for-blasphemy/525990/)

allowed the continued use of Islamic as well as customary legal systems for family law matters. The civil code applied to people of Dutch, European, and Chinese descent. The modern Indonesian state largely maintained this duality, essentially retaining a civil code for non-Muslim populations.

Until 1989, rulings of religious courts had to be confirmed by state courts, a practice that had been instituted by Dutch colonial authorities. After 1989, this is no longer the case, and religious courts now have equal status to state courts. For some time, Muslims had the option of having the civil code, instead of Islamic law, apply to them. But this option was removed by a 2006 amendment that made the application of Islamic law mandatory for Muslim Indonesians.[39] The same year, the jurisdiction of religious courts was expanded to the field of "shariah economic transactions", such as Islamic finance and banking.[40] The result of this legal pluralism is a complete lack of legal coherence: as one scholar puts it, "a range of laws apply different rules to different groups, sometimes conferring rights, sometimes denying them… Overlap and inconsistency between them is common."[41]

The picture in the field of education is the same. Religious education is compulsory, something that is also the case in many secular states. But as Indonesian religious officials make clear, the purpose of religious education differs from secular states. Instead of seeking to ensure that students *understand* religion, Indonesian religious instruction seeks to ensure that religious "teachings and values are not exclusively understood but internalized and …

---

39 Yeni Salma Barlinti, "Inheritance Legal System in Indonesia: Legal Justice for People," *Indonesia Law Review*, vol. 3 no. 1, 2013.
40 Idri Idri, "Religious Court in Indonesia: History and Prospect", *Journal of Indonesian Islam*, vol. 3 no. 2, 2009.
41 Tim Lindsey, "Minorities and Discrimination in Indonesia: the Legal Framework," in Greg Fealy and Ronit Rici, *Contentious Belonging: The Place of Minorities in Indonesia*, Singapore: ISEAS Publishing, 2019.

accordingly acted upon."[42] Thus, it seeks to teach Islam to Muslim children, Christianity to Christian children, and so on – serving to instill religious doctrine in students.

On this basis, Indonesia clearly occupies a place on the continuum of state policies toward religion that is firmly in the "dominant religion" paradigm. The twist is that Indonesia formally establishes not one but several religious traditions, lending it a degree of pluralism that is certainly a positive aspect compared to most countries that have established religions. Still, the Indonesian system largely fails to treat its citizens equally, and maintains different standards, laws, and education for different communities which it enshrines in law.

The Indonesian system undoubtedly has allowed a growing role for political Islam to have an impact on politics and society. In the past two decades, particularly since the democratic transition of 1998, these forces have grown in influence in several ways. First, radical groups have established themselves on the Indonesian political scene. While they have yet to achieve a strong electoral following, their ideology has begun to affect society in broader terms. Not least, they seem to have been able to pull the larger, nominally traditionalist movements in a more conservative direction – as internal disputes have affected both the *Muhammadiyah* and the *Nahdlatul Ulama*, pitting more radical forces against more moderate ones within these organizations. Leaders in these mass movements have been forced to adapt to growing religious ideological fervor in society, for example when seeing many young members ignore their leadership's recommendation not to take part in Islamist protests in 2017.[43] Thus, the Indonesian model

---

42 Kamaruddin Amin, "Evaluating Religious Education," *Jakarta Post*, November 15, 2013. (https://www.thejakartapost.com/news/2013/11/15/evaluating-religious-education.html)
43 "Indonesia," *World Almanac of Islamism*, 2020. (almanac.afpc.org)

is strongly dependent on the continued respect for tolerance and pluralism within Islamic society. Having delegated substantial influence to religious communities, it has little leverage over the internal evolution of the Islamic community.

The Indonesian model, it should be said, has thus far been successful in containing radicalism by promoting moderate, traditional religious communities that have strong following in the population. Its experience suggests that such deeply rooted religious movements can play an important role in maintaining stability and countering extremism. The Indonesian model also presupposes a religious society; and through religious education, it seeks to promote a traditional, tolerant understanding of religion that is expected to inoculate the population against extremist ideology. The success and sustainability of the Indonesian model, however, depends on expectations. If the sole expectation is to counter extremism, it may be judged a success to some degree, although the country has seen a growing trend toward more rigid interpretations of religion and toward more overt Islamist political activity. But conversely, if the expectation is a move toward a more liberal society, it is a resounding failure. A system that differentiates between citizens on the basis of religious identity is becoming increasingly entrenched, and the state has no ambition to overcome such differences. In fact, it bases its legitimacy on their continued persistence. As the example of Lebanon shows, such institutionalized differences only entrench separate identity and thus undermines the possibility of a common national identity. Indonesia, of course, is unlikely to go the way of Lebanon, if nothing else because one group, the Sunni Muslims, so clearly dominate the population. But its model is one that has little ability to develop in the direction of a system that treats its citizens equally irrespective of religious identity.

The lessons of the Indonesian model for Central Asia are limited. There is a consensus in Central Asia and Azerbaijan that a turn toward a system that explicitly seeks to build a religious society and differentiates among its population on a religious basis would be a regression. Furthermore, the model's sustainability is dependent on the continued influence of moderate religious mass movements, which do not exist in Central Asia and cannot be easily replicated there. That said, the notion that moderate Islamic traditions can be cultivated among the population to serve as an inoculation against extremism is very relevant for Central Asia and Azerbaijan, where states similarly seek to develop indigenous religious traditions as an alternative to alien religious ideologies.

Conclusion

The short overview above is by necessity far from exhaustive. But one clear conclusion emerges from this outline of frequently touted models of government approaches to religion in the Muslim world: none of these models resembles what is emerging in Central Asia and Azerbaijan. The closest model is the Turkish model prior to Erdogan's advent to power. This model undoubtedly inspired Central Asian states and Azerbaijan, but they did not simply copy it; and in any case, their history differs significantly. While they share Turkey's moderate Hanafi heritage, they were never the seat of the Caliphate, and do not have the inbuilt confrontation between a revolutionary state and a religious society that is the legacy of Atatürk. The Soviet experience did secularize Central Asian and Azerbaijani societies, but present leaders are not inextricably tied to this history. Neither do these states have a strongly politicized Islamic conservative movement centered around the Naqshbandi order, as does Turkey. This should enable them to adapt their secular model of government without a need to suppress political Islam. Still, the Turkish model does indicate the risks of the state itself embracing Islamic identity as part of its nation-building process, something that helped usher in the victory of Islamism in Turkey.

The other models are considerably different. West African secular states have a cultural and socio-economic context that is very different; but they also have weak states that are incomparable to the situation in Central Asia and Azerbaijan. What they do show is that secular governance can become entrenched as a positive value in Muslim-majority societies, and can stand the test of time and survive Islamist challenges to the constitutional order. This is important for Central Asia and Azerbaijan, as it suggests that current leaders can help their nations transition to a more open political system without necessarily risking the secular nature of the state – but this requires a continued societal buy-in and acceptance of the secular state. Indonesia's peculiar model of several established religions is hardly relevant for Central Asia, as it leads to the entrenchment of religious identity and undermines modern notions of citizenship and equality before the law. Simply put, Central Asia and Azerbaijan have progressed further than such a model. Still, the Indonesian case suggests that the risk of emergent radicalism cannot be dismissed during a process of democratization. Finally, Tunisia and the moderate monarchies do hold value for Central Asian states because they serve as an indication of how states can successfully encourage moderate and tolerant understandings of Islam. Tunisia and Morocco along with the UAE, furthermore, suggest that even in the presence of strongly conservative social forces, it is possible to modernize legal systems to strengthen women and minority rights.

In the final analysis, this chapter shows that the Central Asian and Azerbaijani model of state approaches to religion is truly unique, sharing only limited elements with often touted models in the Muslim world.

8. LOOKING AHEAD

WHAT IS THE FUTURE OF STATE APPROACHES to religion in Central Asia and Azerbaijan? Why does it matter to the United States and Europe? Could this region develop a sustainable, positive form of secular government, and could this be an inspiration for other parts of the Muslim world? These are some of the questions that arise from the preceding pages, to which we shall turn after briefly summarizing the argument made in this book.

Central Asia and Azerbaijan are a clear outlier in the Muslim world. Whereas most other countries have moved toward greater mixing of religion and politics, this region has chosen a secular mode of government and, moreover, doubled down on this approach in the past decade. This approach could easily be dismissed as some form of post-Soviet leftover that carries little intrinsic value. That, however, would be a mistake. As this book has sought to illustrate, Central Asia and Azerbaijan are home to a deep-seated religious tradition that, in the past, proved to be compatible with world-class scientific advances and with a moderate and tolerant approach to religious affairs. This Hanafi-Maturidi tradition, coupled with an influential role for the esoteric practice of Sufism, differs greatly from the core Middle East, which has been under the influence of much more orthodox and intolerant theology. The indigenous religious tradition in Central Asia and the Caucasus nevertheless fell into decline, but in the late nineteenth and early twentieth centuries a school of modernist renewers, the *jadids*, sought to bring it into compatibility with modern science and learning. This exciting experiment was nevertheless brought to an end by Soviet rule, which decimated the indigenous religious tradition of Central Asia and Azerbaijan.

At independence, the situation faced by the leaders of the six new nations was far from enviable. The task of building new, functioning states out of the rubble left by the USSR was exacerbated by widespread poverty, a lack of governing institutions, and in several states, armed conflict as well. Their southern neighborhood was torn apart by violent extremists, who also played a key role in the destruction of Tajikistan. This, and the threat of Iranian-sponsored radicalism, was a formative experience that helped guide the approach that the leaders of these young states took to religious affairs. There was never any question that they would abandon the hollow atheism promoted by Communist ideology; the question was what would replace it. Everywhere in the region, the answer was the same: the six states all embraced a secular form of government that borrowed heavily from the Turkish Kemalist model.

In practice, this meant that the states enshrined secularism into their constitutions and laws, thus ensuring that laws, courts and education systems were shielded from religious influence. The states all took a skeptical approach to religion. In conceptual terms, they followed the French understanding of *laïcité*, which seeks to safeguard the state and society from the oppression of a dominant religious institution, and not the Anglo-Saxon concept of secularism that focuses on the promotion of individual religious freedom. As a result, they took a hard line toward any manifestation of Islamist ideology. Going beyond that, they remained highly skeptical toward *any* novel religious influence that appeared to depart from the indigenous traditions of the region. While they championed the harmonious relations among their traditional Muslim, Christian and Jewish populations, they made sure that challengers to these traditions were made to feel decidedly unwelcome.

There were, especially initially, differences in approach. While Turkmenistan and Uzbekistan took a hard line from the beginning, Kazakhstan and Kyrgyzstan saw less of a danger in religious activism, and tolerated the arrival of proselytizers of various faiths. But over time, the approaches of regional states have become increasingly similar. Whereas Kazakhstan and Kyrgyzstan have imposed growing restrictions, Uzbekistan has begun to liberalize its approaches. Azerbaijan has maintained a relatively steady approach, and in the region today only Tajikistan and Turkmenistan stand out for their highly restrictive approach.

The growing similarity in approaches toward religious affairs does not appear to be the result of any visible coordination between political leaders. While leaders have manifestly discussed religious matters during their many bilateral and multilateral meetings, they appear to have separately come to embrace a largely similar approach to the issue. A remarkable element of this approach is their decision to actively champion the region's indigenous religious tradition, and to assist in the rebuilding of institutions undergirding this tradition. Particularly in the last decade, the Central Asian states have all explicitly come to support the Hanafi-Maturidi tradition as the one supported by the state. Azerbaijan, standing out because of its mixed Shi'a and Sunni population, has similarly supported its indigenous religious traditions but specifically worked to make its Shi'a clergy less dependent on their Iranian counterparts.

This, of course, would appear to contradict the states' simultaneous emphasis on secularism. How can the state be secular if it also explicitly supports a particular religious tradition? While this notion would seem to run entirely counter to secularism as understood by the first amendment to the U.S. Constitution, it is less extraordinary from the vantage point of majority-Catholic countries that have sought to separate religion from the state and regulate relations between state and church. On the basis of France's *Concordat* of 1801, many countries have maintained the secular character of their government, laws and education while regulating their relationship with the country's dominant religious tradition, a process that often includes a recognition of its particular role in society. The difference in Central Asia and Azerbaijan is that the state, following the Soviet era, is not just regulating its relationship with traditional religion but actively assisting in the *restoration* of that tradition.

This peculiar approach is unique to the post-Soviet Muslim-majority states, and a result of their leaders' pragmatic view of religious affairs. Viewing the indigenous religious tradition as part of their national identity, they concluded that it is natural for religion to once again reclaim its role in society and in the lives of individuals. However, they saw an ability – and indeed a need – to influence *what* religious tradition re-emerges in society. Following independence, they were faced with an onslaught of well-funded and confident religious proselytizers from abroad. Indigenous traditional religious forces, decimated by Soviet rule and lacking both funds, confidence and religious knowledge, were at a significant disadvantage against these foreign challengers. If governments had maintained a strict neutrality in religious affairs, they could have witnessed a rapid displacement of their indigenous religious tradition with imported and highly intolerant schools of religious thought from the Middle East and South Asia. Indeed, inklings of such a tendency are already visible in Kyrgyzstan. Seeing this lack of a level playing field, and the potentially destabilizing effect on society of many novel religious forces, governments chose to take an active role and put their finger on the scale. They restricted the ability of foreign religious influences to spread in society and instead sought to champion – and control – the indigenous religious institutions and facilitate their reconstruction.

As a result, the states in the region states exhibit a curious combination: they are at once skeptical of institutional religion while also championing its restoration. In this sense, they combine elements of two ideal types outlined in this book: the skeptical and insulating approach pioneered by Republican France and developed by Kemalist Turkey, as well as the dominant religion approach that has historically been widespread across the world. Still, it is the Skeptical approach that defines them, given their insistence on keeping religion out of their laws, politics and education systems.

The policies adopted by the six states show considerable similarities. Formulations in their constitutions defining the secularism of the state are remarkably similar. Many also establish the secularism of the education system in the constitution itself; other common themes include the prohibition of political parties based on religion, and of clergy engaging in political activities. The six also impose very similar restrictions on religious activity within their borders. They require religious organizations to register with state agencies supervising religious affairs and impose registration requirements that by design are difficult to meet. They also impose restrictions on religious activities by unregistered groups. They seek to impede proselytism – some ban it outright, while others proscribe the promotion of one religion over another. Going further, they supervise and restrict the importation and publication of religious literature, frequently by requiring all such materials to be vetted by state agencies. And in all six states, the security services play a key role in the state approach to religion, taking a direct role in supervising, infiltrating, and prosecuting religious activism that falls outside the boundaries determined by the state.

The approach taken by Central Asian Azerbaijani governments differs considerably from the rest of the Muslim world. The most considerable overlap is with the Kemalist secularism that once prevailed in Turkey, but there are differences: the region's states have taken an, even more, interventionist role in controlling religious proselytism and religious literature. Compared to present-day Turkey, differences are even more profound, given Turkey's slide toward a political system dominated by an Islamist party, with references to religion in politics and the education system now ubiquitous. Compared to other models, similarities are even less pronounced. Central Asia and Azerbaijan share an official commitment to secularism with West African states that were once French colonies, but practical differences abound. Compared to the weak nature of African states, the post-Soviet states have considerably more powerful and activist state institutions, particularly security services. Moreover, West African states have failed to fully secularize their legislation. The notion of family law being adjudicated by customary institutions or according to Islamic principles would appear very foreign to most Central Asians. As for liberal Arab states, both Tunisia and monarchies like Jordan, Morocco and the UAE also seek to combine moderate Islam with modernity and progress. Uzbekistan in particular has taken a page from this playbook by seeking to assertively advocate for a moderate and traditional religious tradition as a counter-weight to extremism. But the similarities end there, as even the most progressive Arab states at the very least pay lip service to Sharia, and recognize Islam as the religion of the state. And while Indonesia is similar to Central Asia and Azerbaijan in championing several different religious traditions and priding itself on the harmony between them, it differs by being a state that actively promotes a religious foundation to education and law, undermining any notion of secular governance.

The differences are not just theoretical, they are meaningful in practice as well. In Central Asia and Azerbaijan, a young woman can go through a fully secular education system, in an environment where religious issues remain a private choice rather than something the state seeks to impose on her. When she reaches adulthood, she enjoys rights that, on paper, are the same as a man's, including in the realm of inheritance and divorce. Elements of these rights exist in several other areas of the Muslim world, but only in Central Asia and Azerbaijan are they all present. Of course, the implementation of these rights continues to leave much to be desired. And while there is a long way to go before everyone in the region enjoys all these rights, the fact that they even exist cannot be taken for granted anywhere else and is a strong foundation for the region to build on.

None of this is to suggest that Central Asian states and

Azerbaijan have found an ideal model, or that it is in any way perfected. This book has pointed to the deficiencies of these states' approach to religion. It has not delved in detail into them, primarily because so many others already have. Anyone seeking detail need go no further than consulting the yearly reports of the U.S. State Department or any number of nongovernmental watchdogs that have spent years cataloging problems and abuses in the region's religious affairs. As these reports amply illustrate, the region's approach suffers from a penchant toward restrictive and often repressive measures, to say nothing of the governments' tolerance of abuses by many of their employees. This is, to a significant extent, a legacy of the Soviet era, as the region's states have continued to accord state security services and the mentality they represent a prominent role in many walks of life, including but not limited to religious affairs. Only very recently have some states begun to curb the role of these services – most dramatically in Uzbekistan – but others have yet to begin that task, and no state is close to completing it.

Even if and when these repressive measures are eased, however, foreign watchdogs are unlikely to be satisfied. That is because there will likely remain fundamental philosophical differences between Western proponents of religious freedom and Central Asian and Azerbaijani leaders. The former – with the exception of France – define secularism in terms of individual religious freedom and as a result, have little acceptance for states that intervene in religious affairs, particularly if this intervention seeks to limit the operation of religious groups. Moreover, western proponents of religious freedom draw the line of acceptable activity in religious affairs at violence or the incitement thereof. As a result, they do not consider it legitimate to proscribe extremist ideology

8. Looking Ahead

unless that ideology overtly calls for violence. By contrast, leaders in Central Asia and Azerbaijan define secularism as a set of safeguards to protect the state and society from religious oppression. They also consider the content and substance of an ideology, not just its violent manifestations, as problematic enough to warrant restrictive measures against it. These differences are unlikely to be bridged anytime soon.

Then again, Western governments have not always spoken with one voice. During the war on terror, for example, the U.S. State Department voiced criticism of the Central Asian states' approach to religion, while representatives of the Department of Defense were considerably more supportive. Furthermore, it should be noted that opinion in America and Europe is itself shifting, and religious freedom activists may not be fully representative of the approaches taken by Western states. The Trump Administration took a much darker view of Islamist ideology than its predecessors, for example. Unfortunately, it did not advance a coherent approach, and sometimes voiced a rhetoric and took measures – such as the travel ban on some Muslim countries – that appeared to target Islam rather than the political ideology of Islamism. In Europe, countries such as Denmark and France have begun to counter the political ideology of Islamism and not just violent extremism. France's new law to "boost republican principles" adopted in fall 2020 is the most recent example. Religious freedom advocates in the West are often highly critical of these measures. But in some ways, Western states are moving closer to the Central Asian approach, setting up a possible future where there is a greater approximation between the two. In the meantime, however, controversies over state approaches to religion in the region are likely to continue.

Accepting that the region's model is imperfect, however, does not mean it is beyond repair. Quite to the contrary, this book has sought to show that the ambition of the regional states is essentially a worthy one that deserves support, even though all methods they employ to implement it might not. This is the main weakness of Western policy on the issue: it has tended to question not just the methods but the aims of state policies in religious affairs. With some exceptions, Western policies have advocated for full religious freedom and only rarely voiced understanding, let alone support, for these states' ambition to maintain secular government. From the region's perspective, Western advice can be summarized as follows: "stop requiring foreign religious groups to register; stop banning Islamist political activity; stop restricting foreign-trained imams from serving in your mosques; stop censoring imported religious literature; and stop banning Islamic dress in schools." Not staying at that, Westerners have confidently argued that if regional states fail to heed this advice, their problem with violent extremism would get much worse. However, these dire predictions, voiced since the 1990s, have failed to materialize. As a result, leaders in Central Asia and Azerbaijan have come to view Western advice in religious affairs as hopelessly naïve at best and outright dangerous at worst. As a result, they have largely tuned out such criticism.

A better approach going forward would be to express understanding and appreciation for the goals set by the regional states' approach and offer to support gradual reforms to it that would, over time, make it less reliant on restrictive measures and more focused on constructive and positive measures. In recent years, the prospect of an improved dialogue on these matters has increased as a result of the renewed urgency for reform that has been visible in the three largest countries of the region – Uzbekistan, Kazakhstan and Azerbaijan. As seen in the example of Uzbekistan, which has already involved the Council of Europe's Venice Commission and the OSCE in the task of writing a new law on religion, this general urge for reform is certain to affect religious affairs. But the region's states are only likely to be willing to internalize Western advice if their Western partners make a serious effort to understand their perspectives on religious matters, and respect their long-term strategic goals.

What is the sustainability of the state approaches to religion in Central Asia and Azerbaijan? As mentioned already in the introduction to this volume, it is an inescapable fact that these states are colored very much by their still recent Soviet experience. It remains an open question, therefore, whether the current commitment to secularism will continue to prevail within the scope of the next two decades, which is as far ahead as it is prudent to produce any forecast. As noted in the introduction, their likely trajectory depends in part on the development of political and religious ideas in the rest of the Muslim world. But it also depends on choices that governments in the region will make in coming years. To a lesser degree, choices by Western states and international bodies in how to approach the question will also play a role. Against this background, there are essentially four likely scenarios for the future. In a first scenario, the region's states have a continued restrictive and defensive approach, something that proves unsustainable. In a second, their continued restrictive approach proves durable over time. In a third, the states liberalize religious policy, but fail to safeguard secular government. And in a fourth, they liberalize religious policy and succeed in maintaining secularism.

Of course, it is entirely possible that different states will follow different scenarios.

In the first scenario, states continue to pursue the current approach but do not engage in significant reform of it. In other words, their approach continues to be centered on restrictive and even repressive measures. But as societies evolve, and as the Soviet generations are replaced with younger people with no memory of the Soviet era or even of the instability and conflict of the 1990s, popular opposition to religious restrictions grows. This is coupled with a continued domination of Islamism across the Muslim world. Furthermore, state efforts to restrict religion fail, because of the impossibility of regulating the spread of information over the internet and particularly social media. Even within the governments themselves, there is increasing support for a more Islamic approach, not least because younger officials themselves no longer believe in the separation of religion and state. Those at the top gradually come to consider secularism as a danger to their position of power, and as a result gradually embrace steps to give greater recognition to Islam. This scenario may occur either under continued authoritarian rule, or under a gradual political liberalization. Central Asia and Azerbaijan would, in this scenario, follow the evolution of Pakistan, Egypt or Malaysia in recent decades. It would lead the regional states to increasingly look to the Islamic world in their foreign policy, and more likely than not lead them to embrace an increasingly antagonistic approach to the United States and Europe.

In the second scenario, the states also continue to embrace an approach heavy on restrictions. The main difference is that they are able to sustain this without generating substantial challenges either from within the government, or from society as a whole.

8. Looking Ahead

In other words, the situation would look very much like it does today. This could be the result of several factors. First, if violent extremism in the rest of the Muslim world continues to be prominently in the news, it may – as it has done thus far – provide popular backing for restrictive approaches, as Central Asians and Azerbaijanis fear being dragged into the Middle Eastern morass. Second, if political Islam peaks in the next decade or two and becomes increasingly unpopular among Muslims everywhere, the same thing could happen. These two possibilities are, incidentally, not mutually exclusive: political Islam could lose support exactly because of its continued association with violence and unrest. Moreover, the efforts of Central Asian states and Azerbaijan to foster a secular ethos in their education systems could actually succeed, and their restrictive measures could prove effective at keeping Islamism at bay.

The third scenario features a liberalization of religious policy that leads to the gradual abandonment of secularism. The regional states, in this scenario, would follow the Turkish or Egyptian trajectory: a transition to multi-party politics coincides with the growth of political Islam as the main political force in society. This could take place gradually, over several decades, as in Turkey; or rapidly, in a revolutionary scenario, as in Egypt in 2011. Most likely, in this scenario states would lose control over the religious bureaucracies they promoted. Politicized interpretations of Islam would get a foothold within the *muftiates* of the region, leading the official *Ulama*, invigorated by state support, to gradually make ever-growing demands for the Islamization of society. This would follow the example of Al-Azhar in Egypt, or the *Diyanet* in Turkey. This scenario also rests on the assumption that Islamism continues to be a dominant force in the Muslim world, and that

Islamist ideas gain a stronger foothold in Central Asia and Azerbaijan in spite of government opposition. In this scenario, it would be likely for the liberalization of these states to be short-lived: as in Turkey, they would be likely to see a restoration of authoritarianism in a more Islamist form, as happened during Erdogan, and in Egypt however abortively under Muhammad Morsi. The alternative would be a Tunisia-like situation, in which Islamist forces are "domesticated" in a secular system. But as viewed in chapter eight, Tunisia has been an outlier and its success thus far has been a result of the strength of its civil society, something that Central Asia and Azerbaijan do not possess at this point. In this scenario, the region's states would in a sense "revert to the mean" of the situation in the broader Muslim world, indicating the failure of the experiment with secular government.

The fourth and final scenario is one in which the gradual liberalization of the region's religious policies does not lead to the abandonment of secular government. It is a scenario that would be likely either if the regional states engage in a gradual liberalization under continued semi-authoritarian rule, or if they make a gradual transition to democracy. It presupposes a commitment to reform that is broader than just the religious realm, as it requires the gradual liberalization of the political system. Still, liberalization and democratization are not synonymous: a state can maintain control over the political system, while liberalizing restrictions on society, including in religious affairs. Such liberalization would, of course, be at least as likely in a scenario that sees greater political participation and contestation of political power. Either way, this scenario is most likely to occur under certain conditions. First, the region maintains political stability and any liberalization is gradual and evolutionary. (As has been seen in the past two decades, revolutionary change tends to open the door to Islamist challenges.) Second, Islamist ideology sees a diminishing appeal across the Muslim world, weakening its appeal in Central Asia and Azerbaijan. And third, as a result, the present support for secular governance continues to prevail in the region, meaning that political Islam gains only the support of a minority of the region's population as political liberalization occurs.

Among these four scenarios, it is clear that the fourth is the most desirable outcome. But how can the region's states achieve it? That will require several important developments in regional affairs. Many variables outside the region will help determine the outcome, and none is more important than the way the Muslim world as a whole relates to the phenomenon of Islamism. Aside from that, three questions will be key. Can the states move on from the Soviet legacy? Can they develop a positive definition of secularism that maintains popular support? And finally, can they phase out their support for dominant religion?

First, for the region's model to be successful in the longer term, it will need to move beyond the Soviet legacy, which manifests itself in a reflexive reliance on state security issues to deal with societal phenomena. A key weakness of the region's approach to religious affairs is what political scientists call "securitization." It is because it defines an issue as a security challenge that the state legitimizes the deployment of repressive measures. In other words, seeing nails everywhere, the state reflexively reaches for the hammer. This was understandable and even perhaps natural for a new, weak state with a poor understanding of religious affairs in a neighborhood replete with very real manifestations of religiously motivated violent extremism. But as time passes, the states of the region have become stronger; and it has become clear that religious extremism does not constitute the mortal challenge it once appeared to.

As this book has argued, states such as Uzbekistan have come to conclude they have the problem more or less under control. Others, like Kazakhstan, have arguably overreacted to terrorist incidents, just as many observers would say the United States did following September 11, 2001. In any case, it has become clear that most regional states continue to securitize matters that do not realistically pose a security threat to either the state or society. Reviewing the application of security measures and reserving them for true security challenges will be an important task for the future. Again, whether this proves possible will depend on whether the challenge of extremism continues to be a manageable one for the regional states. Azerbaijan will continue to have to factor in the role of Iran in supporting Shia radicalism as it finetunes its approach. Weaker states, such as Tajikistan, are likely to be more reluctant to release the pressure than stronger and more confident ones like Uzbekistan. This is why the current reform process in Uzbekistan is of central importance to the region. Should Uzbekistan prove successful in managing religious affairs in a more measured way than in the past, that would in all likelihood lead other regional states to follow suit.

A second key question is whether the regional states can develop a positive approach to secularism that maintains the support of their populations. As this book has shown, the regional states already differ on this question. Some, like Tajikistan, rely heavily on negative, restrictive measures in their approach to religion. Others, like Azerbaijan and Uzbekistan, have begun to articulate a more positive agenda, which centers on the importance of secular government but also embraces the tolerant indigenous religious traditions. Going forward, all regional states will need to develop such positive agendas, and ensure they communicate them to their populations. This will require the development of school curricula, as in Kazakhstan, where a course on secularism and religious affairs has been assigned to high school students. It will also require engagement of civil society to secure the buy-in of the population. Not least, it will require that civil servants are well trained in the concepts underlying the state approach to religious affairs, an area in which much progress remains to be made.

This leaves the question what, exactly, the positive message will be. Again, this will differ from country to country. Azerbaijan, with its need to balance its mixed Shia and Sunni population, is likely to focus more strongly on the conceptual aspects of secular government, and the imperative of the neutrality of the state between these two sects. It is also likely to continue to support theological approaches that bridge the two, as it has sought to do through "unity prayers" that are unique in the Muslim world. Central Asian states will logically continue to stress the compatibility of their Hanafi-Maturidi tradition with secular government, modernity, and the advancement of science. In this regard, they have thus far focused mainly on Abu Hanifa, something that is natural given the scholar's key role in the development of the largest and most moderate of the Sunni schools of jurisprudence. But going forward, Central Asians have a largely untapped resource: the rediscovery of Maturidi's work.

As discussed in chapter four, this medieval theologian remains accepted as a mainstream Sunni scholar, with broad legitimacy across the Muslim world. Yet over many centuries, his theology – including his defense of free will and scientific notions of causality – came to be overshadowed by the more austere

Ashari theology. If Central Asians are looking for a way to boost the legitimacy of their secular form of government, reclaiming the Samarkand-born scholar's legacy will be of crucial importance, and will provide Muslims far beyond Central Asia with a positive alternative. This alternative may not go as far in its embrace of rationalism as the Mutazilite school does; yet it would appear to be an easier lift in many areas of the Muslim world than to restore the role of the widely discredited Mutazilism.

A third key question is how long the states will continue to bolster their indigenous religious traditions. As the preceding paragraph makes clear, it is likely to remain a key element of state policy for some time to come. And because those traditions were so damaged by Soviet rule, this is natural and perhaps even desirable. But over time, the states will run the danger, in supporting religious institutions of a particular kind, of undermining the secularism of the state by allying themselves too closely with that religious tradition. This is an issue that is likely to become increasingly problematic over the next two decades, particularly as a new generation of more self-confident Islamic scholars emerges that may not simply follow the priorities set by governments. In other words, Central Asian states and Azerbaijan will need to find an exit strategy – one that brings them closer to the French model of *laïcité*, which despite the *Concordat* approaches different religious traditions in a more neutral way than do these states, or for that matter Turkey with its *Diyanet*.

In the best case scenario, then, the outlines of a slightly different model would emerge. In this model, the Central Asian states and Azerbaijan continue to be committed to secular government, laws and education. But this secularism would be based on positive underpinnings rather than a defensive and restrictive approach. To boot, the approach would largely be endorsed by the civil society of these countries. Governments would likely continue to take an active role in religious affairs, and continue to promote – though more subtly – indigenous religious institutions that would have restored, to some degree, their historical place in society. Meanwhile, governments would still supervise the activity of foreign religious groups and the publication and distribution of religious literature. But they would do so with a lighter hand, and focus their energies on those influences that are truly extremist in nature, while essentially leaving alone small religious groups that pose no threat to societal stability. In terms of their approach to religion, these states are not likely to become like the United States; but they could become more like France.

Could the secular model of Central Asia and Azerbaijan be emulated by other parts of the Muslim world? To some, this may appear to be neither likely no desirable. Countries in the "core" areas of the Muslim world may feel there is little to learn from what they see as peripheral post-Soviet states that continue to be affected by the legacy of Communism. And even if they would, they may emulate mainly the defensive and restrictive elements of state approaches to religion there.

Yet it is by no means certain that Islamism will continue to remain the dominant ideology in the Muslim world. Islamists have had a certain appeal to the masses, but what has made them powerful is four key factors: their determination and organizational capability; their ample financial resources, courtesy of Gulf funders; their willingness and ability to intimidate or eliminate opponents; and the collapse of alternative ideologies. As noted in chapter two, there are indications that Islamism may, in fact, have passed its peak. When Sudan declared itself a secular state in 2020, it marked the first time that a country having adopted Islamism turned its back to the ideology, implicitly declaring it a failure. The once-mighty Muslim Brotherhood is a shadow of its former self. When several Arab states normalized relations with Israel, the fury of the "Arab street" was nowhere to be seen. Most remarkably, Saudi Arabia, of all countries, has embraced a path to moderation, even purging its textbooks of hatred toward Jews and Christians.

In Iran, the regime is able to maintain its power only through massive and systematic repression. In Turkey, Tayyip Erdogan's rule has turned sour, and his rule is now widely associated with corruption and mismanagement. In both countries, Islamist rule has repelled the population, which is reacting by dissociating itself from religious conservatism and even from religion itself. Two thirds of Iranians want religious prescriptions purged from legislation, and three in five no longer fast during Ramadan. Similarly in Turkey, self-identified religious conservatives are declining rapidly, and a flurry of indicators show the population being more liberal, supportive of women's rights, and tolerant of other faiths.[1] Similarly, a 2019 survey by the Arab Barometer of six large Arab states showed a significant and rapid loss of trust in both Islamist parties and religious leaders.[2]

This is not to say Islamism is not a serious force; it remains the most powerful movement across the Muslim world, and its ideas have been internalized by millions of Muslims around the

---

[1] Terry Daley, "Iran's Secular Shift: New Survey Reveals Huge Changes in Religious Beliefs," *The Conversation*, September 10, 2020; Ragip Soylu, "Turkish Youth Inreasingly Secular and Modern Under Erdogan, Poll Finds," *Middle East Eye*, March 20, 2019.
[2] "Arabs are Losing Faith in Religious Parties and Leaders," *Economist*, December 5, 2019.

globe. But an increasing number of Muslim intellectuals have begun to speak about the decline of Islamism, indicating it may well have passed its prime. The conclusion is that Muslims are gradually tiring of the hatred, unrest and sectarian violence that is being committed in the name of Islam.[3]

If this trend intensifies, as seems likely, Muslims will be looking for alternative models of organizing the relationship between religion and the state. The idea of separating religion and politics, prominent in the Muslim world fifty years ago, is likely to once again gain traction among intellectuals and the public at large. A generation ago, Turkey played the role of an example of successful secular government, which inspired secularists elsewhere and formed an important model for the development of the Central Asian model studied in this book. It no longer plays this role, and no other major state has emerged to replace it. This makes the trajectory of Central Asia and Azerbaijan all the more important. If they fail to build a model that proves sustainable, there will be no example of successful secular government in the Muslim world. Eyes would by necessity turn to the next best example – countries that are not secular, but which are liberalizing under a broad reference to religion, as Jordan, Morocco, Tunisia or the UAE.

Should Central Asia and Azerbaijan refine their model along the lines outlined here, however, it is more than likely that they will catch the attention of those seeking an alternative to the current mixing of religion and politics that prevails in Muslim-majority countries. Just as they once were inspired by the example of Turkey, Central Asia and Azerbaijan can themselves be an example of successful secular government.

---

[3] Mustafa Akyol, "A New Secularism is Appearing in Islam," *New York Times*, December 23, 2019.

ACKNOWLEDGMENTS

MANY FRIENDS AND COLLEAGUES played important roles in making this book happen. First and foremost, among them are the authors and co-authors of the studies on religion and politics in Central Asia and Azerbaijan, on whose work this book draws. They include Victoria Clement, Johan Engvall, Jacob Zenn, Halil Karaveli, Boris Ajeganov, Julian Tucker, and the late Johanna Popjanevski. Several research assistants supported this program over the years, including Braunny Ramirez, Jack Verser, Kamilla Zakirova, Diana Glebova, Paisley Turner, and Jacob Levitan.

The friends in Central Asia and Azerbaijan that have been important interlocutors on the matters at the heart of this book are too many to list. Some deserve special mention, however. They include Elin Suleymanov, presently Azerbaijan's Ambassador to the Court of St. James's; Fariz Ismailzade, vice rector of the ADA University; Abdujabbar Abduvakhitov, former rector of Westminster University in Tashkent, as well as Eldor Aripov, Director of the Institute of Strategic and Regional Studies in Tashkent. Similarly, conversations with a large number of friends in America and Europe have provided inspiration for this work, including Herman Pirchner and Ilan Berman at the American Foreign Policy Council, Niklas Swanström at the Institute for Security and Development Policy, and former Swedish Ambassador to several regional states, Ingrid Tersman. I am also grateful for the many insights from conversations with Gloria La Cava, who graciously consulted with me when leading the World Bank's efforts to counter violent extremism in Central Asia. Professor Brenda Shaffer early on focused my attention on this issue and has provided enthusiastic support for this project.

My gratitude also extends to my father, Erik Cornell, who helped draw my attention to these issues, not least by putting me in French school at an early age, thus exposing me to French republican ideals, and subsequently moving the family to Turkey in the early 1990s. My wife Anna frequently forced me to sharpen my thinking on this issue (and not just this one). Perhaps most importantly, the founding Chairman of the Central Asia-Caucasus Institute, S. Frederick Starr, encouraged me to write this book in a way that hopefully makes it relevant to a broader audience than only Central Asia-watchers. While the list of people who helped this book become a reality is long, the errors that readers will inevitably find in this book are, of course, my own.

ABOUT THE AUTHOR

SVANTE E. CORNELL is Director of the Central Asia-Caucasus Institute & Silk Road Studies Program, a Joint Center whose components are affiliated, respectively, with the American Foreign Policy Council in Washington D.C. and the Institute for Security and Development Policy in Stockholm. Cornell was educated at the Middle East Technical University and Uppsala University. He previously taught political science and Eurasian affairs at Uppsala and at Johns Hopkins University-SAIS. He focuses on national security, regional politics, and conflict management issues in Central Asia, the Caucasus, as well as Turkey. He is the author or editor of eight books and more than one hundred articles.

INDEX

Abduh, Muhammad, 22, 52, 109
Afghanistan, 2, 35, 47, 78, 122, 127-139, 144, 151, 152, 157, 183, 184
Ahmadiyya, 207, 256
Akromiya, 214,
Alash, 110, 111
Al-Azhar, 118, 119, 171, 172, 195, 277
Al-Banna, Hassan, 26, 234
Al-Bukhari, Muhammad, 88, 92, 221
Al-Ghazali, Hamid, 25, 97, 98, 101
Al-Khattab, Samir Saleh Abdullah, 141
Al-Maturidi, Mansur, 94, 95, 97, 98, 243
Anticlericalism, 64, 66,
Anti-Semitism, 28, 211
Ashari, 16, 17, 29, 94, 95, 96, 97, 98, 243, 282
Atatürk, Mustafa Kemal, 29, 68, 226, 232, 233, 262, 123

Azerbaijan, i-iv, 2-5, 9, 10, 52, 84, 85, 99, 105, 108-110, 112, 121-123, 125, 128, 143-146, 158, 159, 161-164, 170, 177-179, 181, 182, 184, 185, 188, 191, 194, 199, 201, 202, 204, 208, 209, 211, 213, 214, 217-220, 224-226, 239, 249, 250, 262, 263, 265-268, 270-283, 285, 288

Babakhan, Ishan, 118, 119
Boko Haram, 251
Bourguiba, Habib, 24, 232-234, 236, 237, 238

Caesaropapism, 12, 74,
Caliphate, 13, 19, 29, 78, 135, 143, 167, 213, 226, 262
Calvinism, 57, 58
Chad, 250, 252, 254, 255,
Chechnya, 139, 140, 141, 142, 143

Dagestan, 139, 140, 141, 143, 144,
Diyanet, 150, 227, 230, 277, 282

Ennahda, 235, 236-238
Erdogan, Recep Tayyip, 10, 30, 38, 50, 52, 55, 70, 214, 228-230, 262, 278, 284,

Family law, 13, 116, 233, 236, 242, 245-247, 253, 255, 259, 270,
First Amendment, 54, 61, 62, 268
Folk Islam, 104, 117, 133, 165, 171, 172, 199.
France, 19, 54-57, 61-63, 65-69, 73-77, 80, 81, 84, 85, 111, 190, 223, 250, 268, 269, 272, 273, 283

Gülen, Fethullah, 207, 214, 228

Hamas, 28, 36, 46
Hanafi school, 88, 90, 91-93, 99, 140, 224,
Hanafi-Maturidi tradition, 81, 98, 118, 119, 219, 267, 281
Hanbali school, 26, 89, 92, 93, 95, 98, 99, 118
Hanifa, Abu, 90, 91, 220, 281,
Hekmatyar, Gulbuddin, 130, 131
Hijab, 68, 149, 150, 171, 190-193, 206
Hindustani, Muhammadjon, 120
Hizb Ut-Tahrir, 36, 135, 153, 213

Human Rights Watch, 3, 157, 191

Iran, Islamic Republic of, i, 8, 14, 19, 21, 30-34, 38, 43, 45, 47, 50, 51, 76, 77, 109, 121, 122, 127-129, 156, 158, 160, 183, 184, 191, 266, 268, 280, 284,
Islamic Extremism, ii, 134, 135, 142, 157, 166, 245
Islamic Jihad Union, 167
Islamic Movement of Uzbekistan, 133, 135
Islamic State, 3, 14, 27, 34, 42, 48, 78, 134, 138, 142, 143, 148, 149, 213
Islamism, 1, 4, 9, 14, 28, 29, 33-36, 39, 40, 44-51, 111, 119, 127, 140, 141, 164, 228, 230, 231, 232, 234, 256, 260, 263, 273, 276, 277, 279, 283-285

Jadids, 140, 142, 143
Jamaat al-Tabligh, 135, 172, 173, 192, 195, 217, 248,
Jamiat-e Islami, 130, 139
Jews, 25, 28, 42, 55, 60, 61, 77, 284
Jordan, 24, 36, 52, 196, 222, 225, 239-243, 245, 246, 248, 249, 271, 285

Karategin, 137, 138, 197
Karimov, Islam, 132, 134, 135, 152, 154, 179, 180, 184, 214

Kazakhstan, i, 5, 52, 53, 100, 109, 110, 118, 119, 122, 143, 144, 146, 164-171, 173, 174, 178, 185, 187-189, 191, 192, 194, 199, 200, 202-204, 209, 210, 214, 216, 217-219, 223, 267, 275, 280, 281
Kemalism, 52
Khalimov, Gulmurad, 148
Kulyab, 137, 138, 197
Kyrgyzstan, i, 5, 53, 118, 122, 132, 135, 136, 139, 146, 164-167, 169, 170, 172-174, 178, 187-191, 195, 199, 200, 204, 214, 216, 217, 219, 223, 257, 259

Laïcité, ii, 54, 55, 63-66, 72, 73, 80, 250, 251, 252, 254, 266, 282
Laïklik, 54, 72, 73, 81

Madrasa Arabia Raiwind, 173, 195
Mali, ii, 14, 21, 249, 250, 251, 252, 254, 255
Masoud, Ahmad Shah, 130, 131, 138
Maturidi, 17, 81, 88, 93-98, 118; 119, 265, 267 281
Mawdudi, Abu A'la, 26, 27
Mirziyoyev, Shavkat, 154, 155-157, 191, 207 218, 221
Morocco, 8, 24, 48, 50, 52, 222, 239-241, 243-248, 263, 271, 285
Mouridiya, 253
Mu'tazila, 15
Muftiate, 167, 171, 173, 197, 199, 205, 222, 277

Muhammad Yusuf, Muhammad Sadik, 198
Muhammadiyah, 257, 260
Muslim Brotherhood, 26, 27, 32, 34, 36, 37, 46, 49-51, 129, 207, 243, 244, 284

Nahdlatul Ulama, 257, 260
Naqshbandiyya, 88
Nazarbayev, Nursultan, 191, 203,

Pakistan, 8, 21, 22, 33, 35, 39, 41, 43, 45, 47, 48, 127, 128-132, 134, 135, 156, 157, 173, 180, 183, 195, 197, 210, 276
Pancasila, 226, 256,
Pashazade, Allahshükür, 159, 160, 194
Personal Status, Laws on, 233, 242, 245, 246, 247

Qatar, 47, 49, 202, 240
Qutb, Sayyid, 26-28, 234

Rakhmon, Imomali, 138, 146-148, 151, 196, 220,

SADUM, 119, 194, 196, 198
Salafi, 16, 23-26, 34, 47, 94, 98, 102, 118-120, 127, 129, 133, 134, 140, 143, 144, 149, 152, 157, 169, 172, 192, 200, 295
Saudi Arabia, 24-26, 34, 42, 43, 47, 49-51, 76, 77, 92, 203, 240, 284
Senegal, 13, 250, 252-255
Shafi'i school, 92, 93, 140

Sharia, 13, 29, 31, 33, 35, 45, 78, 99, 102, 103, 111, 114, 116, 133, 170, 229, 232, 233, 235, 238, 245-248, 259, 271
Shaykh-ul-Islam, 209
State Committee, 150, 160, 162, 188. 201, 202
Sufism, 88, 98, 99, 100-102, 104, 119, 196, 243, 266

Tabligh Jamaat, see Jamaat al-Tabligh
Tajikistan, ii, 53, 99, 112, 118, 119, 121, 122, 125, 128, 129, 131, 132, 134-139, 141, 145-152, 165, 166, 170, 178, 186-189, 192, 193, 196, 197, 199, 200, 205, 206, 207, 217, 218, 219, 220, 223, 266, 267, 280
Taliban, 35, 45, 78, 131, 132, 135, 205, 210
Taqlid, 18, 20, 22, 23
Tokayev, Kassym-Jomart, 218
Toktomushev, Maksatbek, 173, 195
Tunisia, 13, 24, 48, 225, 232-239, 263, 271, 278, 285,
Turkey, i-iii, 8, 13, 14, 21, 29-36, 38, 39, 42, 43, 46-48, 50-52, 54, 55, 67-70, 74-76, 81, 82, 85, 100, 103, 106, 107, 115, 122, 127, 128, 150, 158, 160, 181, 183, 184, 190, 191, 193, 214, 225-237, 255, 262, 263, 269, 270, 277, 278, 282, 284, 285, 288

Turkmenistan, ii, 5, 53, 104, 118, 132, 146, 170, 173, 174, 178, 187, 190, 197, 199, 200, 214, 216, 217, 223, 267

U.S. Commission on International Religious Freedom, 3, 189, 207,
U.S. State Department, 215, 272, 273,
Ulama, 9, 20, 23, 34, 85, 89, 107, 108, 112-114, 118, 166, 193, 196, 200, 233, 244, 246, 257, 258, 260, 277,
United Arab Emirates, 24, 50
United Tajik Opposition, 148, 217
Uzbekistan, ii, 5, 52, 53, 100, 105, 112, 113, 115, 118, 122-124, 131-136, 138, 145, 151-157, 162, 165-167, 170, 174, 178, 180, 185-188, 190, 191, 197-199, 207-209, 214, 216-218, 221-223, 249, 267, 271, 272, 275, 280

Williams, Roger, 59, 60

Yuldashev, Tahir, 134

Ziyoyev, Mirzo, 147, 148

www.ingramcontent.com/pod-product-compliance
Lightning Source LLC
Chambersburg PA
CBHW020325170426
43200CB00006B/269